TRANSACTIONS

OF THE

AMERICAN PHILOSOPHICAL SOCIETY

HELD AT PHILADELPHIA

FOR PROMOTING USEFUL KNOWLEDGE

NEW SERIES—VOLUME 63, PART 4

1973

THE AUSTRO-SLAV REVIVAL: A STUDY OF NINETEENTH-CENTURY LITERARY FOUNDATIONS

STANLEY B. KIMBALL

Department of History, Southern Illinois University, Edwardsville

THE AMERICAN PHILOSOPHICAL SOCIETY

INDEPENDENCE SQUARE

PHILADELPHIA

November, 1973

Auch die Bedientenvölker rütteln
Am Baum, den jeder todt geglaubt,
Die Czechen und Polaken schütteln
Ihr struppiges Karyatidenhaupt.

Friedrich Hebbel, 1861

Library of Congress Catalog
Card Number 73-79575
International Standard Book Number 0-87169-634-7
US ISSN 0065-9746

PREFACE

The vital role language and literature played in the various Austro-Slav national revivals of the nineteenth century has been studied exhaustively and is well known and appreciated. Little, however, has been written about the early literary institutions which promoted and supported the national revivals and which were the earliest national societies among the Austro-Slavs. During the Slav renaissance philology and history were employed as major weapons by the national leaders and almost all literary and scholarly societies had political overtones. Without doubt the most important of such institutions among the Austro-Slavs were the *maticas* or literary foundations which came into being as early as 1826 among the Serbs in southern Hungary.[1]

This study is based largely on a comparative analysis of six Austro-Slav literary foundations in and through which most of the important Austro-Slav national and political leaders participated during most of the nineteenth century. In general the purpose of this work is to show how the politically suppressed and culturally undeveloped Austro-Slavs evolved various kinds of literary institutions to further their national and cultural development, and to assess the role which these institutions, especially the maticas, played in the national revival.

Specifically it is an attempt to discover how and to what extent national literature was disseminated among all strata of the Austro-Slavs, to show how the Austro-Slavs, adopting much earlier Western innovations to their peculiar circumstances, made significant efforts to join that phase of Western cultural life represented by literary and learned societies. More particularly I want to discover the various goals, functions, and common denominators of all these related movements; what the patriots attempted and achieved within the narrow confines in which they were allowed to work, the response of the people at large, what cooperation existed among the Austro-Slavs and finally, in short what were the mechanics of this phase of the "reawakening."

Following an introduction, the study concentrates on the literary foundations of the Serbs, Czechs, Croats, Slovaks, and Slovenes. Three lesser foundations—those of the Poles, Ruthenians,[2] and Lusatian Serbs, are treated briefly in an appendix.

This study does not purport to present complete and detailed histories of either the Slavic revival or of the various maticas, nor is it literary history since the literary merits of the foundations' publications are not treated. Only those periods in their history and those activities which pertain specifically and significantly to the rebirth will be studied in detail. All other activities such as elections, officers, business details, and the like will be mentioned briefly if at all. The basic period is from 1826 (when the Serbian matica was founded) through about 1879. The terminal date cannot be fixed as precisely as the beginning. The year 1879 was chosen because by then the pioneering era of the maticas was over, their most significant national contributions had been made, and the long pro-Slav ministery of Count Edward Taaffe commenced.

Despite the caveats against and the hazards of attempts to cover a subject as great, varied, and complex as the Austro-Slav national revival, this study undertakes such an effort, although on a very modest scale. Each chapter offered unique problems of presentation and organization and, since the various national movements were not equal in significance, variety, interest, and success, the desideratum of writing chapters of equal length and proportion became impossible. The chapter on the Slovaks, for example, is quite long because of their many small literary societies.

In spite of these and other problems inherent in such a study it is hoped that the benefits of having this synthesis pass through the filter of only one mind will outweigh the defects of such a venture which otherwise might have been carried out by a committee—an undertaking which would have generated its own problems and defects.

The different alphabets, dialects, and transliteration schemes presented a problem. As far as possible I have kept the original spelling of the names

[1] The term *matica* or *matice* is difficult to translate. It is a generic term meaning many things such as matrix, queen bee, mother, riverbed, record book, and screw, and implies protection or embracing care. Its probable origin is from Old Slavonic *Mat'* (mother) plus the diminutive ending *ica*. In modern Serbo-Croatian, Slovak, and Slovenian it is spelled *matica*, in Czech *matice*, *macierz* in Polish (*maćica* means uterus in Polish), and *matytsia* in Ukrainian. (In Russian *matitsa* means a girder.) Since the Serbian matica was the prototype of all the others, this study uses this spelling.

It can also signify a society, association, or more precisely a foundation—an institution for applying private wealth to public purposes. During the nineteenth century the term was used to denote various kinds of foundations—religious, educational, and even popular commercial publishing ventures. The foundations discussed in this book, however, were basically cultural with the primary functions of fostering the national language and literature, and putting cheap copies of good national "entertaining and informative" books into the hands of as wide a reading audience as possible.

[2] From the Latin word for Russian, Ruthenus. Later the word came to designate Russians living out of Russia. In this work it is used to indicate Ukrainians living in Habsburg lands.

of people, places, and things, and have in all cases avoided such orthographic innanities as Chafrjik (Šafařík), Vouk Karadgitch (Vuk Karadžić), Lyoodevit Schtur (L'udevit Štúr), or Layosh Koshut (Lajos Kossuth).

Where there were important dialectal differences, such as between central and western Slovak, I have used the dialect which was preferred at the time and have not modernized the spellings. All Cyrillic names have been transliterated according to the Library of Congress system. With respect to the complications of Ruthenian orthography and transliteration, however, I have followed the *Ukraine: A Concise Encyclopaedia* (2 v., Toronto, 1963, 1971).

There must be, of course and unfortunately, some exceptions to these tidy rules. Some names are so well known by their Latinized equivalents such as Vienna for Wien, Prague for Praha, Francis Joseph for Franz Josef, that it would be difficult or pedantic to change now. A few borderline cases have been left in the original. The Czech Václav, for example, is usually rendered by the ugly and unnecessary form Wenceslaus which this study avoids.

All Slavic cities and place names are rendered in their Slavic forms and, where appropriate, the German, Magyar, or Italian equivalents are given in parentheses. This system works admirably with but one exception—Lwów, Lviv, or Lemberg. Here is one case where the Latin Leopolis would be welcome. In deference to national sensitivities this study will use Lwów in reference to things Polish and Lviv in connection with Ruthenian affairs.

This book is based primarily on research done and materials collected during the year 1964–1965 in Europe, when I worked in Prague, Brno, Bratislava, Martin, Lviv, Ljubljana, Zagreb, Beograd, Zadar, Novi Sad, Vienna, and Munich and where as far as possible I worked in the libraries and archives of the existing maticas, and in modern academies and libraries, and conversed with many individuals acquainted with the institutions of this study.

Portions of this text previously appeared in the *East European Quarterly* and in the Odlozilik *Festschrift—The Czech Renascence of the Nineteenth Century*, published by the University of Toronto Press. I wish to thank the editors for permission to reprint some of this material.

I would particularly like to acknowledge the financial help and encouragement of the Alexander von Humboldt Stiftung which enabled me to live and study in Munich during the academic year 1964–1965, and of the Graduate School of Southern Illinois University, Edwardsville, for additional funds to travel widely in the Slavic world. Everywhere I went in Germany, Austria, Yugoslavia, Czechoslovakia, and Russia courteous and helpful secretaries, directors, scholars, and librarians went out of their way to answer questions and help me locate necessary materials. Without such help this study would have been impossible.

I would also like to acknowledge the help and encouragement of Joseph F. Zacek of the State University of New York at Albany, who read and criticized constructively an earlier, incomplete draft of this study; Radko K. Jansky of Maryville College, St. Louis, for a close reading of the entire manuscript and many helpful suggestions; and my colleague at Southern Illinois University, Rudolf Wierer, for similar advice. The same gratitude is extended to Živan Milisavać of the Serbian Matica in Novi Sad for reading the chapter on the Serbs, to Jiří Kořalka of the Czech Academy of Science in Prague for help with the chapter on the Czechs, to Milan Kudělka of the Institute for the History of European Socialist Countries in Brno for reading the chapter on Moravia, to Štefan Baranovič of the Slovak Matica in Martin for helpful criticism of the chapter on the Slovaks, and to Fran Zwitter of the University of Ljubljana for reading the chapter on the Slovenes.

I profited greatly from the advice of these friends and colleagues. All errors of fact, interpretation, and concept must, however, be laid at my door.

S. B. K.

THE AUSTRO-SLAV REVIVAL: A STUDY OF NINETEENTH-CENTURY LITERARY FOUNDATIONS

STANLEY B. KIMBALL

CONTENTS

I. THE INEVITABLE BACKGROUND AND SOME ORDERING GENERALITIES

During the late eighteenth and early nineteenth centuries, the Austro-Slavs, after centuries of political and cultural subjugation by Germans, Magyars, Turks, and Italians, experienced a reawakening, a national revival. This was caused by three things: an internal and latent remembrance of their historic past (especially of medieval independence and putative glory), which was kept alive and treasured by savants, clergymen, members of the *literati*, and in folk literature; and two external forces—the Enlightenment and the Romantic movement.

The first of the outside forces influencing the Austro-Slavs was the Enlightenment, which came from France and Germany and which had both an intellectual and, later, a political effect. Intellectually, it fostered an increased appreciation and revival of Austro-Slav cultural traditions and progress in education which led to the founding of several cultural, economic, and learned institutions during the late eighteenth century. Such societies were German in language and spirit, scholarly, conservative, aristocratic, and at best patriotic, but certainly not national and popular.

They were organized and led by cosmopolitan members of the "Austrian" nobility, and a few middle-class Austro-Slav savants, wealthy businessmen, and members of the clergy for the purpose of transmitting to their areas the advanced ideas and humanitarian and practical reforms of the Enlightenment. The nobility in particular (especially those in Bohemia), also hoped thereby to effect some kind of safe opposition to the centralizing efforts of Maria Theresa and Joseph II. By fostering a limited form of *Landespatriotism*, they strove to maintain their provincial privileges.

The Enlightenment also released powerful political ideas which were carried to the Austro-Slavs primarily as a result of the French Revolution. It was only natural that the French effort to provide for the constitutional "rights of men and citizens" would be interpreted by the Austro-Slavs to mean also national freedom from foreign domination.

The second external influence on the national revivals was Romanticism. This movement (among other things) was essentially a rejection of the rather cold formalism and rationalism of the "Classicism" of the Enlightenment in preference for a more free and emotional form of expression. Since Romanticism lauded and encouraged the study of the past, popular language, folklore, and national individuality, it had a great influence on the Austro-Slavs. (Herder's concept of Romantic nationalism, for example, and his doctrine of the sacredness of "hereditary idiom," was so powerful that he became known as the *praeceptor slavorum*.)

After 1815, the much more nationally minded second generation of Austro-Slav national leaders not only wished to transmit the ideas of the *Aufklärung* to the masses for their improved educational and economic conditions, but wanted also to fashion a national language adequate to the task. They also desired to provide all kinds of national literature for the purpose of awakening the masses to national consciousness. To this end, it was necessary to organize literary institutions, to publish journals and the essential books of the revival—grammars, dictionaries, histories, encyclopedias, school texts, collections of folk songs, popular and polite literature, and reprints of the "classics."

Where possible, as among the Czechs, Croats, and Slovenes, this new generation successfully used the earlier eighteenth-century patriotic institutions as bases from which to found more popular and national organizations. Elsewhere, among the Serbs and Slovaks, these early national societies had to be organized practically *ex nihilo*. Their most fundamental activity was to put cheap copies of good national literature in the hands of as many readers as possible. To this end they collectively developed a great variety of activities including, in addition to publishing books and journals, awarding prizes for manuscripts, supporting authors, making book grants, promoting libraries, reading rooms and literary salons, forming collections of various kinds, granting stipendia to students, administering trusts, organizing scholarly activities, establishing publication exchange programs, raising standards of literature and literary criticism, promoting orthographic reforms, fostering the national tongue in schools and public life, and promoting Slavic mutuality.[1]

Following the pattern of the Serbian prototype, however, they were all organized in basically the same way—with executive committees, various boards, and several kinds of membership such as honorary, sustaining, contributing, and general. All members, including those in the general category paying dues of 2 to 5fl.,[2] received free (or at reduced cost) copies of all publications. The maticas were, therefore, a kind of stock company the dividends of which were publications.

They all, furthermore, were closely allied with and affected by most all other national, cultural, and intellectual societies of that time—the reading rooms, museums, learned societies, academies, Catholic publishing societies, and other literary societies.

Their membership was made up largely of the urban middle classes and the clergy—the two classes which led and promoted the whole national revival. Especially numerous were educators and parish priests—the natural leaders of the masses. For a variety of reasons which will be pointed out in succeeding chapters, none of them succeeded in attracting many members of the proletarian and peasant groups. They were, therefore, never at any time really popular, and only the Czechs had any significant support from the nobility. In addition to German and Magyar opposition they had to work also against the lethargy, distrust, indifference, backwardness, and divided allegiances of the peoples they were striving to serve, and against native competing societies organized by individuals and groups who, for various reasons, opposed their programs. In spite of these difficulties, during the height of their influence they became the most important (sometimes the only) literary-national-cultural societies among their respective groups.

The political and intellectual atmosphere in which these national activities took place was that of a largely Germanized, centralized, bureaucratic police state ruled by Francis I; his Staatskanzler, Prince Klemens Metternich; Count Josef Sedlnitzky, chief of the Polizei-und Censor Hofstelle; and Count Franz Anton Kolowrat, Minister des Innern. These men rigidly opposed the political aspirations and many civil liberties of their subjects, especially the non-Germans. At a time when Europe was vibrating with many new ideas and "isms," the empire was surrounded with a Chinese wall to keep them out.

The French Revolution had contributed the powerful ideas of popular sovereignty, self-determination of peoples, equality of rights, and nationalism. There were also liberalism, rationalism, individualism, constitutionalism, romanticism, socialism, and other new and disquieting ideas. Sedlnitzky sent a memorandum to Metternich indicating some of those most repugnant to Austria: "philosophical materialism, religious rationalism or mysticism, so-called liberalism, the revolutionary principle, and the corporative."[3]

In spite of censorship, outside ideas did seep into Austria. Some were imported by members of the nobility and wealthy class who studied and traveled abroad, others by students who had studied abroad, especially at the university in Jena which at that time was in the forefront of the German patriotic movement and was considered by Vienna to be a source of infectious national and social unrest. Furthermore, even though all cultural life was overshadowed by official control, German-Austrian cultural contributions were not negligible, as the names of Beethoven, Schubert, Grillparzer, and Raimund prove.

The vast real-estate holdings of the House of Habsburg, over which Francis I ruled, was an artificial conglomerate of peoples including Germans, Magyars, Italians, Rumanians, and all or parts of seven Slavic peoples—Czechs, Poles, Slovaks, Ruthenians, Slovenes, Croats, and Serbs. Since the time of Joseph II, the "Hereditary Lands of the House of Habsburg" had been divided into thirteen *Kronländer* ruled by appointed *Staathalters* or governors. Each province was divided into *Kreise* or districts and ruled by a *Hauptman* or captain. German was the sole administrative language.

In place of an Imperial Council or Reichsrat in which representatives of the various peoples of the monarchy sat, there was a centralized chancellery and a little-used council of state and conference of ministers. In the *Kronländer*, the non-Germans had little control over their affairs, for the *Landtage* or provincial diets were but shadowy and powerless relics of the Middle Ages, dominated by the German-

[1] The Czech *vzájemnost* and the Serbo-Croat *uzajamnost* mean mutuality or reciprocity. While neither term is common in English, the former seems to be the clearer.

[2] A florin (fl.) or gulden (Krone after 1892) was the basic coin of the empire until 1900. It was divided into 100 kreuzers. Some idea of its value and buying power is suggested by the following facts: In 1848 one florin was worth about $.48 and the average weekly wage in the empire was about 5.22fl. Šafařík came to Prague from Novi Sad in 1833 for a guaranteed salary of 480fl. a year, or about 9.23fl. a week. A 5fl. membership fee then would represent about the average weekly workingman's pay or about half of the weekly income of an educator.

[3] As quoted in R. W. Seton-Watson, *A History of the Czechs and Slovaks* (London, 1943), p. 170.

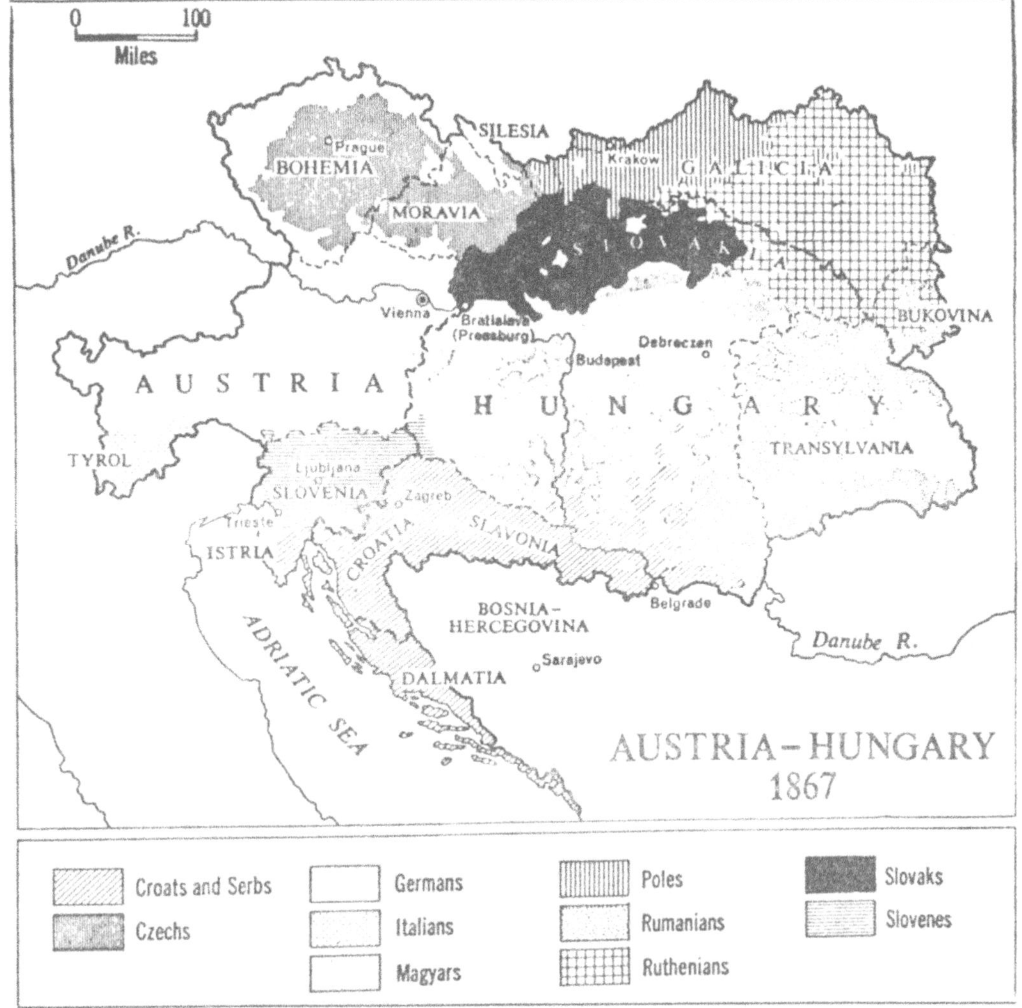

MAP 1. From Charles and Barbara Jelavich, *The Habsburg Monarchy: Toward a Multinational Empire or National States?* (New York, Rinehart, 1959).

ized privileged classes, and restricted to administrative responsibilities. This system changed little from 1815 to 1848. Francis I was a narrow-minded reactionary who set his face against all progress, and advised others to "Hold yourselves to the positive, honor the old ways. The Old is good. I will have no musings." Metternich, encouraged by his ultra anti-nationalist secretary, Friedrich von Gentz, considered autocratic absolutism the best form of government, and Sedlnitzky's enormous spy system prohibited everything considered to be detrimental to morals and religion or hostile to the existing political and social system.

In spite of this (and of the fact that the Slav revivals were usually led by such important and frustrated political aspirants as the Serb Jovan Subotić, the Czech František Palacký, and members of the *literati* like the Croat Ljudevit Gaj), there was some tolerance of non-German cultural and intellectual activity. Vienna at times even encouraged the Slav revival in the hopes that cultural and practical studies would lessen their political aspirations and would be less dangerous than various sorts of pan-Slavism.

Francis was not opposed to the national tongues as long as they were not used to foster discontent. Metternich was an intelligent, cosmopolitan, international "Romanized" German, who was proud of being a patron of the arts and sciences. He was tolerant of non-German culture and language and patronized the Czech literary revival and promoted South Slav Illyrianism. As Srbik records, he was "an advocate of the progress of Slav national and cultural efforts."[4] He would have liked to have continued the intellectual progress promoted by Joseph II (and best exemplified by the famous medical faculty of the Allgemeines Krankenhaus and also by the famous Orientalische Akademie) and to have given Vienna the cultural and intellectual atmosphere of Paris. Unfortunately, neither Leopold II nor Francis I had followed Joseph's example, and Metternich was never able to realize his expectations or Vienna's potential in this respect. Moreover, the sterile bureaucracy and censorship affected him. He was, in the words of Kraehe, an "enlightened, but thwarted reformer."[5]

Kolowrat, of Czech ancestry, was also tolerant of Slavic cultural activities. Prior to coming to Vienna as minister of the interior, he had been the highest burgrave (*Nejvyšší purkraví český*) of Bohemia and had done much to bring about the founding of the Gesellschaft des vaterländischen Museums in Böhmen (see below, p. 24). Even Sedlnitzky (also of Czech extraction) was lenient regarding Slavic cultural activities. A telling example of his attitude in this respect is the paucity of police documents in the Viennese archives regarding Slavic cultural activity.[6] Furthermore, even some of the imperial and royal court contributed financially to the success of these early national societies. In the 1840's, for example, Archdukes Franz Karl and Stephen contributed to the Czech matica.

The slow beginning of the Austro-Slav revivals in the *Vormärz* era can be attributed only in part to the slings and arrows of some outraged German centralists and Magyar chauvinists. As will be shown below, the revivals were impeded in the main by social, cultural, and economic realities: a largely Germanized middle and upper class; a generally suspicious, illiterate, indifferent, and poor lower class; and a time of material hardship, low pay, rising prices, and technological unemployment.

Furthermore, as late as 1825 the Austro-Slavs had no national institutions. Before the founding of the Matica Srbska in 1826, the few institutions to which Austro-Slavs went or looked for education and cultural advancement were the universities in Prague, Vienna, Graz, Pest, Cracow, and Lwów, a few gymnasia or secondary schools, lycea, and Theologenseminaren, the museums in Graz (the Johanneum named after Archduke Johann), and Pest (Budapest only after 1873, Magyar Nemzeti Múseum). There were also the Königlich-böhmische Gesellschaft der Wissenschaften, the K. K. Patriotische-ökonomische Gesellschaft, and the Privatgesellschaft Patriotische Kunstfreude in Prague, the Mährischschlesische Ackerbaugesellschaft in Brno, the Slovene Academia Operosorum (Academy of [Learned] Works) in Ljubljana, the Slovak Erudita Societas Kis-hontensis (Malahont Learned Society) in Nižný Skálnik, and the Polish Towarzystwo Naukowe Krakowskie (Cracow Society of Learning).

These institutions, however, as has been noted above were patriotic at best, certainly not national. Almost the sole exception to these learned-patriotic institutions in the monarchy were a few small Slovak literary societies such as the Protestant Institutum Linguae et Literaturae Slavicae (Institute of Slavic Language and Literature) in Bratislava, and the Catholic Literata Slavica societas (Slavic Literary Society) in Trnava which were slightly national in character.

Elsewhere in the Slavic world there were few such institutions. The Croats, Serbs, Lusatian Serbs, Ruthenians, Ukrainians, and Bulgarians had no important institutions of any kind. In the Russian Empire there was the Imperatorskaia Akademiia Nauk (Imperial Academy of Sciences, founded in 1724 by Peter) and the Imperatorskaia Rossiiskaia Akademiia (Imperial Russian Academy, founded in 1783 by Catherine II) in St. Petersburg, universities in Moscow and Vilna, and the Towarzystwo Przyjaciół Nauk (Society of the Friends of Science) in Warsaw, but these societies had little effect on the Austro-Slavs.

There was a corresponding dearth of journals among the Austro-Slavs. Before the appearance of the Serbian journal, *Ljetopis* (Chronicle) in 1825 there were no national journals and hardly any learned journals among the Austro-Slavs. Four important learned journals—the *Prager gelehrte Nachrichte*, the Moravian *Monatliche Auszüge*, and the Slovak *Annales* and *Staré Noviny Literního Umění* (Old Journal of Literary Arts) had ceased for lack of support by 1803. In 1815 there were only two important learned journals published among the Austro-Slavs—the *Abhandlungen* of the Königlich-böhmische Gesellschaft der Wissenschaften in Prague,

[4] Heinrich Ritter von Srbik, *Metternich: der Staatsmann und der Mensch* (2 v., Munich, 1925–1954) 2: p. 188.

[5] Enno E. Kraehe, ed., *The Metternich Controversy* (New York, 1971), p. 110.

Although mainly concerned with post-1848 intellectual developments, William M. Johnston does discuss briefly the Metternichan period in his *The Austrian Mind: An Intellectual and Social History, 1848–1938* (Berkeley, 1972).

[6] Some documents may have been destroyed in the fire of 1927, but even the various indexes list few references to these societies.

and the *Solennia* (Yearbook) of the Malahont Learned Society by the Slovaks.

Although between 1815 and 1821 three new and important museums were founded—the Gesellschaft des Vaterländischen Museums in Böhmen, in Prague; the Francisceum (named after Francis I) in Brno; and the Landesmuseum im Herzogthume Krain in Ljubljana, not until after the founding of the Matica srbska in 1826 did a new era, an era of national institutions, fostered by the growing number of increasingly nationally minded Slav intellectuals, commence among the Austro-Slavs. From then until 1848–1850 the whole revival was advanced by literary societies of various sorts. Not only did the Czechs, Moravians, Croats, and Ruthenians soon found their own maticas, but there came into being Czech, Croatian, Slovene, and Serbian reading rooms, a Croatian national theater in Zagreb, the Polish Ossolineum (named after Count Ossoliński) in Lwów, the Slovak Tatrín (from Tatra Mountains) in Liptovský Sv. Mikuláš, and the Sub-Carpathian Ruthenian Literaturnoie Zavedeniie Priashovskoie, or Priashiv (Prešov) Literary Institute, and even the Lusatian Maćica Serbska in 1847.

As would be expected there was a corresponding increase of literary and learned journals. In addition to the journals of the various maticas there appeared in the empire, for example, the Serbian *Bačka Vila* (Fairy of Bačka), the Czech *Včela* (Bee), and *Květy* (Flowers), the Croatian *Danica Ilirska* (Illyrian Morning Star), the Slovak *Zora* (Aurora), *Orol Tatranski* (Eagle of the Tatras), and *Slovenskej Pohladi* (Slovak Views), the Slovene *Krajnska Čbelica* (Carniolan Bee), the Polish *Czasopism naukowy* (Journal of Science), and the Galiacian-Ruthenian *Rusalka Dnistrovaia* (Dniester Nymph), an almanac.[7]

So nationalistic in fact did the Austro-Slavs become that in 1848 there were revolutionary movements in Bohemia, Moravia, Galicia, Dalmatia, Croatia, and among the Slovaks, as well as in Hungary, Lower Austria, and Lombardy, against old Austria. Under Czech leadership the first pan-Slav Congress was held in Prague, and a flood of national literature was published throughout the empire. Metternich was forced to flee to England, the young and promising Francis Joseph replaced his weak-minded uncle on the throne, an Act of Emancipation (*Bauernbefreiung*), which relieved the peasants of the vestigial remains of feudalism (especially the *robota* or statutory labor), was passed in principle and a Reichstag (the first and only Austrian imperial diet) was called to sit at Kroměříž (Kremsier) in Moravia to draft a constitution for the empire.

[7] For a detailed and interesting study of "the poetics of periodical names" see William B. Edgerton, "The Poetics of Periodical Names (from Aurora to Zarja)," *To Honor Roman Jakobson: Essays on the Occasion of his Seventieth Birthday* (The Hague, 1967), pp. 594–614.

This revolutionary phase of the "spring of the peoples," however, had no summer. By March, 1849, the conservative new chief minister, Prince Felix Schwarzenberg, crushed the revolutions (except the Magyar which lasted until August) and the Slav Congress; overshadowing the new emperor, he unceremoniously dismissed the Kroměříž Reichstag, and began to restore absolutism. Prague, for example, was placed under a state of siege until 1853. Not even the Croats who had supported Vienna by sending an army against the Magyars, escaped the ensuing harshness of absolutism. All that remained of 1848–1849 was the Act of Emancipation.

A decreed (but not enacted) constitution of March, 1849, began a process of extreme centralization. This was not harsh enough, however, and it was repealed by the *Sylvesterpatent* (New Years' Eve Patent) of December 31, 1851, which insured a rule of German centralism by dividing the empire into seventeen *Kronländer* (without diets) which was to be governed by the emperor through a nominated and weak Reichsrat, an imperial ministry, appointed governors or *Statthalters*, and a vastly enlarged police and spy system.

After the death of Schwarzenberg in April, 1852, Alexander Bach, minister of the interior, functioned as the real head of government. His administration, called "Bach's absolutism," was far more severe than Metternich's. One contemporary characterization of Bach's absolutism is very apt. It said that the empire was maintained by a standing army of soldiers, a sitting army of officials, a kneeling army of priests, and a creeping army of denunciators.

Under Bach's absolutism, especially as a result of his repressive laws regarding the press and societies (*Pressordnung* and *Vereinsgesetz*), all manifestations of political national life were suppressed or stagnant. The four maticas, though severely curtailed, managed to stay alive, but their leaders had to hide their political aspirations under a cultural cloak. Palacký and Gaj, for example, were treated especially harshly and were forced out of positions of leadership. For a while, Gaj was even imprisoned, and Palacký's friends dared visit him only at night. Throughout the decade of Bach's absolutism, the maticas, led by conservatives, were under strict police surveillance and were officially required to reject all kinds of political activity and restrict themselves strictly to the scholarly fostering of language and literature. Even so, the maticas continued to operate and to increase in membership. In fact, because of the general lack of other political and cultural activities, they became through their modest efforts the main representatives of Austro-Slav nationalism at that bleak time. In spite of censorship, a shortage of funds and members, and general fear and apathy, each of them continued to publish books and journals throughout the 1850's. Of the books published, those on Slav history and literature were the most effective in keeping alive the sparks of the revival.

Fortunately, Bach's absolutism did not last long. As a result of the defeat of Austria by Italian and French troops during the Austro-Italian war, especially at the decisive battle of Solferino in June, 1859, Francis Joseph ended absolutism. In an effort to strengthen the empire he dismissed Bach and formed a new imperial cabinet under the leadership of a conservative Pole, Count Agenor von Gołuchowski, who initiated a series of halting steps towards liberalism or constitutionalism. He drafted the so-called *Oktoberdiplom* of 1860 which was a kind of a federal constitution. It called for a real Reichsrat of constitutionally limited powers, reconstituted and elected *Landtage*, and wide autonomy for the *Länder*. This promising beginning, however, lasted less than twelve weeks and Francis Joseph, giving in to German pressure, dismissed Gołuchowski and scrapped the October Diploma.

The new chief minister was Anton von Schmerling, an advocate of moderate centralism which he tried to conceal under a cloak of liberal phrases. His contribution to constitutional experimentation was the *Februarpatent* of 1861, which emphasized the unitary character of the empire and preponderant German influence. Both the Reichsrat and the reconstituted *Landtage* (presided over by nominated governors) were controlled by a special electoral system, often called *Wahlgeometrie* or electoral geometry, which assured control to the wealthy and the German elements. Even this limited form of constitutionalism, however, greatly improved the general political and cultural conditions of the Austro-Slavs. Political life revived in the provinces and nationalism began to flourish again. After this new beginning the national revivals of most of the Austro-Slavs continued to grow in strength and effectiveness culturally and politically throughout the rest of the nineteenth century to 1914.[8]

Since many new national activities of all kinds were quickly organized it at first seems paradoxical that the first four maticas which so successfully had pioneered the national revival under adverse conditions did not experience renewed and sustained growth and activity after 1860, but rather declined and became simply publishing houses. Though surprising, this development is easily explained. First, the maticas had been seriously weakened by Bach's absolutism. Second, after 1860 there were so many real political opportunities and freedoms for Slav patriots that they did not have to rely so much on previous cultural substitutes for political activity. This was characteristic of the whole Austro-Slav national revival; as soon as new political tools became available, the old cultural tools were no longer considered so nationally important.[9] Third, after 1860 many new national societies and institutions such as the Srbsko Učeno Društvo (Serbian Learned Society), the Czech Umělecká Beseda (Artists' Union), the Hrvatska Akademija (Croatian Academy), the Galician-Ruthenian Prosvita (Enlightenment), the Bukovina-Ruthenian Ruskaia Beseda (literally, Russian Conversation), and some popular publishing houses such as the Czech Matica Lidů (Peoples Foundation) and the Croatian Društvo sv. Jeronima (St. Jerome Society) were organized (*cf.* the Bulgarian Učeno Družestvo (Bulgarian Learned Society), 1850). Most of these new national societies drew away members and financial support from the maticas and, in some instances, took over and specialized in one or other activity of the maticas.

Although the first four maticas declined after 1860, two new ones were founded. In 1863 and 1864 the Slovaks and the Slovenes founded their maticas, both of which immediately became the most important national institutions among these peoples.

The final major constitutional change which affected the maticas during the time period covered in this study was the *Ausgleich* or compromise between Austria and Hungary in 1867. The *Ausgleich*, the result of continued Magyar intransigence and demands for their historic privileges and rights of the Crown of St. Stephen, and the ignominious defeat of Austria by Prussia during the Seven Weeks War of 1866, caused Francis Joseph to come to terms with the Magyars in the hopes of strengthening Austria for a war of revenge against Bismarck. Count Richard Belcredi, who succeeded Schmerling in 1865, laid the foundation for the compromise, which was actually effected by Count Friedrich von Beust, who became chancellor in February, 1867.

The *Ausgleich* established a dual system with Francis Joseph as emperor in Austria and king in Hungary, and restored Hungary's freedom under very favorable circumstances, making her an independent kingdom with her own diet, constitution,

[8] After 1867, however, Magyar chauvinism crushed the Slovak revival, hastened the shift of the center of the Serbian revival from Novi Sad in Hungary to Beograd in the Principality, and curtailed the Croatian revival.

[9] During the revolutionary period of 1848–1849, for example, the various maticas accomplished very little. Many of their leaders, who were as politically as culturally minded, eagerly seized this opportunity to pour their energies into real political activity.

Perhaps a "law" (or at least a trend) of the Austro-Slav national revival may be formulated: During the Austro-Slav national revival of the first two-thirds of the nineteenth century there is a direct and inverse relationship between new political freedom and old cultural activity. As will be shown below, almost all early national-cultural activities were also substitutes for forbidden political activity. Therefore, when political activity was freer the older cultural activities were generally neglected. This trend, however, did not affect new cultural activity, for, as will also be shown below, the comparative freedom of the 1860's brought many new national and cultural societies into being.

and government. Except for the common ministries of Foreign Affairs, War, and Finance the two halves of the empire were independent.

The *Ausgleich* was a great boon to the historic Magyar nobility who since their defeat by the Turks at Mohâcs in 1526 had been agitating and fighting for their rights and privileges against the Turks and, after the Habsburgs conquered Hungary from the Turks during the late eighteenth century, against the Germans. Since the Peace of Szatmâr in 1711, the Magyar nobility had enjoyed a diet in Pozsony (Bratislava, Pressburg), a constitution, their own chancellery in Vienna, and many of their antiquated privileges, especially Magyar control of local affairs through their *comitates* or county councils. By 1825 they had, furthermore, founded a national museum and an academy, and were taking steps to make Magyar the official and national tongue in place of German or Latin. Unfortunately Magyar nationalism was almost always anti-Slav and thus the Serbs, Croats, and Slovaks not only had to contend with German centralism, but with xenophobic local Magyar officials as well.

This political and geographic division left the Czechs, Moravians, Slovenes, Poles, and the Galician Ruthenians in Austria and the Slovaks, Croats, Serbs, and some Ruthenians (in the Bukovina and Sub-Carpathian Hungary) in Hungary. With the advent of the *Ausgleich,* two separate policies toward the Slavs in the empire must be followed—the Austro-German and the Magyar.

The greatest changes this compromise made in the Austrian half were incorporated in the *Grundgesetze* or fundamental laws of December 21, 1867. These laws, which remained in force until the end of the empire, retained the structure of an emperor and Reichsrat in Vienna with appointed governors in the *Länder* and *Landtage* presided over by *Landmarschälle.*

The fundamental laws also guaranteed equality before the law and in public service, freedom of press, speech, and assembly, and the inalienable rights of all peoples of the Austrian half to the preservation and cultivation of its nationality and language. Although these laws were not always enforced, national, political, and cultural-national advancement continued to increase in Austria, especially under the short pro-Slav ministry of Count Karl Hohenwarth (1871) and the long ministry of Count Edward Taaffe (1879–1893), who followed the policy of moderate Slav appeasement. Even so the nationality problem was never solved and the Slavs in both Austria and Hungary entered World War I greatly frustrated by their lack of autonomy. Austrian internal policy from 1860 to 1918 has been well characterized by May as confused parliamentarianism versus awakening nationalism.[10]

In Hungary, under the guidance of the enlightened prime minister of Hungary (1867–1871), Count Gyula Andrâssy, a progressive nationality law of 1868 was adopted which promised far-reaching privileges to the non-Magyar minorities. Unfortunately, this law remained largely a dead letter to which the Slavs appealed in vain as their rights were continuously curtailed and infringed by Magyar chauvinists. After 1871, as a result of the death of such moderate leaders as Baron József Eötvös (minister of education, 1867–1871), the near retirement of Ferencz Deák (leader of the Liberal Reform Party), and the transfer of Andrâssy to Vienna to become minister of foreign affairs, the proponents of ruthless Magyarization came to power. According to Sinor, "Blind nationalism alone survived, narrow, stupid, and corrupt." [11] Following an unstable interregnum of several weak cabinets, Kálmán Tisza, a Slavophobe, became prime minister and for sixteen years (1875–1890) waged a ceaseless campaign against the minorities.

As a result both the Slovak and the Hungarian-Serb national movements nearly died out. The Croatian national movement, however, was at first relatively unaffected. The Magyars, in deference to Croatia's traditional rights, which rested on the disputed terms of the union of Hungary and Croatia in 1102, effected their own compromise or *Nagodba* with the Croats, granting the latter some restricted autonomy. They were to be ruled by a *ban* (governor), appointed by Budapest, but responsible to the Croatian sabor (diet) which would be generally autonomous in four areas—education, religion, internal administration, and judicial affairs. Croatian became the sole official language and was permitted in the joint diet in Budapest (when common affairs were discussed) to which the Croats sent about forty delegates.

The resulting decline of the importance of the Croatian matica after 1867 was more a result of new institutions (such as the Croatian Academy) and political opportunities than of Magyar oppression, which did not become severe until 1880 when a Magyar chauvinist, Khuen Héderváry, became *ban* for twenty years. After 1880 the Croatian national movement, while never as dormant as the Slovak or Hungarian-Serb, declined.

After the maticas passed the peak of their influence and importance, they all (with the exception of the Slovak matica which the Magyars closed in 1875) continued into the twentieth century as quiet publishers of books and journals. After 1918 they were all reorganized and again began to play an

[10] Arthur J. May, *The Hapsburg Monarchy: 1867–1914* (Cambridge, Mass., 1951), p. 434.

[11] Denis Sinor, *History of Hungary* (New York, 1959), p. 275.

important role in the cultural development of their people. With the exception of the Czech matica they are still active and important today.

II. THE SERBIAN MATICA, 1826: THE ELDEST SISTER AND PROTOTYPE

The reason for this organization is solely love and zeal for the general welfare; and the purpose is the dissemination of literature and enlightenment to the Serbian nation, which is to publish original and pious Serbian books now and in the future without end.

From the original constitution.

At the time of the Serbian national awakening in the early nineteenth century the Serbs were under four different administrations—the Austrian (especially in the Vojvodina [Duchy] of southern Hungary), the Turkish in Bosnia, their own prince-bishops in Montenegro, and the semiautonomous supreme *knez* or prince of the Belgrad *pashalik*. Three of these groups—those in Bosnia, Montenegro, and the *pashalik*—made at first little contribution to the Serbian awakening.[1] Centuries of Turkish domination had made the Serbs in Bosnia and Montenegro nationally inert, while those of the *pashalik* poured their energies into a struggle with the Turks for full autonomy.

It was left to the Serbs in the Vojvodina, the "cradle of Serb nationalism," with their schools, presses, and intellectuals under the relatively enlightened and tolerant rule of the Habsburgs to save the Serbs in general from ignorance and cultural and national extinction as the other three groups of Serbs had sought (and were still seeking) to save them from political and military destruction.

One of the most important acts of the Serbs in the Vojvodina for the purpose of advancing their cultural-national rebirth was the founding in 1825 in Novi Sad (Neusatz, Ujvidék) of the literary-scholarly journal called *Ljetopis* (Chronicle), the first such journal among the Austro-Slavs. Although a small and modest publication, it soon led to the establishing of the most significant Serbian national institution (and in fact the first national institution of all the Austro-Slavs of the nineteenth century), the Matica Srbska in Pest in 1826.[2] This event also initiated a movement which led to the founding of similar institutions among all the Austro-Slavs.

By 1825 there had been a large Serbian minority in southern Hungary for at least 135 years. During the latter part of the seventeenth century Leopold I, wishing to colonize and rebuild southern Hungary, which had been devastated and almost depopulated by the Turkish wars, began to invite Serbian colonists from the Turkish-occupied Balkans to settle there.

In April, 1690, he issued his famous proclamation to the Christians of the Balkan peninsula offering them protection, religious freedom, and the privilege of electing their own *Vojvody* (dukes). Seeing in Leopold's proclamation an opportunity to recoup some of their political and national rights denied them by the Turks, Patriarch Arsenije Crnojevic of Ipek (Peć) led about 30,000 Serbs across the Danube and settled in the area of southern Hungary between the Theiss and Danube rivers where other Serbs from Turkey had previously settled. There they developed a lively cultural, political, and religious center which was (as a result of their Byzantine Orthodox religious and cultural background and their patriarchal and agrarian social structure) somewhat alien to the surrounding area. Numerically, at least, the colonies in the monarchy flourished. By 1850, there were more Serbs (1,000,000) in Austria than in Serbia proper (956,893).

Many of Leopold's promises, unfortunately, were not fulfilled. In the southern Hungarian part of the monarchy the Serbs did obtain full recognition of their religious rights, but their political and national rights were forgotten and ignored, and they slowly fell under the control of the Magyars, who, as a result of the extensive privileges they won from Charles VI in the early eighteenth century, had become the dominant people in the Vojvodina. After 1825, the successful Magyar national movement became, in spite of the views of enlightened liberals such as Count István Széchenyi, increasingly intolerant of non-Magyars. As Stavrianos points out, however, "The Serbs counterbalanced this setback with notable economic gains in the eighteenth and early nineteenth centuries. Commerce expanded rapidly during those decades and the Serbs took advantage of the opportunity to gain control of most of the trade of southern Hungary." [3]

Since centuries of warfare with and suppression by the Turks had denuded the Serbs of most of their native nobility and since the lower classes were culturally and nationally inert, it was these well-to-do middle-class Serb businessmen, cattle and hog breeders, and a few intellectuals, clergymen, and professional men in the Vojvodina who played the most important role at the time of the reawakening.

Not only did the wealthy Serbian middle classes have money to help finance the cultural rebirth, but they also had, through their business dealings, close contact with Western culture. In commenting upon this, Jaroslav Bidlo has written, "Of all the Slav

[1] The medieval Serbian state, founded by Stefan Nemanja in the twelfth century, had been defunct for over two hundred years. Its demise began with the defeat of the Serbs by the Turks on the plain of Kosovo in 1389. By 1463 Serbia had become a mere *pashalik* in the Ottoman Empire and what little Serbian national feeling existed was kept alive by the Orthodox clergy, with headquarters at the Patriarchate at Ipek (Peć) which had been founded in 1557.

[2] In Serbian it was "srbska" to 1869, thereafter, "srpska."

[3] L. S. Stavrianos, *The Balkans since 1453* (New York, 1958), p. 235.

peoples, the Serbs in Habsburg lands matured first to their cultural rebirth. The wealthy classes (businessmen, hog and cattlebreeders) came into close contact with western culture, convincing themselves (already in the middle of the eighteenth century) that only through culture could they be supported effectively in their political struggle with the Magyars and Vienna. Their struggle centered at that time above all in their schools and publishing houses." [4] Bidlo was referring, apparently, especially to the two Serbian gymnasia in Sremski Karlovci (Karlowitz Karlóca) (founded 1791) and in Novi Sad (founded 1810), the chief cultural centers of the Vojvodina Serbs, and to the Matica Srbska of Pest (which later moved to Novi Sad).

The first important step taken in the Serbian rebirth was the founding of a journal—*Ljetopis*—in 1825 in Novi Sad. This event was the result of several factors, including the mildly tolerant attitude of Vienna regarding cultural activities, the existence of European models such as the German *Blätter für litterarische Unterhaltung*, founded in Weimar in 1818, and the coming together of three savants in Novi Sad—Lukijan Musıčki (1777–1837), a distinguished monk and writer and the most cultivated Serb of his time; Georgije Magarašević (1793–1830), a writer and professor at the Serbian gymnasium in Novi Sad; and the famous Slovak, Pavel Josef Šafařík (1795–1861), who since 1818 had been the director of the gymnasium.[5] They had determined that the best course of action to awaken the masses nationally, to foster Serbian national and cultural life, to promote the Serbian (as well as other Slavic) languages and literature, and to strengthen Slavic mutuality, would be to do what had already been done in Western Europe—to found a literary-scholarly journal. This journal was to be dedicated to Slavic, especially Serbian, history and national tradition and was to be instructional as well as scholarly. In the preface to the first issue of *Ljetopis* Magarašević stressed the early pan-Slavic orientation of the publication by announcing that it would "be concerned with everything that pertained to the Slavs from the Adriatic to the White Sea, and from the Baltic to the Black . . . ."

At the time of the founding of *Ljetopis* Serbian culture, though not supressed by Vienna was, nevertheless, on the verge of extinction in Hungary. What little cultural life that existed was provided mainly by the conservative Orthodox church. The Serbs had no newspaper, theater, journal, or cultural or national institutions, and very little national consciousness. The literary situation was particularly poor. In neither of their two cultural centers of Novi Sad and Karlovci, for example, was there a Cyrillic printing press; there were in fact only two in the whole empire, one in Vienna and one at the University of Pest. Few books were in circulation and readers were few. Most book sellers and publishers would not risk the cash outlay to publish for so limited a market. Among the people there was insufficient wealth and interest to support literature and culture in general. There was also the vexing question of the proper Serbian literary language—was it to be the old, conservative Slavo-Serb, or Church Russian, or the new reformed language advocated by Obradović and Karadžić (see below pp. 14, 16).

Furthermore, there were only a few intellectuals, who for the most part were either connected with the Orthodox church, living in Pest, or with the gymnasia in Karlovci and Novi Sad, which since the Serbs had no other institutions of higher learning, played a very important role in the Serbian rebirth.

The first few issues of *Ljetopis*, edited by Magarašević, were printed only because of the enthusiasm of the triumvirate of savants who founded it and the generosity of a Novi Sad book seller who assumed the financial risk, for in the beginning it only had about hundred subscribers. Since the authorities would not permit a Cyrillic press to operate in the Vojvodina, *Ljetopis* had to be printed at the University of Pest.

At first *Ljetopis* appeared as a quarterly, later semi-annually, and still later as an annual. It was not only one of the earliest such Slavic publications, antedating the Czech *Časopis Českého Musea* (Journal of the Bohemian Museum) of 1827 and the Polish *Czasopism Naukowy* (Journal of Science) of the Ossolineum in Lwów of 1828, but is today the oldest continually published journal of the former Austro-Slavs. It was a typical miscellany, carrying articles about Serbian history, language, and literature, bibliographies, necrologies, biographies, genealogies, maps, announcements, membership lists, and such materials. After five issues, however, it became apparent that there was not yet sufficient interest or audience among the Serbs to enable such a venture to be self-supporting. Its editors and publishers found themselves in the awkward position of needing the support of a body of people which did not yet exist—a sufficiently numerous group of the nationally conscious. They required the backing of a group they were trying to bring into existence. This, of course, was an almost impossible position. By the third issue it became obvious that *Ljetopis* would have to have financial support from outside Novi Sad and the immediate area.

[4] Jaroslav Bidlo, "Historický Vývoj Slovanstva," *Slovanstvo*, ed. by Jaroslav Bidlo *et al.* (Prague, 1912), p. 85.

[5] Since the middle of the seventeenth century Slovaks had been trying to better themselves by moving down into southern Hungary. By the time of Šafařík's arrival there were about 15,000 Slovak Protestants living in ten or twelve communities in the Vojvodina.

1826–1835

Fortunately this help came quickly through the efforts of a nationally minded lawyer in Pest named Jovan Hadžić (1799–1869). (Hadžić is also well known by his pen name, Miloš Svetić, and is, therefore, often referred to as Jovan Hadžić-Svetić.) He may have learned of the straightened conditions of *Ljetopis* through his relatives in Novi Sad or from his friend Magaraševič. In any event he took quick and decisive action to save it. He was familiar with and influenced by The Magyar Academy, newly founded by Count István Széchenyi in 1825, with its aim of fostering the Magyar languages,[6] and he apparently considered the existence of *Ljetopis* an opportunity to found some sort of similar society with a like aim for the Serbs.

Hadžić-Svetić, with modest financial backing of 700 florins from a group of six young Serb businessmen in Pest, organized in 1826 a literary-scholarly and national society called the Matica Srbska. Among those that served with him were several of his businessmen backers—Josif Milovuk, Jovan Demetrović, Gavrilo Bozitovac, and Djordj Stanković.[7]

The aim of this small group was not only to take over the publication and support of *Ljetopis* and the program of its founders, but also to publish books (especially the works of Serbian authors) in cheap editions so that the young and the poor could afford them and thereby help combat backwardness and illiteracy. Furthermore, they hoped to discover and encourage new and young authors by offering prizes. Later they founded a library, administered trusts, provided stipends to students, and collected items for a museum.

The by-laws of the new organization were prepared by Hadžić-Svetić, who based them somewhat on those of the Magyar Academy. He also served as the first president. The matica was organized as a society, the members of which contributed a minimum of 40fl. and received copies of the publications of the matica. In this way it became a company the dividends of which were its own publications. It grew slowly at first, gaining only twenty-one members in two years. During the following two years no one at all joined, and at the end of its first ten years it had a total membership of only about fifty members who were mainly from the upper middle classes—certainly a modest beginning for a society which was to become the prototype for all other Austro-Slavs. As modest as it was, however, it soon became and remained for decades the most important cultural institution of all the Serbs in and out of Hungary.

There were several good reasons for this slow and humble beginning and success of the Serbian matica. The chief one, of course, was its dependency upon that which it was trying to create—a nationally conscious public and a coterie of individuals who would and could support such a venture. In commenting on the initial slow growth of the matica, Šafařík wrote to his friend, Ján Kollár, "There are few members of the gentry among the Serbs. To accomplish something alone in Novi Sad is impossible. Other than a few merchants everything is rustic and wild." [8]

The leaders of the matica were also rather conservative businessmen and intellectuals, not especially representative of the masses. One example of this conservatism is that the matica clung to the old-fashioned and artificial Slavo-Serb language which was favored by the Orthodox clergy and considered sacrosanct and characteristic of "Serbianism." It also reflected the Russophilism of these men, who like many other Slavs of the early nineteenth century expected great things from Russia. Such adherance, however, caused the matica to take an unfortunate position against both the literary reforms of Vuk Stefanović Karadžić (1789–1864); the founder of the modern Serb literary language and the most prolific and influential Serbian writer of the nineteenth century[9] and the Croatian inspired "Illyrian" move-

[6] The necessary action to organize the Magyar Academy was taken during the Hungarian Diet of 1825. This, the first Diet since the end of the Napoleonic wars, convened in Bratislava in September. On the following October 25 Széchenyi, the first member of a Diet to depart from the traditional use of Latin, made a speech in Magyar (partly because his Latin was inadequate). On November 3 the subject of the Magyar tongue was brought up and the establishment of an academy urged. Count István Széchenyi, familiar with such institutions as a result of his extensive travels in Western Europe, made the suggestion a reality by offering a year's income of 60,000fl. to help found it. In so doing he emulated his father, Count Ferencz Széchenyi, who had founded the Magyar National Museum (Magyar Nemzeti Múzeum) in 1802.

Soon contributions by others, including Counts Károlyi and Andrássy, brought the total to 154,000fl. The goal of this new Magyar Academy of Science (Magyar Tudos Torsasay) was stated by Széchenyi: "To promote the sciences and arts in the language of the country; thereby the language becomes more magnificent and expressive, and the national spirit, strengthened by noble and useful knowledge, will live in brightness forever." Francis Wagner, "Széchenyi and the Nationality Problem in the Habsburg Empire," *Jour. Central European Affairs* 20 (Oct., 1960): p. 294.

[7] The earliest extant police report regarding any of the maticas is one dated Vienna, September 5, 1827, which refers to the Serbian matica. This short document, a quarter of which was destroyed during the fire in the Verwaltungsarchiv in Vienna in 1927, is almost unreadable, but the gist of it is a statement about the help received by "Magarasevitz" from a "Johann Hadschitz" and several others connected with the publication of *Ljetopis* through organization of the "Maticza" and a question about the validity of this society and its authorization. Allgemeines Verwaltungsarchiv, Polizei-Hofstelle, 184/1827.

[8] Jaroslav Vlček, *Pavel Jos. Šafařík* (Prague, 1896), p. 63.

[9] While at the university in Vienna, Karadžić, urged by the great Slovene philologist, Jernej Kopitar, began to collect and edit Serbian folk songs, stories, and ballads as Bishop Thomas Percy, James Macpherson, J. G. Herder, and the Grimm brothers had done previously in England and Germany. His

ment (see below, chap. V). There was also the relatively neglected condition of Serbian letters and general indifference to literature. Membership in the matica was, furthermore, too expensive for most Serbs. Finally there was the opposition of the Magyars, who resented its existence and continually tried to curtail its activities. In reference to this Magyar opposition Šafařík reported to Kollár.

Troubles are developing over the matica and *Ljetopis*. I will tell you about it. Someone in Vienna has charged that the matica is against the government. So far nothing official has come from Vienna to the archbishop, but an agent has already reported everything to him. The archbishop immediately ordered a secret "inquisition" (although I know all about it). Magaraševič has been forbidden to publish *Ljetopis* or anything else without the archbishop's permission or be sentenced to prison.[10] About two weeks later Šafařík reported to Kollár that, "The archbishop is just waiting for an opportunity to curtail this beginning of national literature and culture." [11]

In spite of this unpromising beginning (and even its temporary suppression by the Magyars in 1835), the leaders of the matica had sufficient confidence in themselves and in their society to enable them to build the matica slowly into a real power in the Serbian national awakening.

The first activity of the newly founded society was to assume the direction, editing, and publishing of *Ljetopis*. Freed now from financial worries, Magaraševič continued to edit *Ljetopis* until he died in 1830. Under his editorship the journal offered a wide variety of useful and interesting articles and contributions. A breakdown of the contents of the first fifteen issues includes the following quantity and types of materials: 26 articles on Serbian history and biography, 17 on history, 9 on biography, 144 articles on literature, 52 poems by Serbians, 19 articles on Slavic literature, 14 articles on Serbian literature, 12 prose works by Serbian authors, 47 translations from classical authors, 79 miscellaneous reviews and reports on literature and literary activities.[12] Other than the evidence of pan-Slav interests (which would later cause trouble) there is nothing surprising or unusual about this breakdown. It simply provides a good idea of what this early prototype of many other Slavic literary-scholarly journals was like. Basically it offered its readers scholarly, literary, and useful information, especially on Serbian history and literature. The most important contributors were Mušicki, Hadžić-Svetić, and the physician, Jovan Steić. The classical authors most translated were Horace, Virgil, Seneca, and Cicero. The biographies were, of course, of important Serbs such as their twelfth-century ruler, Stefan Nemanja.

Considerable interest was manifested in the other Slavs. Šafařík, who himself was much interested in Slavic mutuality, had earlier written to Kollár, "The Serbs are the most Slavic-minded of all Slavs." [13] Six of the nineteen articles on Slavic literature, for example, concerned Russia. Among the reviews and reports on literature and literary activity the Czechs and Slovaks were best represented. In this category were articles on the works of Dobrovský, Jungmann, Bernolák, Kollár, Šafařík, Herkel, and Čelakovský. There was also material on the Russian Pogodin, and the Pole Mickiewicz, the Czech *Časopis*, the Polish *Czasopism Naukowy*, and the German *Blätter für Literarische Unterhaltung*. Among the miscellaneous items (*smesice*) were official announcements, correspondence, and useful information about the number and location of other Slavic peoples, Serbian monasteries, schools, and lawyers.

While Magaraševič had not been completely committed to the Slavo-Serb language and favored a more liberal attitude on the language question, after his death in 1830 the conservative Hadžić-Svetić took over the editorship of *Ljetopis* in addition to his duties as president, whereupon *Ljetopis* became and remained for many years the voice of conservative Serbian nationals and of a few well-known, but not great, Serbian authors. Šafařík, who had never been happy in Novi Sad, called the matica a " 'merchants society' which printed books without consideration for the needs of the masses." [14]

After seeing six issues through the press, Hadžić-Svetić found his task as president and editor too demanding.[15] So he turned *Ljetopis* over to the priest and writer Pavel Stamatović (1805–1864). After only two issues, however, Stamatović gave up

first publication was *Mala Prostonarodna Slavenosrpska Pjesmarica* (1814).

Along with his collecting and editing he tried to elevate the vernacular of his people to the position of a literary language to supersede the conventional Slavo-Serb. He introduced phonetic reforms into the Cyrillic alphabet and insisted that the language be written as it is spoken. His first grammar appeared in 1814 and his more important dictionary (*Srpski Riječnik*) came out four years later.

Unfortunately his reforms were bitterly resisted by many Serbs, especially the old and the conservative. Hadžić-Svetić in particular was against the reforms of Karadžić and used his position as president of the matica to make this society the center of opposition to Karadžić until the latter's ideas finally triumphed in the 1860's in spite of the opposition of the matica and others.

[10] Jos. Hanuš, *Pavel Josef Šafařík v Živote i Spisich* (Prague, 1895), pp. 88–89.

[11] *Ibid.*, p. 89.

[12] From a study of the first fifteen issues of *Ljetopis*.

[13] Hanuš, *P. J. Šafařík v život i spisich*, p. 44.

[14] Karel Paul, *Pavel Josef Šafařík: Život a Dilo* (Prague, 1961), p. 92.

[15] During that same year Hadžić-Svetić had also assumed the directorship of the gymnasium in Novi Sad, following the dismissal of Šafařík, a Protestant, by ultra-conservative Orthodox school officials.

Ljetopis and was succeeded in 1832 by Teodor Pavlović (1804–1854), a young lawyer in Pest who had been called in to assist Hadžić-Svetić with the work. He became the first secretary of the matica as well as editor of *Ljetopis*. He was five years younger than Hadžić-Svetić and had somewhat more liberal ideas about what the matica should be and about its policies. He was also the first editor to stay with the job for very long—for ten years, until 1841.[16]

During its first decade the matica gained sixty members and published thirty-nine issues of *Ljetopis* and eighteen other items most of which reflected the aims of its leaders—to foster national consciousness and to advance education among the masses.

The most important of the nationalistic publications were good examples of the spirit of early nineteenth-century Serbian literature—a strong feeling for Serbdom, love of their past, pride in their medieval state, and a fanatic hatred of the Turks.[17] The first of such works, published in 1827, was *Kassia Carica* (Empress Kassia) by Milovan Vidaković (1780–1841), a professor at the Novi Sad gymnasium. This highly nationalistic and romantic novel, based loosely on Serbian history, had little artistic merit. It was entirely popular and appealed to the unsophisticated masses and encouraged them to read Serbian literature. A similar work published that same year—*Svetislav i Mileva* (Svetislav and Mileva), a drama by Jovan Sterija Popović (1806–1856), the most important Serbian playwright of that period.[18] The following year his novel *Boj na Kosovo* (Battle of Kosovo) appeared. This drama was the first of several publications about this Turkish victory of 1389 which ended the medieval Serbian Empire. The following year the matica published *Car Lazar* (Czar Lazar I), a verse tragedy by the poet and playwright Isidor Nikolič. It was based on the life of Lazar I, a fourteenth-century Prince of Serbia, his war against the Turks, and his defeat and death on the Plain of Kosovo. In 1839 they published Theodor Petronović's *Kosovski Boj* (Battle of Kosovo) to commemorate the 450th anniversary of the event.

The most important of the instructional works were two volumes of the writings of Dositej Obradović (1742–1811), the "Father of Serbian Education." Obradović was a minor *Philosophe*, the best representative of the Enlightenment among the Serbs, and one of the most influential Serbian writers of his period. He anticipated the language reforms of Karadžić by writing in the popular idiom and strove to promote literature and education among the masses. The two volumes, both edited by Magarašević, were *Pisma Dositea* (Writings of Dositej) and *Duch Spisanija Dositea* (Spirit of the Writings of Dositej). Two other instructional works appeared during this period—Magarašević's *Kratka Vsemirna Istoria* (Short Universal History), and Jovan Steić's *Ogledi umne Nauke* (Survey of Science).[19]

Such was the beginning of the Matica Srbska, the modesty of which completely belies its real significance not only among the Serbs, but among the Austro-Slavs. The Magyars, always suspicious of their minorities and fearful of any step toward their unification, suppressed it in 1835 because of its alleged pan-Slav tendencies. According to Popović, the only evidence of such tendencies was the receipt of a single letter from Moravia.[20] This was not the whole story, however. Budapest was also disturbed over the number of articles which had appeared in *Ljetopis* about Russian literature, museums, Serbo-Russian unity, and even the theory that Russian and Serbian were the same language. Furthermore Hadžić-Svetić had never even asked for, let alone received, official permission from Vienna to organize. It is possible also that the founding of the Matice Česká in 1831 might have caused the Magyars to fear similar movements among the Croats and the Slovaks. In any event, the Serbian matica was dissolved. The charge of pan-Slav tendencies in 1835 may be the first example of that convenient all-purpose charge which the Magyars used to hinder Slavic nationalism for the rest of the century.

[16] Pavlović was a capable editor and through his office he hoped to overcome indifference to literature, to help solve the question of orthography and language reforms and the resulting quarrels and contention among the Serbs. While he was editor and secretary the first prizes and awards were offered in 1834 for original Serbian manuscripts—50fl. for the best drama, 20fl. for the best poem, 20fl. for the best prose contribution, and 10fl. for the best translation into Serbian. The contest was a total failure. Not only were no awards made, not even one manuscript was submitted. Furthermore, when Pavlović appealed for original or translated manuscripts to be printed in *Ljetopis*, not one Serbian writer responded—ample evidence of the neglected condition of Serbian letters, and of the maticas lack of stature. It also probably reflects the results of the conservative stand the matica took regarding literary reforms.

[17] Most references to the publications of the matica have been taken from the official *Bibliografija Izdanja Matica Srpska, 1826–1949* (Novi Sad, 1950).

[18] Popović later moved to Beograd, where he became head of a government ministry and founded the Serb National Theater in 1841 and the Družstvo Srpske Slovesnosti (Serbian Grammatical Society) in 1842, which became a strong competitor of the matica and eventually in 1886 became the Royal Serbian Academy of Science and Art.

[19] They also published the following translations: Voltaire's philosophical tale, *Zadig*; I. F. Jinger's *Odlazek iz Trsta* (Departure from Trieste), Kotzebue's drama *Žertva na Smert* (Sacrifice unto Death), Archbishop Janos Imre's *Mladi Mudrac iz Madžrske* (Young Philosopher from Hungary), and Konstantin Popović-Komoraš's reworking of Kotzebue's tragedy *Die Spanier in Peru*, which was retitled *Turci u Bosni ili smrt Miloša žalostna* (Turks In Bosnia or the Sad Death of Miloš).

[20] Dušan Popović, *Srbi u Vojvodini, 1790–1861* (Novi Sad, 1963), p. 164.

1836–1849

For two years after the dissolution Pavlović worked to convince the Magyar authorities that the matica posed no pan-Slav threat. Finally, the matica's constitution was approved and in December, 1836, the society was permitted to reorganize and recommence the publication of *Ljetopis* (which thereafter dropped its pan-Slav orientation).

After this experience Pavlović realized that what the matica needed quickly and most importantly was more members, especially some wealthy and influential ones. During 1837 he induced fifty-one individuals to join—mainly from the ranks of scholars, wealthy officials, and businessmen—bringing the total membership to 101. Of these new members the most important was the great patriot and wealthy landowner, Sava Tekelija.

Tekelija (Tökeli, Tekeli, Tököly, 1761–1842), as a result of his study of law and philosophy in Vienna, had long been concerned with the problem of higher education of young Serbs. He had, for example, in 1810 set up a fund of 10,000fl. to support Serb students at the Military Academy in Vienna. He succeeded Hadžić-Svetić as president of the matica in 1837 when the latter moved to Beograd to serve as a legal adviser to Prince Miloš.[21] One of Tekelija's first official acts was to assume personally the pressing financial obligations of the matica by providing office space and paying the salaries of the secretary (200fl.) and the editor of *Ljetopis* (500fl.). Of equal importance was his broader concept of what the matica ought to be. He conceived of it more as a learned society or academy than as a simple book-publishing and distributing society. Unfortunately, he died too soon, 1842, to realize much of this concept, but during his five years as president the matica did expand and improve considerably.

In 1838 he made his greatest contribution to the matica and to the Serbian awakening. He set up a fund of 100,000fl. plus land and houses in Pest and Arad, to be administered by the matica for the education of poor Serbian students at the University in Pest. In addition to this fund, which initially supported about twenty stipendiaries, he bought a building in Pest as a home for the students and for the matica and its editorial offices. This building was soon dubbed "the Tekelijanum."

The innovation of the Tekelija Fund instituted a type of activity which soon became one of the chief characteristics of the matica and which for a time overshadowed its publishing activities. A second fund of 5,000fl. was set up by a wealthy patriot, Jovan Nako, in 1855, the income of which was to be used to award prizes for literature. By 1864 the matica was administering four such funds and during the 1870's fifteen of them.

Aside from administering the Tekelija and Nako funds, the activities of the matica for the next thirteen years (through 1850) consisted almost solely of publishing. During this period the matica printed sixty items—forty-one issues of *Ljetopis*, nine official publications, and ten works of Serbian polite literature.

Ljetopis was by now established as a quarterly and, because it had only two editors during this period, was much more stable. Pavlović remained as editor until he died in 1841. He was succeeded by Jovan Subotić for the period 1842–1853. The journal improved considerably under Subotić (1817–1886), an important lawyer and author, especially in the field of literary criticism, and the first politically important person connected with the matica.

Of the original works published the most important were by Subotić, Mušicki, and Nikolić. Three works of Subotić were published: a collection of poems, *Lyra*, in 1837; his *Nauka o Srbskom Stihotvorstvu* (Study of Serb Versification) in 1845, and finally his epic poem, *Kralj Dečanski* (King Dečanski or Stefan Uroš, 1275–1321, one of Serbia's medieval rulers) in 1846. In 1840 a second volume of Mušicki's verses (*Mušicki Stihotvorenija, Kniga Druga*) and in 1843 Isidor Nikolic's *Spomeni Naroda Srbskog* (Remembrances of the Serb Nation) were published. As mentioned above, Petronović's *Kosovski Boj* was published in 1839.[22]

Had Tekelija lived longer he would undoubtedly have accomplished much more in developing the matica into a learned society. His death, however, not only deprived the matica of its leadership, but left a vexatious legal quarrel with Tekelija's heirs over the disposition of the land and houses which had been willed to the society. This quarrel lasted for three years and absorbed all the energies of the matica. Even though in 1845 it was decided in favor of the matica, the society had been so weakened by the quarrel that it had no real opportunity to recoup its strength and position before the events of 1848 were upon it. During this revolutionary time the matica was further seriously weakened. The Magyars oppressed it, many members quit, not one meeting was held, only two issues of *Ljetopis* appeared, and there was not one stipendiary at the Tekelijanum.

1850–1863

After the concessions Hungary won from Vienna in March, 1848, representatives of the Vojvodna

[21] A position Hadžić-Svetić held for nine years, until 1846. After the matica moved to Novi Sad in 1863 he became one of its vice-presidents from 1864 until his death in 1869.

[22] During this period the matica initiated its program of awarding literary prizes. The first one went to Petronović in 1839 for his *Battle of Kosovo*. In 1846 the first award made from the Nako fund was granted to Subotić for his *King Dečanski*.

Serbs appeared before the Hungarian diet in Bratislava in April to work for their own national rights. Upon being rebuffed by Lajos Kossuth, revolutionary governor of Hungary, the Serbs, like the Croats, joined with the Habsburgs and took up arms against Magyar intolerance. After the Magyars were finally defeated with Russian help in 1849 and Kossuth fled to Turkey, the only concession Vienna granted the Serbs was to detach the Vojvodina from Hungary and make it autonomous, with its seat of government at Temesvár. Since this autonomy was extremely restricted, all that really happened was that Austrian rule replaced Magyar, and even this lasted only until 1860 when the Vojvodina was returned to Magyar domination.

The matica had not participated in the "spring of the peoples" and when it finally did begin activity again in August, 1851, it had to operate under very changed conditions. Not only was the blighting effect of Bach's absolutism fairly well established, but Pest had ceased to be an important center of Serbian national life in Hungary.

The main decision of the August meeting directed by Bishop Platon Atanacković (1788–1867) of Novi Sad, a writer, patron of Serb culture, and past president of the matica (for the years 1842–1844), and Pavel Trifunać, president for the years 1844–1853, was to continue to publish as much as possible and to make every attempt to move as soon as possible to Novi Sad which, especially after 1848–1849, was rapidly improving as the Serbian intellectual center. Since local Magyar officials in Pest, however, did not wish the matica to remove to Novi Sad, where it would be more difficult to control and harass, the leaders of the matica sought in vain for years to secure permission to move. Furthermore, the same local officials stifled the foundation by the petty, but effective means of ordering various changes in the by-laws and then taking years to approve them or by taking years to answer a request.

In spite of such obstacles the matica continued to publish, make literary awards, and receive and administer funds. The publication of *Ljetopis* (which by then had from 500–600 subscribers) remained its most important contribution. In addition to twenty-eight issues of *Ljetopis* and sixteen official publications there were nine works of some literary, cultural, or national value.

Of the publications at this time the most important by far was *Seoba Srbalja* (Migration of the Serbs) by Djura Jakšić (1833–1878), a dramatist, poet, and painter. It was a good example of Serbian literature from the earlier literary models. The subject matter was still much the same (Serbdom, its past grandeur, strivings for freedom, and unification), but the style was pretty much along the lines of European Romanticism, exhibiting sentimentality and fantasy.

A noteworthy translation published by the matica was Wacław Maciejowski's *Historija Prawodawst v Slowiańskich* (History of Slavic Law, originally published in Warsaw in 1832). Among other things this work supported Slovak claims against the Magyars and in general supported the Slavic legal status against Germans and Magyars. Five other publications also dealt with Serbian history; four awards were made and a third fund came in.[23]

This third phase of the matica ends with Francis Joseph's *Dekret* of June, 1863, which (as a result of constitutionalism) finally approved the removal of the matica to Novi Sad. Thus after nearly thirty years the matica moved to the real center of Serbian culture in Austria.

1864–1875

The matica began the new era with a meeting April 30, 1864. It was no longer under the nose of Pest officials, but not because of a change of government. After Austria's military defeat during the war with Piedmont and France in 1859, Vienna, in order to placate long-standing Magyar demands, turned the Vojvodina back to Magyar administration. Novi Sad was, therefore, again under Magyar control. The initial success of the matica in Novi Sad was due rather to new leadership and the influence of being in a Serbian cultural center. This new era, unfortunately, lasted for only a few years. The *Ausgleich* of 1867 established a dual system and restored Hungary's freedom under very favorable circumstances. Thereafter, the Magyars became increasingly anti-Serb, so much so that by 1875 the matica was all but dead. In spite of this sad reverse, however, the efforts of the leaders of the matica at this time are both interesting and important.

Novi Sad, the "Serb Athens," had become not only the political, institutional, and cultural center of the Vojvodina, but also one of the most important of all South Slav cultural centers. Many of the leading Serbian intellectuals such as Svetozar Miletić,

[23] The other publications of this time were: *Djuradj Branković: Krv za Rod* (Djuradj Branković: Blood for the Nation), a novel by the first Serb realist, Jakov Ignjatatović (1824–1888) who was also editor of *Ljetopis*, 1854–1856; a drama, *Kraljević Marko i Vuča Djeneral* (Crown Prince Marko and General Vuča) by Atanasije Nikolić (1803–1882); *Istorija Srbskog Naroda* (History of the Serb Nation) by Nikola Krstić (1829–1902); and two works by Joksim O. Nović (1807–1869), *Dušanija ili Znati Dogadjaji za Vremena Carstva* (Dušan and the Facts of the Serbian Empire) and *Moskovija, Rat u Krimu* (Crimean War). There were two other translations, Lessing's *Nathan der Weise*, and the poems of Horace.

The four awards were made to Stefan Lazić for his translation of Horace, to Krstić for his *History*, to Jakšić for his *Migration of the Serbs*, and to Subotić for volume eight of his collected works (not published by the matica).

The third fund was a bequest of 23,862fl. left to the matica by Pavel Jovanović. The income, about 1,000fl. annually, was used to help students at the Polytechnic School in Vienna.

Mihajlo Polit-Desančić, Jovan Jovanović-Zmaj, and Laza Kostić had moved there after the failure of 1848–1849.[24] There were also nine political and literary journals published and printed there on Cyrillic presses which had sprung up after the fall of Bach. Since 1842 an important *čitaonica* or reading room [25] had operated there and a national theater was founded in 1861.

At the time of the transfer and for some years afterwards some of the old Pest leadership continued to direct the matica. Bishop Atanacković was re-elected president in 1864 and held this office until his death in 1867. He not only provided continuity in leadership, but also headquarters for the matica in his palace until more suitable quarters could be secured. Antonije Hadžić, secretary since 1859, served in this capacity until 1895. In 1865 he also assumed the editorship of *Ljetopis*, a post he also held until 1895. Furthermore, Hadžić-Svetić, then returned from Beograd, served as vice-president until his death in 1869, and Dr. Jovan Subotić, former editor of *Ljetopis* during the 1840's, succeeded Atanacković as president after the latter died in 1867, and served from 1868 to 1872. While this continuity provided stability it also perpetuated the older, conservative type of leadership.

There were, however, a few young and more liberal personalities to help guide the matica after its move to Novi Sad, such as Svetozar Miletić (1826–1901), an important journalist, a deputy in the Hungarian diet, founder and leader of the Popular party, and the most significant political leader of the Serbs in Hungary during the mid-nineteenth century, and Jovan Jovanović-Zmaj (1833–1904), the most distinguished and prolific Serb writer of the last half of the century.

At the time of the move to Novi Sad the matica had about 200 members and funds totaling 271,942fl. (the total of the monies collected by the matica and the Tekelija, Nako, and Jovanović funds), plus property consisting of two houses in Pest, nine houses in Arad, vineyards and fields. There were about 250 subscribers to *Ljetopis*. The real (though short-lived) potential of the matica now began to show.

During its first year in Novi Sad, for example, its membership almost doubled when 160 new members joined, including some of the best Serbian scholars and writers. Membership continued to grow and thereafter to 1879 the matica averaged about 500 to 600 members, reaching a high of 1,400 in 1880. Subscribers to *Ljetopis* rose to about 700 in 1873 and to 1,000 in 1874.

The first important thing the matica did after moving to Novi Sad was to organize in 1865 a literary board to concern itself with the purely literary matters of the matica as distinct from financial and administrative duties. The responsibilities of the board were to supervise all publications, to commission and acquire manuscripts for publication, and to award literary prizes. The leader of this board was also to serve as vice-president of the matica.

The first person elected to that office was Svetozar Miletić, who held the position for nineteen years, 1865–1883, and with the help of Jovanović-Zmaj did more than anyone else during the fifty-three years of the history of the matica treated in this study to widen its scope of activities, to make the matica more popular and democratic, and achieve its original goals.

He resented the fact that the Slovak and Slovenian maticas, organized more than twenty-five years after the Serbian, had many more members than the Serbian prototype. In 1866 the Slovene matica had 1,200 members, the Slovak matica 1,482 in 1868, and the Serb 460 in 1868. In addition to his work as vice-president and director of the literary board he founded a political newspaper, *Zastava* (Flag) and solicited the support of the Omladina, which he received.[26]

[24] Most of the early national cultural leaders such as Mušicki, Magarašević, Šafařík, and Pavlović were by this time dead.

[25] Reading societies had been known in Western Europe since the beginning of the eighteenth century. Among the earliest were the French Cabinets de Lecture, one of which is known to have existed in 1701. The first English reading rooms or circulating libraries were founded in Edinburgh in 1726. Among the Germans, *Lesegesellschaften* were organized as early as 1771 in Vienna and in 1779 in Stralsund, Prussia.

The basic idea of these societies was to arrange with one or more publishers to buy copies of books at reduced prices. Such books would then circulate among members and later be placed in a library, along with journals and newspapers to which the society subscribed, for the future use of members.

Apparently the first Austro-Slavs to found reading rooms were the Czechs, who established some as early as 1818. From the Czechs the idea spread to the South Slavs—to the Croats in 1837, the Austrian Serbs in 1841, and to the Slovenes in 1860 (the Bulgarians organized their first reading room in 1856)—who, having no great center like Prague, or important learned societies, founded dozens of these simple and easily organized centers throughout their territories.

Taking their inspiration from the Czechs and the Croats, the Serbs in the Vojvodina founded their first reading room in Irig (a few miles from Novi Sad) in 1841, five years before the first one was established in Beograd. The idea spread and by 1870 there were twenty-one such societies in the Vojvodina alone. The most influential was the one in Novi Sad, which like all the others worked to halt Magyarization. In 1847 Hadžić-Svetić became its president. At that time it had 200 contributing members, a library of 1,500 volumes, a fund of over 2,000fl., and subscribed to eighteen different newspapers and journals. It was closed during the revolution of 1848–1849 and reopened only after the fall of Bach.

[26] The Omladina, the United Serbian Youth Movement, resembled the Young Italy and Young Germany movements. It was founded in 1866 in the Vojvodina and flourished there for a few years. It encouraged the Serb peoples to develop according to their own characteristics and requirements and nurtured Serbian nationalism. It later spread to the principality where, because its democratic ideals conflicted with Prince Michael's regime, it was soon banned.

Even though the matica was never as popular as some of its sister organizations, Miletić could take comfort from the fact that it was certainly far richer. Shortly after the move to Novi Sad a patriot, Peter Kostić, died and left 30,000fl. for the support of Serbian students, and in 1866 another patriot, Ilija Kolarać, donated 2,400fl. to help found a law academy in Novi Sad. So many various funds were turned over to the matica that by 1874 it was administering fifteen of them totaling almost 500,000fl. Such wealth, however, did have a negative effect on the matica for, while it needed funds to operate, the administration of so many trusts required so much time and energy that it slowly turned into more of a society for handling estates than a literary institution for spreading national literature and culture. The main activities of the matica for the period 1864–1879 were financially supporting about twenty students a year, granting literary prizes, and publishing.

During the twelve years following the move to Novi Sad and through its fiftieth anniversary in 1876, the matica published fifty-two items, including ten issues of *Ljetopis*, sixteen official reports, twenty various kinds of books, and six volumes of a new journal, *Matica*, for the general public. This trimonthly magazine carried all kinds of articles on literary activities as well as news about conditions and activities of all Serbian cultural institutions and societies, literary criticism, and opinions. It printed materials not only about Serbian works, but also about the South Slavs and foreign literary activities as well. It also printed bibliographies of Serbian and non-Serbian works about Serbia.

Matica was initiated by Miletić in an effort to attract a wider interest in the society. It had a larger format, and was much more popular than the scholarly *Ljetopis* which was published irregularly and not at all during 1868–1870 and 1876. The first edition appeared October 10, 1865, edited by A. Hadžić (who was also editor of *Ljetopis*). *Matica* lasted only for six years (180 issues), through June, 1870. Unfortunately, there were not sufficient funds to support it and it took up too much of the editor's time.

Of the twenty other publications during this period, only a few were of much importance. The only noteworthy book published was Laza Kostić's five-act tragedy, *Maksim Crnojević*, based on a folk tale of the same name, in 1866. Kostić (1841–1910) is regarded as the most learned Serbian writer of his time.[27]

This short-lived success and limited output of the matica subsequent to its move to Novi Sad can be explained primarily by the fact that it hardly had time to resettle there before the dire effects of the *Ausgleich* were upon its leaders. Although for a few years after 1867 Hungary was led by moderate and enlightened leaders such as Count Gyula Andrássy, the prime minister; baron Jozsef Eötvös, minister of education; and Ferencz Deák, leader of the Liberal Reform Party; and although far-reaching privileges were promised the non-Magyar minorities by the progressive Nationalities Act of 1868, this liberal era did not last long. After 1871, as a result of the death of Eötvös, the near-retirement of Deák, and the transfer of Andrássy to Vienna to become minister of foreign affairs, the Nationalities Act became a dead letter and the proponents of ruthless Magyarization came to power.

In 1872, for example, the slavophobe August Trefort became minister of education and inaugurated a new wave of Magyarization by closing the gymnasium in Novi Sad in 1873 and by ordering the confiscation in 1876 of the matica's greatest source of income, the Tekelija fund. Furthermore, following an unstable interregnum of several weak cabinets, Kálmán Tisza, an extreme conservative, became prime minister and for sixteen years (1875–1890) waged a ceaseless campaign against the minorities.

1876–1888: EPILOGUE

By 1876 the matica ended a half-century of activity and had, in part at least, achieved many of its original goals. It had grown from a nucleus of about 20 to over 600 members. Though never large in membership or really popular it had acquired fifteen funds totaling over 489,000fl. with which it financed the education of from twelve to twenty students annually at the university of Pest and of several in Vienna. It had also awarded some literary prizes and, initially at least, advanced Slavic mutuality. Its main activity of course was publishing. During this half-century it had published 390 items: 180 issues of *Matica*, 118 issues of *Ljetopis*, 3 issues of *Srbska Pčela*, 41 official reports, and 48 books.

Whatever joy and comfort its leaders could derive from this, however, were quickly dissipated by two developments which caused the matica to decline from being a pioneer of the Serbian cultural and national movement to a quiet publisher of innocuous books.

---

[27] For six years after 1867 nothing more significant than a few national songs, a translation of Demosthenes' *Philippics*, a Latin grammar, and a medical handbook appeared. Then in 1874 there appeared *The Collected Works of Jakov Ignjatović, Part I*. Ignjatović (1802–1888) was a publicist, lawyer, and a one-time editor of *Ljetopis*. Also in 1874 appeared Kosta Trifković's drama *Ljubavno Pismo* (Love Letter) and a study of Serbian music, a Latin reader, and a work on magic. Other than two issues of *Ljetopis* nothing significant was printed during 1875–1876. There was some effort to publish an encyclopedia for all the South Slavs, but it was stymied by insufficient funds and writers for such an undertaking. The first encyclopedia among the South Slavs was not published until after World War. I. This was Professor St. Stanojević's *Narodna Enciklopedija Srpsko-Hrvatsko-Slovenačka* (4 v., Zagreb, 1925–1929).

The first development was a very successful move on the part of the Magyars to curtail the matica further by confiscation of the Tekelija fund. As early as the time of the move to Novi Sad there were members of the matica who considered that this fund tied up too much cash in real estate and that the matica would be able to do much more if the fund were converted to cash. They thought that not only could the number of grants be increased from eighteen to fifty a year, but that those receiving the grants should be able to attend any university of their choice and not have to live in Pest and therefore be limited to the university there. They also argued that the matica was not set up primarily to educate doctors and officials, but for the spreading of culture among the Serbs. Another point was that since the university in Pest had changed from Latin to Magyar for lectures that this would seriously disadvantage Serbian students.

In 1872, therefore, the matica began work to convert this fund into cash. Trefort, who assumed office that same year, was of course against such a change and the Serbs again fought in vain. In 1874 Trefort insisted that all recipients of grants from the matica must study in Pest and he also required the matica to return the large Tekelija library of 2,861 volumes to Pest at its own expense. A special governmental official was appointed to watch the matica carefully. He demanded a complete inventory of its possessions, a list of all who had applied for and received grants from 1860 through 1874, and detailed information about all publications since 1864. The whole year of 1875 was taken up in the preparation of these reports. Finally in December, 1875, the matica was given the choice: return to Pest or give up the Tekelija fund. The return to Pest would have meant the rapid extinction of the matica (still the only Serbian literary society in the Vojvodina) and giving up the fund would mean the end of grants to students—the future hope of the Hungarian Serbs.

The protests of the matica were in vain. It finally concluded that the lesser of two evils was to give up the fund which then totaled over 256,000fl. or more than half of its total funds of 489,000fl. A few patriots tried to help make up this loss by small gifts, but only about 30,000fl. came in, about 12 per cent of what was lost.

A second factor in the decline of the matica during the 1870's was the emergence of Beograd as a national and cultural center of the Serbs, both in the Principality and in the Vojvodina. Since the early 1840's Beograd had been developing the necessary institutions to foster culture and nationalism. In 1842 the Društvo Srbske Slovesnosti (Serbian Grammatical Society) was founded and began publishing in 1847 a journal, *Glasnik* (The Herald), to promote language and history. In 1864 this society was turned into a state institution by Prince Michael and became the Srbsko Učeno Društvo (Serbian Learned Society). Finally in 1886 it became the Srpska Kraljevska Akademija Nauka i Umjetnosti (Royal Serbian Academy of Science and Art). In 1842 there had also been established a national theater, which like the Grammatical Society had been organized, as mentioned above, by the playwright Popović.

By 1900, the matica was no longer significant in Serbian cultural and national life and development, and Novi Sad was fast declining to a mere provincial center. From that time until after World War I, the matica existed simply as a publishing concern bringing out about ten publications annually. For over fifty years, however, even though its whole existence had been one of struggle against ignorance, indifference, backwardness, and Magyar suppression, it had done more than any other institution to advance Serbian cultural and national life, not only in the Voyvodina, but among all Serbs in general.

After World War I, the matica slowly won back its original significance. In Novi Sad today it functions somewhat as an academy with its own publishing house which has printed an average of thirty books a year since 1945, as well as *Ljetopis* (now a monthly devoted to literature); a library of over 250,000 books, and 50,000 letters and documents concerning Serbian history and civilization; an important and impressive art gallery of about 2,000 pictures, drawings, and pieces of sculpture (especially of the eighteenth and nineteenth centuries); and various literary and scientific divisions. It also grants stipendia to 500 students in secondary schools. It is without question one of the most important institutions in modern Yugoslavia.

III. THE CZECH MATICA, 1831: PALACKÝ'S DEFENDER OF THE CZECH LANGUAGE

This fund is established for the purpose of aiding and facilitating the publishing of good Czech books whether they be of general interest, scientific, or esthetic.

From the original by-laws.

Probably the most important thing about the Serbian matica was the example it set for all other suppressed Austro-Slavs to follow. The Czechs were the first of the other Slavs in the empire to realize the importance and significance of the Serbian innovation. The great historian František Palacký was especially responsible for the founding in 1831 of the Matice Česká, the first modern Czech national institution and, even though learned societies had existed in the lands of St. Václav for nearly a century and in spite of the fact that Czech savants for more than thirty years had been trying to organize formally a "Czech [language] Society" (Společnost Česká), the matica became the first institution to promote successfully the revival of the Czech language. It was also the first independent Czech cultural institution to advance nationalism, the first modern institution of a purely Czech character, one of the first and strongest supports of the modern Czech nation, the most important legal center of the Czech national movement to 1848, or, as one Slovene scholar so nicely and succinctly puts it, the *"foyer de toute l'activité de la renaissance nationale."* [1]

By 1829 a group of Czech savants and writers led by Palacký, the physiologist Jan Svatopluk Presl, and the philologist Josef Jungmann came together informally to consider ways and means of promoting the revival and survival of the Czech language, which at that time was full of inconsistencies and foreign phrases and in great need of modernization, standardization, and fashioning into a fit instrument for the national rebirth. They also decided to try to publish an encyclopedia to bring the reviving Czech culture and intellectual life more into line with western European developments. Subsequently, on January 6, 1830, Palacký went before the Museum Board for Czech Language and Literature with a proposal to organize formally as a committee of the museum. He pointed out that such a committee could and should be created in accordance with the museum's by-laws of 1818, especially section 12 which stated that the museum would advance knowledge of all kinds, and 13 which insisted that "All members of the museum must [at least] understand Czech and the secretary must [also] be able to read and write it." [2]

His proposal was quickly adopted and on 11 January a Committee for the Scholarly Fostering of Czech Language and Literature (Sbor k Vědeckému Vzdělávání Řeči a Literatury České) was made an agency of the Museum Board. To further their goals more effectively the new committee set up a foundation called the Matice Česká which commenced activity on January 1, 1831.

Palacký's sources and inspiration for the matica came from domestic and foreign institutions going back nearly one hundred years. Among the domestic sources the earliest was the Societas Incognitorum (Gesellschaft der Unbekannten, Society of Unknowns), the first learned society in the Czech lands. It was founded in Olomouc (Olmütz) in 1746 (see below p. 32).

Close on twenty years later another learned society was organized in the Czech lands—the Gelehrte Privatgesellschaft (Sourkrommá Společnost Učená, Private Learned Society), which was organized in 1770 in Prague by Ignaz, Ritter von Born and a few like-minded friends.[3] Their most important activity was the publication of the first scholarly journal in Bohemia—the *Prager Gelehrte Nachrichten*, a book-review periodical which reviewed publications throughout the empire. The journal, however, lasted only two years, 1771–1772. This society also published an important journal of research, *Abhandlungen*, from 1775.

Until 1784 the society was simply a private organization embracing a small group of men influenced by the spirit of the English and French Enlightenment (rather than the romantic nationalism of Herder), who were interested in intellectual pursuits. Even so it contributed considerably to the cultural reawakening of Bohemia. In 1784 it received permission from Joseph II to organize as a public institution with the name Böhmische Gesellschaft der Wissenschaften (Česká Společnost Nauk, Societas Scientiarum Bohemica, Bohemian Society of Learning), whereupon Prince Karl Egon von Fürstenberg became its first president. Finally in 1790 it took the name by which it is generally known, the Königlich-Böhmische Gesellschaft der Wissenschaften (Královská Česká Společnost Nauk, Royal Bohemian Learned Society), and became one of the earliest academies in Central Europe.

From the beginning, this society was strictly aristocratic, intellectual, and patriotic rather than national in spirit. It was patriotic to the extent that it was interested in producing a critical history of the Czechs, but not national enough to foster Czech language and literature. Despite its non-national character it became and remained the center of Czech intellectual life until the museum was founded in 1818, and even thereafter it continued to grow and flourish. In 1840 it was divided into four sections: mathematics, natural history, history, and Czech philology.[4]

Toward the end of the eighteenth century, other similar societies for special interests were organized—the K.K. Patriotisch-ökonomische Gesellschaft, (C. K. Vlastenecká Hospodařská Společnost, Royal-Imperial Patriotic Economic Society) in 1769, for example;

[1] Fran Zwitter, *Les Problèmes Nationaux dans la Monarchie des Habsbourg* (Beograd, 1960), p. 52.

[2] These by-laws are reprinted in Josef Hanuš, *Národní Museum a Naše Obrození* (Prague, 1881) 2: pp. 102–104 and in František Kop, *Národní Museum* (Prague, 1941), pp. 177–179. The stipulation in section 13 seems absurd today, but it is very revealing of the neglected condition of Czech at the beginning of the national revival.

[3] See Arnošt Kraus, "Kdy Byla Založena 'Soukromná Společnost v Čechách'," (When was the "Private Society" Founded in Bohemia?), *Český Časopis Historický* 42 (April, 1936): pp. 56–76. Other writers give the date of the founding of this society as 1769, 1771, 1772, and 1774.

Czech purists may prefer Ignác, rytíř Born to Ignaz, Ritter von Born, but I have kept the German forms throughout this chapter: thus Jan Norbert, Ritter von Neuberg and not Jan Norbert, rytíř Nerberk, and Petr, Ritter von Chlumecký, not Petr, rytíř Chlumecký.

[4] Even after the Czech Academy of Emperor Francis Joseph I for Science, Literature, and Art was organized in 1890 (after 1918 called simply the Czech Academy of Arts and Sciences) the Learned Society held its own. Finally, in 1952, both the Learned Society and the Czech Academy were merged into the newly organized Czechoslovak Academy of Science.

and somewhat later the Privatgesellschaft Patriotischer Kunstfreunde (Společnost Vlasteneckých Přátel Umění, Society of the Patriotic Friends of Art) in 1796. Since these societies were largely aristocratic and provincial rather than national in spirit, and since their language was German, a group of Czech savants including the philologist Josef Dobrovský, the historian František Martin Pelcl, and the publicist Václav Matěj Kramerius began at the end of the eighteenth century vain attempts to found a "Czech Society" (mentioned above) in order to promote the sadly neglected and deteriorated Czech language and literature in the same way as the other societies were promoting science, economics, and art. They also hoped to publish a Czech dictionary and to improve the unsatisfactory conditions of book publishing in the Czech lands.

At that time most publishing was in the hands of booksellers who were interested mainly in profit and not in advancing any cause. Not many Czech books were printed, because of the small market for them, and those few which were printed were mainly of the type which would sell fast—almanacs, religious works, and popular songs and stories. Often even these books were published only if there was a prepaid subscription list.[5] Nor was there much financial inducement for authors to produce manuscripts. They were seldom paid for their work, usually receiving only a few free copies. Another domestic activity which may also have influenced Palacký was that of the reading societies (sing. Čtenařský spolek, Leseverein, see fn. 25, chap. II). An early attempt among the Czechs to emulate this Western European idea, but for the fostering of nationalism, was made by Antonín Puchmajer, a priest and poet, in 1818 in the town of Radnice near Plzeň in western Bohemia.[6] A professor in Plzeň, Josef Vojtěch, became very enthusiastic over the work of Puchmajer and through the pages of Kramerius's *C. K. Vlastenecké Noviny* (Royal-Imperial Patriotic Journal) he appealed to his countrymen to follow this example and set up other reading societies. Not much came of this suggestion, however. Only about ten or so were founded in small cities and towns throughout the Bohemian countryside. Their activities were very tame and consisted mainly of subscribing to Czech books and journals and making them available to all members in a central reading room. They also provided a few modest and innocuous social and cultural activities with only slightly nationalistic tendencies. Their main significance was to unite the countryside more closely with the great cultural and national center in Prague.[7]

Palacký also may have been influenced by the Dědictví Svatojanské (Heritage of St. Jan Nepomuk), a Catholic publishing society organized in 1829 to distribute good, cheap books in Czech, such as Bibles, catechisms, legends, and other useful and entertaining literature. This venture was very popular. It sold membership cards at prices ranging from ten to forty florins and soon had over 20,000 members of all classes throughout the Czech lands.[8]

Among the foreign influences on Palacký were the eight or ten literary and learned societies organized by the Slovaks since 1785 (see chap. VI)—especially the Catholic Anton Bernolák's Literata Slavica Societas (Slavic Literary Society) organized in 1793 in Trnava, and the Protestant Spolek Literatury Slovenské (Slovak Literary Society, Institutum Linguae et Literaturae Slavicae), founded in Bratislava in 1801 in connection with the Lutheran Lyceum (an autonomous secondary school) there where Palacký had studied prior to going to Prague in 1823.

Palacký may have also been influenced by the linguistic reforms of the Serb Vuk Karadžić and the Croat Ljudevit Gaj. By far the most important foreign influence on Palacký, however, was the older Matica Srbska. Palacký was acquainted with this foundation both through correspondence with his friend, Šafařík, who had been connected with the organization of the Serbian matica (see above p. 13) and through the gift copies of its publication, *Ljetopis*, which were sent to the Czech Museum.

However much all these domestic and foreign societies and activities may have influenced Palacký,

[5] Such lists are helpful today in reconstructing the history of the early Czech national revival.

[6] For the earlier history of related activities see Josef Volf's *Dějiny veřejných půjčoven knih v Čechách do r. 1848* (Prague, 1931).

[7] From at least 1780 to the union of Buda and Pest in 1873 Prague was the second largest city in the Monarchy (except during the years 1815–1859 when Milan belonged to the Habsburgs). Partly because of its size Prague played a much greater role in the Czech national movement than Zagreb in the Croatian, Ljubljana in the Slovenian, Lwów in the Polish and Ruthenian, Bratislava in the Slovak, or Beograd in the Serbian. None of the other Austro-Slav groups was so centralized or compact a national, ethnic, political, and geographic group as the Czech. The others were divided geographically and politically, sometimes into as many as six divisions.

There is a partially burnt document in the Verwaltungsarchiv in Vienna from the Prague police to Police Chief Sedlnitzky about a *Lesegesellschaft* in Prague. This document, dated February, 1820, states that although such organizations are not illegal this particular one may have "some secret goals and should be carefully watched." It is not clear, however, whether the author means a Czech or German society. Polizei Hofstelle, 1485/1820. It could not have been the liberal and mildly reformist Juridisch-Politischer Leseverein which was established only in 1842.

[8] See K. Borový, *Dějiny Svatojánskeho Dědictví* (Prague, 1885). The first such society was organized in Bohemia as early as 1699 by the Jesuits. During the nineteenth century similar societies were organized by the other Austro-Slavs: the Slovene Society of St. Hermagoras, 1852; the Ruthenian Society of St. Basil, 1865; the Croatian Society of St. Jerome, 1868; and the Slovak Society of St. Adalbert, 1870.

it was the founding of the Bohemian Museum which gave him the first real opportunity to act and to institutionalize his ideas. The hopes of those working for the "Czech Society" had indeed almost gone, when their cause was resuscitated by the founding of the museum in 1818.

The museum was organized by certain members of the Czech nobility who, though largely Germanized, had been working carefully for some time to secure more autonomy from Vienna and had developed a kind of *Landespatriotismus*—a territorial or Bohemian patriotism which was neither German nor Czech in orientation. In 1783, to give one example of this attitude, Count Franz Anton Nostitz-Rieneck, the highest burgrave (*Nejvyšší Purkrabí Český*) of Bohemia, built the Gräflich Nostitzsches Nationaltheater—in 1797 renamed the Estates Theatre (Standestheater, Stavovské Divadlo)—as an act of moderate resistance to Joseph II's centralization. These nobles slowly and cautiously began to cooperate with the growing number of middle-class intellectuals, who were becoming increasingly nationalistic and who were beginning to challenge the centralist, absolutist, and Germanized Austrian state through the only means possible, cultural activity.

In 1814 another highest burgrave of Bohemia, Count Franz Anton Kolovrat, inspired by the founding of the Magyar National Museum in 1802 and the Johanneum (a museum founded in Graz in 1811 by Archduke Johann) as symbols of provincial autonomy, requested Count Kašpar Sternberg to investigate the Johanneum and report whether such an institution could be organized successfully in Prague. Count Sternberg's report was in the affirmative and in 1808 Kolovrat (spurred to action by the organization of the Francisceum, a museum named in honor of Francis I in Brno earlier that same year) petitioned Vienna for permission to organize a museum in Prague.

The cumbersome and suspicious Austrian bureaucracy took two years to process the petition, but finally in June, 1820, granted permission to organize a Gesellschaft des Vaterländischen Museums in Böhmen (Společnost Vlastenského Musea v Čechách, Society of the Patriotic Museum in Bohemia), which, although as conservative, aristocratic, and patriotic as the earlier learned societies, differed significantly from them in that its leaders insisted that all members must at least understand Czech.

Count Kašpar Sternberg was elected the first president and provided space for it in his palace. In 1847 it moved to the Nostic palace, and finally in the 1890's to the present monumental structure at the top of Václav Square in the heart of Prague.

For the first few years the Museum Society accomplished little. Its first significant activity was in 1827 when it began publishing two journals—a monthly in German, the *Monatschrift der Gesellschaft des Vaterländischen Museum in Böhmen*, and a quarterly in Czech, the *Časopis Společnosti Vlastenského Museum v Čechách* (Journal of the Society of the Patriotic Museum in Bohemia).[9]

As editor of both publications the leaders of the museum chose the Moravian Palacký—evidence of the growing rapprochement between some of the patriotic nobles and the nationally minded intellectuals. Palacký had come to Prague in 1823 at the age of twenty-four with the desire to write Hussite history. There he made friends with Dobrovský, who helped him secure employment as keeper of the family archives of Count František Sternberg, older brother of Kašpar. Through Sternberg's influence Palacký was later (in 1829) appointed by the diet to the honorary position of "Historian of the Bohemian Estates."

Through Palacký's efforts as editor, *Časopis* fostered Czech and became the first real "beach-head" of the Czech campaign for national rights, the first organ for the fostering of the Czech language, the official representative of Czech culture and scholarship, and one of the chief means of spreading knowledge of past and present Czech culture and history among the people.

It was not edited, as other journals such as the *Abhandlungen* of the Royal Bohemian Learned Society were, for a small group of scholars, but for the widest possible audience of intelligent readers in Bohemia, Moravia, and Slovakia. It carried all kinds of articles, not only scientific ones, especially contributions on literature—samples of old Czech literature, new poetry and prose, translations from German and other Slavic tongues—and such features as "news" and book reviews. No other Czech journal has ever had such a deep and lasting influence.[10]

Following the organization of the Czech matica as a committee in 1831 the Museum Board appointed the prince-patriot Rudolf Kinský as its agent or curator of this new committee and called Palacký, the philologist Josef Jungmann, and the physiologist Presl to work with Kinský as an "agency" (*jednatelství*) or sort of executive committee. Thus the Museum Board turned the direction of the matica over to leaders of the new national Czech spirit who, though genuinely interested in promoting Czech language and literature, were also politically minded

[9] The short-lived German journal in 1830 changed its name to the *Jahrbücher des Böhmischen Museums für Natur- und Länderkunde, Geschichte, Kunst und Literatur*, and then ceased publication for lack of subscribers. Few Czechs, of course, subscribed to it and Germans were apparently satisfied with the *Abhandlungen* of the Royal Bohemian Society of Learning. In 1831 the Czech journal became the *Časopis Českeho Museum*, in 1855 the *Časopis Musea království Českeho*, and finally in 1923 the *Časopis Národního Musea*—the name it still bears.

[10] For the complete bibliography of this journal see Provoslav Kneidl, *Časopis Národního Musea 1827–1956, Rejstřík 125 Ročníků Muzejního Časopisu* (2 v., Prague, 1961–1963).

and who realized the necessity, in the police state in which they lived, of disguising their national and political efforts as literary activities. This fact proved as fortunate for the institutionalizing of Palacký's ideas as it was further evidence of the cautious but real support given to the Czech revival by some of the Czech nobility at that time.

The matica officially began its activities immediately by issuing on January 1 a public announcement to "the Patriots of National Literature"[11] calling for a general collection of funds to establish a treasury called the Matice Česká (a name which was soon applied to the whole committee). This was to be used for the publishing of "good scholarly and useful books of all kinds in the Czech language." Those who contributed at least 50fl. were considered as supporting members entitled to one free copy of each publication. The first announcement also stressed that the initial major goals of the matica would be to publish a large Czech-German dictionary and an encyclopedia.

The most important and active period during the more than 100-year life of the matica was from 1831 to about 1861. After that the relative freedom of constitutionalism enabled so many new societies to form that it slowly shrank in importance and activity to a mere publishing house. This study will therefore concern itself with the pre-1861 period, which may be broken into three roughly equal ten-year periods: 1831–1840 was a period of organization and development, 1841–1851 represented the time of its greatest flourishing and significance, and 1852–1860 was a period of severe curtailment by absolutism. During these thirty years the matica engaged in most of the above-mentioned activities to foster the Czech language and literature, to increase national consciousness, and to raise cultural standards among the masses.

1830–1840

During its first decade membership and contributions grew rapidly. From a beginning of 169, membership rose to 1,217 in 1834 and to 2,277 in 1840. The matica's funds correspondingly increased from 2,363fl. to 11,795fl. to 18,794fl.—a considerable amount, but far short of the 50,000fl. considered necessary to publish an encyclopedia.

This was a dramatic beginning considering that national life was just starting to stir, that few of the nobility committed themselves wholly to the national cause, that the matica limited its appeal to the public almost exclusively to announcements in *Časopis*, that its program and publications did not appeal to the masses, that the 50fl. membership fee was beyond the budget of most Czechs, and that some overzealous members of the museum worked against the matica for fear it would compete with the museum, and finally that Vienna did not favor the rise of Czech nationalism and harassed the matica in the beginning. The committee, for example, was not even allowed to use the term Matice Česká during the years 1835–1841.

A detailed analysis of membership figures reveals that throughout this decade most support came from the clergy and from students. About 40 per cent of all support came from the clergy (especially the lower clergy—the priests, chaplains, and theological students); about 20 per cent from students, mainly at the university level; and the remainder came from businessmen, officials, professional men, the *literati*, and the nobility. Peasants, workers, and tradesmen were hardly represented at all.[12]

Among the noble founding members were Thuns, Kolovrats, Kinskýs, Sternbergs, Krakovskýs, Černíns, Lobkovices, Clam-Martinices, Schwarzenbergs, and Fürstenbergs. But they made no large gifts to the matica comparable to the 118,000fl. contributed in 1825 to found the Magyar Academy by Counts Széchenyi, Károlyi, Vay, and Andrássy, or even to the 10,000fl. donated by Bishop Strossmayer to found the Croatian Academy in 1867. Even Prince Kinský gave only 1,000fl. while Counts Kašpar Sternberg and Alois Kolovrat-Krakovský, archbishop Prague, gave only token gifts of 100fl. each.[13] Most donations were between 5fl. and 50fl. Other important early founding members, besides Palacký,

[11] Reprinted in Karel Tieftrunk, *Dějiny Matice české* (Prague, 1881), pp. 264–266.

[12] See M. Hroch and A. Veverka, "K Otázce Sociální Skladby České Obrozenské Společnosti: Rozbor Společenského Složení Vlastenců Kolem Českého Musea a Matice České v Letech 1827–48," *Dějepis ve Škole* (April 4, 1957), pp. 153–159. See also Miroslav Hroch, *Die Vorkämpfer der Nationalen Bewegung bei den kleinen Völkern Europas*, Prague, 1969, pp. 41–61 and the same author's "The Social Composition of the Czech Patriots in Bohemia, 1827–1848," *The Czech Renascence of the Nineteenth Century*, eds. Peter Brock and H. Gordon Skilling, Toronto, 1970, pp. 32–52.

[13] Further evidence of the well-known difference between the highly nationalistic Polish and Magyar nobility and the conservative, provincially patriotic at best, Czech (and Bohemian nobility) is provided by the following figures concerning the contributions to the Czech Museum during its first four years. At the end of the first year, 1818, all contributions totaled only 98,079fl. Four years later, at the end of 1822, the figure was 168,113fl.—or only about 40 per cent of the amount to be contributed to the Magyar Academy in the one year 1825 by only four noblemen.

The largest single contribution to the Czech Museum in the beginning was 10,000fl. from Prince F. Kinský. Other large gifts during the first four years came from Prince V. L. Chlumčanský (8,000fl.), Count J. Vratislav (7,500fl.), the Duchess Katherin of Sagan or Žahăń (7,500fl.), Prince F. Trautmannsdorf (5,000fl.), Count M. Kaunic (5,000fl.), Count J. F. Stadion (5,000fl.), Prince J. Schwarzenberg (4,000fl.), and Archduke Karl (4,000fl.). All the Černíns, Fürstenbergs, Harrachs, Sternbergs, Thuns, Kolovrats, Lobkovices, Nostics, and Kolovrat-Krakovskýs together contributed only 18,350fl. by the end of 1822. These figures are based on membership lists given in Hanuš, *Národní Museum a Naše Obrození* 1: pp. 51–56.

Jungmann, and Presl, included the poet and philologist Václav Hanka, the physiologist Jan Evangelista Purkyně, the strong nationalist Josef Frič, the future political leader František Ladislav Rieger, and the Slovak poet Ján Kollár.

The publishing activity of the matica began in 1832 when it assumed direction of *Časopis*, which at that time became the mouthpiece of the matica as well as the organ of the museum. Further evidence of the neglected state of Czech book production is the fact that this journal was printed in Hradec Králové (Königgrätz) by Ján Pospíšil, who published as many Czech books as all the Prague printers together. Its first two editors were Palacký (1827–1838) and Šafařík (1838–1842). Under their editorship its circulation increased from 500 to 1,000. They worked hard to purify and standardize the language and to initiate some modest spelling reform, against the wishes of antiquarians who wanted to preserve some old-fashioned elements from the sixteenth century. In all only four orthographic changes were made in the early 1840's: *j* for *g*, *i* for *j*, *ou* for *au*, and *v* for *w*.

Because of lack of sufficient funds, the condition of the language, and the need for a great deal of preparatory work, little further was said about the publishing of the encyclopedia. In addition to nine volumes of *Časopis* the matica published six other works during its first decade, of which two were of such importance that they established its scholarly reputation. They were Jungmann's five-volume *Slownjk Česko-německý* (Czech-German Dictionary), 1835—1839, and Šafařík's *Slowanské Starožitnosti* (Slavic Antiquities), 1837.[14]

Jungmann's work, which fulfilled one of the original major goals of the "Czech Society" and the matica, was the result of over thirty years' labor. It became one of the foundation stones of the language rebirth, considerably enriching the native vocabulary and demonstrating its latent potential as a living literary language. Šafařík's work, the first publication in the Czech language to have important European influence, became a source of arguments and ammunition for the Czechs in their struggle against the Germans. Its main thesis was that before the Christian era the Slavs had settled all lands between the Baltic, Black, and Adriatic seas and between the Vistula and Danube rivers, thus giving them an old and respectable pedigree. The work was soon translated into Russian, Polish, and German. The publication of the *Dictionary* and *Antiquities* had some negative side-effects, however. Their cost was so great that the matica actually acquired a debt of 750fl. in order to complete their publication, and furthermore their very scholarly character hindered mass participation in the matica.

The merits of the matica at this time, however, did not lie entirely in its publishing activities. One of its greatest achievements was to bring Šafařík from Novi Sad to Prague. In 1830 Šafařík had been dismissed as director of the Gymnasium because he was a Protestant. In correspondence with his friend Palacký he indicated his interest in coming to Prague if he could make a living and support his family there. Palacký, realizing what an important contribution Šafařík was capable of making to the Czech rebirth and national movement, secretly arranged with nine wealthy patriots to guarantee that the matica would make him an offer of 480fl. a year for five years to assist with the publishing of *Časopis*. The offer was accepted, and Šafařík moved his family to Prague in May, 1833, where he remained until his death twenty-eight years later in 1861. Because of his influence and his many Russian, Polish, and South Slav connections he helped make Prague the main center of Slavic studies and Slavic mutuality.

While these negotiations had been underway Palacký wrote to Kollár that he was "doing everything possible to bring Šafařík to Prague," and Jungmann also wrote to Kollár that "The arrival of our Šafařík in Prague will be a new Spring in our literature. . . ."[15] There was, however, one disagreeable requirement Šafařík had to accept—to change his name from the Slovak Šafárik and German Schaffrik to the Czech Šafařík and to publish in Czech rather than his native Slovak.

1840–1849

The 1840's proved a new and much more vigorous decade for the matica, in fact the most important in its history of more than one hundred years. In December, 1841, the matica published a new announcement or appeal written by Šafařík for more support, contributions, and members.[16] Jan Norbert Ritter von Neuberg, a nationally minded and sympathetic member of the Czech nobility, became the new curator. Prince Kinský had died in 1836 and Count Hanuš Kolovrat-Krakovský, his successor, had resigned in 1841 because of "frequent traveling." The executive committee was enlarged in 1841 by adding leading patriots, scholars, and writers such as Šafařík and Hanka, and later Count Lev Thun, Josef Frič, Václav Vladivoj Tomek, František Ladislav Čelakovský, Karel Jaromír Erben, Johannes Evangelista Purkyně, Josef Čejka, Václav Staněk, and Jan Erazim Vocel (who also edited the *Časopis* from 1843 to 1849).

In an effort to improve its publishing program

[14] All bibliographical citations are from Antonín Grund, *Sto let Matice České* (Prague, 1931), and are given in their original spellings.

[15] Tieftrunk, *Dějiny*, p. 49.

[16] Reprinted in *ibid.*, pp. 266–267.

and to attract a wider audience and membership than such scholarly works as the *Dictionary* and *Antiquities* had done, four new publishing series were inaugurated in 1841.[17] They were intended not only to aid Czech literature and science, but also to meet the more popular and general needs of the people. These were the Staročeská Bibliothéka (Old Czech Library) of standard classics up to the eighteenth century, the Novočeská Bibliothéka (New Czech Library) of new works in the fields of science and belles-lettres, the Bibliothéka Klassiků (Classical Library) of translations of important past and present world literature, and finally the Domácí Bibliothéka (Domestic Library) for popular and useful works. In the following year another series, the Malá Encyklopaedie Nauk (Small Encyclopedia of Science), was commenced, to function as a sort of a substitute until the matica could produce a real encyclopedia.

During this decade the matica also began new activities such as awarding prizes to authors, making book grants, and arranging exchanges of books and journals.

A good gauge of the success of all these activities, and evidence that this was a fruitful period, can be found in the detailed membership and financial records, which show that the number of new members (who after 1840 paid as little as 5fl.) rose during the year 1841 from an all-time-low of 10 in 1840 to 48, and increased steadily thereafter to 490 in 1851, when there was a grand total of 3,773 individual and 95 institutional memberships. A few important non-Czech members such as Prince Miloš Obrenović of Serbia and the Russian minister of culture, S. S. Uvarov, joined during this decade.

Finances showed a commensurate growth from 19,309fl. in 1841, to 62,912fl. by the end of 1851. Furthermore, the matica's publications were now being printed in increasingly large numbers—from 1,000 copies in the beginning to 3,000 copies.

In 1832 and 1835 pamphlets were printed in honor of Francis I and Ferdinand I. In 1833 a useful and popular book *Domácj Lékař* (Home Physician), by J. F. Paulický was published, and in 1832 it produced a seven-page survey by Palacký about court and provincial officials of the Czech kingdom from earliest times (*Přehled Saučasný Neywyšších Důstognjků a Auřednjků Zemských i Dworských we Králowstej Českém . . .*). Slowly it earned for itself the position of the chief representative of Czech scholarship and culture in general, not only at home but also abroad, especially among the other Austro-Slavs. It also began to approximate an academy of science in spite of the existence of the Royal Bohemian Learned Society.

Of some interest is the official response of Vienna. Even though during the 1830's the matica published pamphlets in honor of Francis I and Ferdinand I, not a kreutzer was donated to the matica from Vienna. It was not until 1840 that Archduke Franz Karl gave a niggardly 100fl. The only other gift from the Haus, Hof und Staat was a trifling 50fl. from Archduke Stephen in 1845. Nevertheless the matica was required, as were all other publishing concerns throughout the empire, to send one copy of all its publications to the Imperial Court Library and the Imperial Academy of Science in Vienna and to the libraries of the University of Prague. Of much more significance than the little note which Vienna did take of the matica is the fact that the government did not seriously hound and persecute it.[18]

In 1844, at the suggestion of Palacký, the matica initiated a program of offering prizes for worth-while books written in good Czech. The books could be written anywhere or published anywhere. There were two classes of prizes: for books about Czech language and literature, 50fl., and for books on other subjects, 25fl.[19]

During this period the matica also began a program of book grants. The first was made to a Czech regiment in Mainz in 1844. Others followed to the Imperial Hospital in Vienna, to the Soldiers' Hospital in Prague, to the Protestant Theological Seminary in Vienna, and to a local library in Celje, Styria. During the revolutionary era of 1848–1849, books were distributed to poor students, and a copy of each publication was donated to a group of revolutionary students called Slavia (Slavic Brotherhood).

Similarly the matica began exchanging books and journals with institutions such as the Ossolineum in Lwów, the Johanneum in Graz, the Francisceum in Brno, the library of the University of Cracow, the Kievan Society of Antiquities, and with such Polish publications as the Lwów *Rozmaitości* (Miscellanies), the Przemyśl *Tygodnik* (Weekly), and the *Biblioteka Warszawska* (The Warsaw Library). Similar book exchanges were arranged with the Royal Academy in Munich, the Imperial Society of History and Antiquities of the University of Moscow, the St. Petersburg Archeological Society, and the Upper Lusatian Society of Science. The matica was also careful to set up exchanges with sister maticas in Moravia, Croatia, and among the Ruthenians.

[17] This step was taken partly as the result of Frič's criticism that the matica was too narrow in outlook and ought to return to the idea of the founders. J. V. Frič, *Paměti J. V. Friče* (Prague, 1939), p. 256.

[18] A search in the Haus-, Hof-, und Staatsarchiv and the Verwaltungsarchiv in Vienna failed to turn up any significant documents on the matica.

[19] During that initial year no first prize was awarded, but the dramatist Josef Kajetán Tyl received a second prize for his novel *Poslední Čech* (The Last Czech), written in the historical spirit of Sir Walter Scott. For a detailed study of these prizes during the 1840's see František Svejovský, "Počátky literárních cen v českých zemích," *Sborník Národního Muzea v Praze*, Řada C. 11, 3 (1966): pp. 87–108.

Through such exchanges it furthered and strengthened Slavic reciprocity and solidarity.

In 1849 an exchange program was worked out with the recently (1846) established Smithsonian Institution in Washington, D.C. By 1852 the matica had received among other things volumes I and II of the *Smithsonian Contributions to Knowledge*, the *History, Conditions and Prospects of the Indian Tribes in the United States*, a *Report on the Discovery of Neptune*, and the *Ephemeris of Neptune for 1852* from the Smithsonian Institution and had in turn sent to Washington some of its publications by Palacký, Jungmann, Čelakovský, Tomek, Vocel, and a nearly complete run of its journals published to that date.[20]

In 1845–1846 the matica began specific activities to help Czech students in the Germanized middle schools become better acquainted with their mother tongue, chiefly by publishing special cheap editions of appropriate books. They made available, for example, a completely new edition of Jungmann's *Slowesnost* (textbook with literary excerpts, first published in 1820) costing 1 florin, 1845; volume I of J. F. Smetana's *Wšeobecný Dějepis Občanský* (Universal History) for 36kr. in 1846, and a special German-Czech dictionary of scholarly terminology in 1851. In addition, a few years later, in 1856 the matica entered the lists as a champion of the preservation of a common Czech and Slovak literary language by publishing a work entitled *Hlasowé o Potřebě Jednoty Spisowného Jazyka pro Čechy, Morawany, a Slowáky* (Voices Concerning the Need for a Unity of the Written Language for Czechs, Moravians, and Slovaks). This remarkable little book cited a formidable list of thirty-one Czech, Moravian, and Slovak authorities and their arguments against a separate Slovak language. Its publication was to combat the efforts by various individuals and groups among the Slovaks, especially Anton Bernolák and L'udovít Štúr, to substitute either a western Slovak dialect (*bernoláčina*) or a central Slovak dialect (*štúrovčina*) for Czech.[21] (For the Slovak reactions see below p. 54.)

The matica also began in 1844 to collect manuscripts and rare books for the museum. Among their acquisitions was a manuscript of the fourteenth-century Tomáš of Štítný, and a copy of the rare fifteenth-century Krumlov Bible. They also provided funds to help support the research and work of Šafařík in preparing a font of Glagolitic type, which at that time did not exist in Europe.

Towards the end of this decade the matica once again seriously began to work on the encyclopedia. It commenced by preparing an index of all the articles to be included, and by the end of 1851 had about 700 covering "A" through "Al." The following year, however, when Bach's absolutism began in earnest, the government refused to let the work proceed. Aside from political considerations, the matica was constantly frustrated in its attempt to produce an encyclopedia, because it lacked funds, co-workers, and editors for such an enormous undertaking. Furthermore, the chief proponent of the encyclopedia, Palacký, turned more and more from this frustrating task to the successful preparation of his *History*. The matica never did fulfill its goal. The first Czech encyclopedia was the *Slovník Naučný*, published between 1860 and 1874 without matica support and under the editorship of Rieger.

The most important activity of the matica during this decade was, of course, its publishing. For the first time there began to appear regularly original and scholarly works in various fields in Czech. Between 1841 and 1851, in addition to *Časopis*, it printed thirty-seven books. The subjects of history, natural history, and polite literature dominated, and some works were published in the fields of law, geography, travel, and pedagogy. Some important maps and atlases were also published. The most representative and important publications were works of the famous poet, Čelakovský, *Spisu Básnických Knihy Šestery* (Six Books on Poetic Writings); Jungmann's *Sebrané Spisy Weršem i Prosau* (Collected Writings: Poetry and Prose); an anthology of Czech literature; four historical studies by Tomek; Presl's greatest work, *Wšeobecný Rostlinopis* (General Botany); and, above all, two volumes of Palacký's *Dějiny Národu Českého* (History of the Czech Nation)—the most important publication of the matica since Jungmann's *Dictionary* and Šafařík's *Antiquities*. Volume I, part 1, of the History appeared in Czech in 1848 and volume III, part 2, in 1851. This history, Palacký's real life work, which made him the "father of his people," restored to the Czechs their forgotten history, gave them pride in the past, and hope and courage for the future. Each volume of this monumental work, of course, had to be approved by the office of the censor, but even so it became one of the great foundation-stones of the whole Czech rebirth.

Palacký began publishing his history in German as *Geschichte von Böhmen*, the first volume of which appeared in 1836. The first part of Volume I of the Czech edition in 1848 was a rewriting of the German. Thereafter, Palacký wrote in Czech and the parallel German version was translated from the Czech. By 1864 four volumes of the work had been

[20] The documents pertaining to this exchange are in Prague, in the Archiv Národního Musea, Registratura NM, S-7, 20, 49, 51, 64. Correspondence with the Smithsonian Institution has failed to turn up any further documents on this interesting Czech-American exchange of publications. Most likely these documents were lost in the fire of January, 1865, which destroyed all of the official records of the Smithsonian Institution.

[21] Frič records that Štúr was in Prague when this pamphlet appeared and complained to him about it. Frič, *Paměti*, p. 145.

published. These were volumes I, III, IV, and V, which brought the story to 1526, the beginning of Habsburg rule in Bohemia. Between 1874 and 1876 Palacký finished the Czech edition by bringing out the missing volume II covering the period 1252–1403, from the beginning of the reign of Otakar II to the early career of Jan Hus.

For various reasons Palacký never went beyond 1526. He had not intended in the first place to go beyond the Czech loss of independence in 1620. Furthermore, he assumed that the authorities would make access to the requisite documents for the critical century between 1526 and 1620 difficult. And finally, by the time censorship was relaxed in the 1860's, he was too involved in public affairs to continue his historical researches.

The matica also published other important works during this period. In 1841 a fifteenth-century Czech legal classic was reprinted. This was *Knihy Dewatery o Práwiech a Súdiech i o Dskách Země České* (Nine Books on Laws, Verdicts, and Records of the Land of Bohemia, first edition 1499 and enlarged 1502–1508) by the great Czech humanist Viktorín Kornel of Všehrd. In its day this book was considered the official compendium of Bohemian law and its ninteenth-century appeal to Czechs was its insistence that Czechs were the only lawful inhabitants of the land and that the Germans were foreigners. Also in 1841 was published the first of three works by Jungmann during this decade—his *Sebrané Spisy Weršem i Prosau* (Collected Writings: Poetry and Prose). In 1845 and 1846 the matica brought out revised and corrected second and third editions of his important *Slowesnost.* Finally, in 1849 there appeared a second, enlarged and revised edition of his famous *Historie Literatury České* (History of Czech Literature, first published in 1825), the first modern history of Czech literature written in Czech.

In 1842 the first of four works by V. V. Tomek, the historian and disciple of Palacký, was published. This was his *Krátký Wšeobecný Dějepis* (Short Universal History), which was followed in 1843 by his *Děje Země České* (History of the Czech Lands), and in 1845 by his *Děje Mocnářstwí Rakauského* (History of the Austrian Empire) and finally in 1849 the first volume of his important *Děje University Pražské* (History of the University of Prague) in honor of its 500th anniversary.

The most important publication of 1845 was Volume I of *Výbor z Literatury České* (Anthology of Czech Literature), which was intended to range from oldest times to the present. It was collected and edited by Palacký, Šafařík, Hanka, and by Jungmann, who served as the chief editor. This first volume, covering the period up to the beginning of the fifteenth century, is still considered one of the best anthologies of early Czech literature.

One year later, in 1846, the first of two important works in the field of natural history was published—Presl's greatest work *Wšeobecný Rostlinopis* (General Botany). In 1848 the matica also published his *Počátkové Rostlinosloví* (Introduction to Botanical Terminology) as a companion of the first work.

In 1847 the most important of the several books of belles-lettres published during this decade appeared. It was *Spisů Básnických Knihy Šestery* (Six Books of Poetic Writings) by the famous Czech poet, Čelakovský.

Three important translations were published during this period: Milton's *Paradise Lost* by Jungmann in 1843, Shakespeare's *Romeo and Juliet* by F. Doucha in 1847, and Virgil's poems by Karel Vinařický in 1851. Jungmann's translation of *Paradise Lost* was extremely important in that it proved conclusively that Czech was capable of grace and power and could express lofty thoughts.

During the revolutionary period of 1848–1849 the matica as an institution accomplished little. Many of its leaders, who were as interested in politics as in culture, eagerly seized this opportunity to put their energies into genuine political activity. At least five members of the Executive Committee, Palacký, Šafařík, Vocel, Čejka, and Staněk, were members of the Kroměříž diet. As a result they temporarily neglected the cultural activities of the matica.

1850–1860

After the failure of the revolutionary phase of the spring of the peoples, the political-cultural leaders of the matica returned to its offices in the Nostitz palace to preserve and advance the national movement as best they could through purely cultural activities. The new absolutism which was instituted by the end of 1851 by Bach, proved to be much more rigid than that of Metternich. Prague lay under a state of siege until 1853, Czech "home rule" was negligible, Bach's Press Law and Law of Associations firmly curtailed all political and many national activities, and all forms of particularism were suppressed.

The most feared problem of the monarchy at this time was nationalism and one of the most alarming varieties was that of the Czechs. The leaders of the matica, especially Palacký and those who had been to Kroměříž, were closely watched. Leopold von Sacher-Masoch, director of the Prague police, was particularly interested in forcing Palacký out of the museum and matica.[22] Not only was Sacher-

[22] Because of the political activities of some of its leaders and because of articles about the Slavic Congress of 1848 and letters of Hus which had appeared in *Časopis*, the matica was compromised in the eyes of Vienna. Palacký, as editor of *Časopis*, and as an active participant in the Slavic Congress, was particularly watched by Vienna. Furthermore, the publication in 1851 by the matica of Volume III, part 2, of his

Masoch successful in this, but in 1852 he also arranged for the conservative Count Kristián of Valdštejn, who had previously not even been a member of the museum, to replace Neuberg as its president. Even after Sacher-Masoch was transferred to Graz in 1854, things did not improve, for Vienna saw to it that his place was taken by Anton Paumann who was just as thoroughly anti-Czech as Sacher-Masoch. He saw to it that the museum and matica were directed by conservatives and that its more liberal members were muzzled.

Although the matica never regained the unique position it had held during the 1830's and 1840's, the relative lack of other political and cultural activity during the bleak 1850's caused it, because of its publishing activities, to become (along with the committee to build the national theater) the chief defender of the Czech national movement during the 1850's.[23]

One of the first acts aimed at curtailing its importance and influence occurred in April, 1852, when it was told that henceforth it would be required to notify the Municipal Captaincy (*Hejtmanství*, *Hauptmannschaft*) of its meetings, so that a representative of the *Hejmanství* could be present. This form of police supervision lasted until 1866.

In July, 1852, Neuberg resigned as curator and was replaced by professor Purkyně, who was assisted by Šafařík, Erben, Frič, Hanka, Tomek, Vocel, and Nebeský who then served as secretary and editor of *Časopis*. Jungmann, Presl, and Čelakovský were dead and Palacký had been forced out.

The new by-laws of this period necessarily stressed that the main goal of the matica was the scholarly fostering of the Czech language and literature. The government required that it become completely subservient to the museum and that it request permission from the latter for each publication. Thus, by strictly controlling the conservative museum, the government also controlled the matica.

The Law of Associations in 1852 required that the name of the museum be changed from that of National Museum to the Museum of the Bohemian Kingdom and that the matica be reduced from an independent committee to a subordinate section.

The negative features of absolutism are clearly revealed by the records of the matica. Membership fell from a total of new members for the year 1852 of 327 to 31 in 1860, and contributions correspondingly fell from 14,635fl. in 1852 to 3,542fl. in 1860. The modest support of the patriotic nobility all but ceased after 1849. Still, in spite of the decrease of the annual number of new members and contributions the total membership grew from 4,105 members in 1852 to 4,655 plus 142 corporations in 1860, and the total funds from 57,791fl. in 1852 to 79,120fl. in 1860.

The annual decrease reflects not only the ravages of absolutism, but also the discontent of many Czechs with the greatly curtailed activities of the matica, and the general discontent with all national life at this time, while the overall increase suggests the importance of the matica as one of the few outlets for Czech national aspirations.

Apart from the publication of books and journals the activities of the matica were extremely limited in this period. It made a few book grants and arranged for some exchanges of books and journals. For example, books were given to several Czech gymnasia and to some Slovak libraries. Books were also sent to the Bavarian Academy, the Lusatian Maćica, and the Royal Bohemian Society of Learning. Exchanges were arranged with the St. Petersburg Academy, the Danish Archeological Society, the Ossolineum in Lwów, and the Society of Learning in Cracow.

As a result of Bach's absolutism it is not surprising that most of the publications in this period were scholarly, practical, and neutral. The matica had to be very careful to avoid political and religious subjects. For example, in 1856, when it wanted to publish Jan Krejčí's *Geologie* (Geology), it had to take care that there was nothing in the manuscript against religion, and even then it was not finally published until 1860–1863. Works about and by Hus were, of course, not permitted.[24] Under the dead hand of absolutism the matica restricted its publishing primarily to harmless works on botany, health, travel, and translations of Shakespeare's plays. It did, however, manage to bring out Volume IV, parts 1 and 2, of Palacký's *History*, which brought the narrative through the reign of Jiří of Poděbrady, the last native Czech king, and to his death in 1471.[25]

History, which treated the Hussite Wars (from the death of Žižka in 1424 to the beginning of the reign of Ladislav Posthumus in 1439) and thus did much to revive national feelings, angered Vienna. So complete was Sacher-Masoch's victory over Palacký that, after Palacký had been a member of the museum board for thirty-four years, he was not even thanked formally or recognized for his service by the museum.

[23] In 1850, to help compensate for the failure of 1848–1849, a committee was founded to build a Czech national theater, of which Palacký was also president. By the time of the first opening of the National Theater in 1881 (it burned and had to be reopened in 1883), the committee had raised nearly two million florins. See my study *Czech Nationalism: A Study of the National Theatre Movement, 1845–1883* (Urbana, Ill., 1964).

[24] Apparently Michail Petrovich Pogodin, professor of history at the University of Moscow, had written to Šafařík regarding the works of Hus, for in 1853 Šafařík answered that "No one in Austria may publish Hus's works, only works against him . . . . Let the dead rest." Tieftrunk, *Dějiny*, p. 169.

[25] By 1859 eight of Shakespeare's plays had been published. They caused no problems with the censor's office, and extended the Czechs' acquaintance with a great poet of the non-German world; they did not do much to increase interest and participation in the matica, which became more and more a simple printing society.

The matica also initiated the publication of two new journals in addition to *Časopis*—*Živa* and *Památky.* In 1852 the great scientist Purkyně had suggested that something practical be published, primarily on science for the use of teachers in the Czech middle schools. This led to the founding of a natural history journal for which permission was received in December, 1852. It was called *Živa* (from *život,* meaning life)[26] and was edited by Purkyně and Krejčí. Although called a "natural history magazine," it was actually a yearbook averaging about 300 pages an issue. It was an immediate success and soon had 1,500 subscribers; indeed it was largely self-supporting, and lasted for twenty-five years, 1853–1878.

The success of *Živa* stimulated the archaeological section of the museum to set up its own journal. This section complained that *Časopis* did not devote enough of its space to archaeology and claimed that its members had all kinds of articles to publish. Therefore, two years later, in 1855, the museum authorized, and the matica published, another learned journal devoted to archaeology and geography. It was called *Památky Archeologické a Místopisné* (Archaeological and Topographic Relics) and like *Živa,* it appeared anually and was sold at half price to matica members. *Památky,* edited by Karel V. Zap, was also successful, but not nearly as popular as *Živa,* because of its more specialized materials. By the end of 1854 it had 569 pre-paid subscribers. It continued to be published by the matica until 1892, after which the Czech Academy took it over. In 1855 the matica tried to stabilize the number of copies of each of these two journals—publishing 1,000 of *Živa* and 800 of *Památky. Časopis* was still appearing, and naturally the two other journals competed with it, so much so that in 1857 the number of copies of *Časopis* was cut from 4,000 to 3,500.

Slowly the three journals began to specialize: *Časopis* concentrated on literature, philology, and philosophy; *Památky* published primarily archaeological and historical articles, while *Živa* took the field of natural history. Such were the activities of the 1850's.

EPILOGUE

Because of its important pioneering activities it may seem surprising that the matica did not experience a period of great growth and activity after the fall of Bach in 1860 and with the subsequent freedom of the age of constitutionalism.

Though surprising, this development is rather easily explained and was mentioned in the introduction to this study. After 1860 there were simply too many political opportunities and freedoms for Czech patriots to continue to rely so much on cultural substitutes for political activity. This is a characteristic feature not only of the Czech national movement but of the whole Austro-Slav national revival—while cultural advancement remained as important a desideratum as ever, as soon as political tools became available, cultural tools were no longer considered so politically and nationally important. Furthermore, by 1862 other societies and institutions, such as the Umělcká Beseda (Artists' Union), the choral society Hlahol, the gymnastic society Sokol (Falcon), and the literary society Svatobor were founded, each of which either took over a part of the activities of the matica or drew away members from it. New popular publishing concerns were founded. One of the most important of these was the Matica Lidů (People's Foundation), organized by several patriots in 1867 for the purpose of publishing good popular books as cheaply as possible; for 1fl. members received six publications annually. Soon the Matice Ceská was reduced almost exclusively to the publishing of scholarly books.

Thereafter, under the aegis of men of the caliber of K. J. Erben, Rieger, Tomek, Alois Jirásek, Jan Jakubec, and Lubor Niederle, the matica continued to contribute to the mainstream of Czech cultural development by publishing books and journals; it advanced education by making generous book grants to schools in Bohemia, Moravia, and among the Slovaks, and it strengthened Slavic mutuality by developing publication-exchange programs with other maticas, libraries, and institutions throughout the Slavic world. After the post-World War II restructuring of Czech intellectual and cultural life the matica ceased to exist, though its name is still preserved by a lecture society.

IV. THE MORAVIAN MATICA, 1836: A FRAIL OPPONENT OF GERMANIZATION

> The purpose of the matica should be the publication of books which can find a publisher neither at the Czech matica nor at Moravian publishers, especially books written in Moravia about Moravia which merit publication.
>
> A. V. Šembera

The seeds of the Matice Moravská were carried from Prague to Moravia in 1830 (during the same year that the Matice Česká was founded) by the young Bohemian Czech, Alois Vojtěch Šembera (1807–1882), who moved to Brno to take a position as a minor official of the government. His success

---

In addition the matica published Čelakovský's *Mudrosloví Národu Slovanskeho ve příslovích* (Wisdom of the Slavic Nation in their Proverbs) in 1852, Štúr's *O Národních Písních a Pověstech Plemen Slovanských* (National Songs and Stories of the Slavs) in 1853, and Volume One of the twelve-volume *Dějepis Města Prahy* (History of Prague) by Tomek in 1855.

[26] *Živa* was also the Czech name for the Roman deity Ceres (Demeter), the goddess of agriculture and harvest, and the protector of peace and of plebeian freedoms.

in eventually founding the Moravian matica somewhat repaid the Bohemian debt to Moravia for having sent one of her native sons, Palacký, to Prague in 1823.

The Margraviate of Moravia was a small province, half the size of Bohemia and about the size of Massachusetts, with a population in 1857 of 1,867,000, of which 70 per cent was Czech, 28 per cent German, the remainder consisting of a few Jews, Slovaks, and Croats. The people were 95 per cent Catholic. The main cities were Brno (Brünn) with a population in 1857 of about 61,000 and Olomouc (Olmütz) with 14,000.

For several reasons the task of the awakeners in Moravia was much more difficult and less rewarding than in Bohemia, but since so much less is known about the Czech revival in Moravia than in Bohemia, it deserves more study than it has heretofore received. Moravia had no national center comparable to Prague. Brno, only 40 per cent the size of Prague, had so few important institutions or centers of learning that it neither produced nor attracted many nationally minded intellectuals. Throughout the province there was not a single publisher of Czech books, no literary or scholarly journals, no university or academy, and not even a Czech-language secondary school until 1867. Consequently Moravian Czechs lacked a strong national center and had few patriots and scholars to push the revival, to foster scholarly activities, or to unite those of Czech sentiment. There were, furthermore, few members of the "historic" nobility to sponsor and financially support patriots. The German element was stronger in Moravia than in Bohemia and the two national groups did not live in blocs as in Bohemia, but were closely intermingled throughout the province. Not only was Brno geographically closer to Vienna than Prague, but Moravia's economy was more oriented to Austria than to Bohemia.

There was also a strong separatist feeling in Moravia, among those who were jealous of the Bohemian Czechs and resented Moravia's tie with Bohemia.[1] At times the Moravian Estates had regarded Prague as dangerous to their independent development as Vienna and many *Moravane* considered their nationality to be distinct from the Czech. The Germans naturally exploited to their advantage the weakness of national consciousness among the Moravian Czechs and the feelings of separatism.

Under such circumstances there were of course no national societies to foster the Czech revival. There were in fact only two scholarly societies in all Moravia, the Mährisch-schlesische Ackerbaugesellschaft (Moravsko-slezská Společnost pro Zemědělství, Přírodu, Vědy, a Vlastivědu, Moravian-Silesian Society for Agriculture, Natural History, Science, and Home Science) founded in 1769,[2] and the museum which this society founded in 1818 in honor of Francis I, the Francisceum. Both societies were not only completely Germanized, aristocratic, scholarly, and provincial rather than national, but were also in a state of vegetation, and neither published a journal.

The Societas Incognitorum (Society of Unknowns), the first learned society not only in Moravia, but in all Czech lands, founded in 1746, had long since ceased to exist. It had been founded in Olomouc chiefly through the efforts of Josef Freiherr von Petrasch, who was well educated and had traveled widely in Western Europe. Acquainted with the activities of learned societies there, he wanted to do something similar for his own country and people. He gathered around him some like-minded individuals, who founded the society, which was housed in his home in Olomouc, where it met quarterly.

Its most significant activity was the publication of a monthly journal, the *Monatliche Auszüge Alt- und Neuer Belehrten Sachen*. This journal was a frank imitation of similar Western journals such as the *Journal des Sçavans* and the *Philosophical Transactions* of the Royal Society of London, both of which were published as early as 1665, and the German *Acta Eruditorum*, published from 1682 in Leipzig.

The *Auszüge* printed the papers of the society's members, necrologies, news, and similar information. The society and the journal lasted only until 1751 when Petrasch left Olomouc. It was not a national society at all, nor even necessarily patriotic, and it was strictly German in spirit. In reality it was the extension of one man's desire to see a learned journal published in his homeland.

The purpose of the Agriculture Society was strictly utilitarian and the aim of the Francisceum was to study critically and pragmatically the history of Moravia and to advance culture and knowledge, certainly not to foster the Czech revival. By 1850 it was divided into four sections: history, apiculture,[3] natural history, and gardening and agriculture. Even though it was founded prior to the Czech museum it never had the influence of the latter nor the support and leadership of many scholars and nobles. Patriots like Dobrovský, Palacký, and Count Sternberg did not exist in Moravia.

The Francisceum was directed by one of its founders, the former governor of Moravia (1815–1827)

[1] Moravia had at one time (during the period of the shadowy Great Moravian Empire of the ninth century) been independent, but from 1029 on it has been incorporated with Bohemia and was usually ruled by younger members of the royal house—facts which rankled some Moravian patriots.

[2] The great geneticist, Gregor Johann Mendel (1822–1884), was a member of this society, before which he read his pioneering work *Versuch Über Pflanzenhybriden* on February 8 and March 8, 1865. This paper was printed by that society in 1866 but was generally ignored until the 1890's.

[3] Most of the maticas also published works on apiculture, an important aspect of peasant life, producing the staples of wax and honey.

Count Anton Friedrich Mitrovský (1770–1842), leader of the separatist movement in Moravia. Once in 1833 Palacký wrote to the important Czech Moravian historian Antonín Boček (1802–1847) about cooperating with historical materials. It is said that Count Mitrovský advised Boček (who at the time was tutor to the count's family) to sever all connections with Bohemia, "for Moravia is an independent province and need pay no attention to Bohemia." [4]

As close as Moravia ever came to acquiring a Czech-oriented academy or national society was through the efforts of Šembera and other patriots to organize a Moravian matica. Although this particular foundation was quite tame and colorless in comparison with its sister organizations, its accomplishments modest and publications few, and although it was usually in financial straits, as the only Czech literary or national society in Moravia it did more than any other organization to promote the Czech language and national consciousness in Moravia, to overcome disinterest, Germanization, and lethargy, and to advance scholarship. By 1869 it had published or distributed thirty-seven scholarly and popular works, founded the second most important scholarly journal in Czech lands, organized some libraries, exchanged publications throughout the Slavic world, and garnered over 700 members. Its history can be divided into several distinct periods: from 1836 to 1848 when it existed as a private organization, from 1848 to 1849 when it was known briefly as the Jednota Moravská (Moravian Union), from 1849 to 1853 when it was called the Národní Jednota Moravská sv. Cyrilla a Methoda (National Moravian Union of Saints Cyril and Methodius), and since 1853 to the present, when it again took the name of the Moravian matica. This study, however, will treat its history only to about 1869 by which time its pioneering activities were over.

1836–1848

Coming from Prague, Šembera was understandably dismayed at the lack of Czech national and cultural life and activity in Moravia. He soon became convinced that the main reasons for the weakness of national consciousness in Moravia were the insufficiency of the Czech book market, the lack of a single publisher of Czech books, the non-existence of a literary or scholarly journal published in Moravia, and the lack of an institution to support and foster Czech language and literature. His efforts over twenty years (until he left to take the chair of Czech language and literature at the University of Vienna in 1850) as a literary historian, editor, and leader of the matica made him one of the most important of the early "awakeners" in Moravia.

Patriot though Šembera was, he was not one to rush precipitously into something, for he took no action to remedy the situation until 1836, when he began collecting money from a few friends and patriots and organized a society along the lines of the Czech matica, to publish books for Moravian Czechs to acquaint them with Czech and especially Moravian culture and history. Among those who worked with and supported Šembera was professor Jan Helcelet (1812–1876), a professor of economics and natural history at the Imperial Technical School in Brno[5] and one of the most important national leaders and scholars in Moravia.

Šembera's society, the Matice Moravská, was private, for he thought Czech nationalism in Moravia too undeveloped to support a public venture. Up to 1845 it consisted only of a small circle of like-minded friends and patriots. Thereafter, in an effort to give the organization more permanance and strength, Šembera turned it into a sort of stock company into which members paid a minimum of 5fl. and from which they received publications in proportion to the number of shares held. Even so the matica remained a private concern and limped on for three more years until the events of 1848 eclipsed it.

There was some opposition to this form of operation, for some members wanted the society to be fashioned into a public organization after the manner of the Czech matica. Šembera, however, was against such a move; as he wrote to his friend Václav Stanek (a member of the Executive Committee of the Czech Matica), "Moravia lacks a center. If there were only a university or an academy it would be much better. Even the museum [Francisceum] could support research and publication, [but] Brno lacks scientific activity and patriots who could unite and join our scattered strength." [6] Šembera also complained about the lack of any publicity regarding his organization: "Up to now there has not been the smallest mention of the founding of the Moravian matica." [7]

Throughout this eleven-year period the matica, always operating on a shoestring, published twelve items, mainly national songs and handbooks. Its

[4] Hanuš, *Národní Museum* 1: p. 291. Boček had been the official historiographer of the Moravian Estates since 1837. Zacek believes that this lack of cooperation also may have been due to the fact that Boček forged some of his documents. See Joseph Frederick Zacek, *Palacký: The Historian as Scholar and Nationalist* (The Hague, 1970), p. 47.

[5] This was essentially a German institution, but some of the professors there such as the mathematician Karel Kořistka and the natural historian Friedrich Kolenaty, worked with Helcelet to further the development of nationalism in Moravia.

[6] H. Traub, "Dějiny Matice Moravské," *Časopis Matice Moravské* 34, 3 (1910): p. 200.

[7] Part of the reason for lack of publicity was a latent fear in Bohemia of Moravian literary separatism similar to Slovak separatism. Furthermore the main Czech language newspaper in Moravia, *Moravské Noviny* (Moravian News), was an official government paper hardly inclined to foster Šembera's activities.

first two publications reflected the general aim of all the maticas—to put into the hands of their countrymen good original literature in the native tongue and to provide the masses with practical handbooks. In 1836 Šembera published František Matouš Klácel's *Lyrické Básně* (Lyric Poems).[8] Klácel (1808–1882) was an important poet, philosopher, and a rather free-thinking Augustinian who during the preceding year had become a professor at the Philosophical Institute in Brno. (See below, p. 35.) Also in 1836 the matica published Karel Slavoj Amerling's handbook on horticultural grafting, *Štěpařství pro Lid* (Grafting for the People).

Several other noteworthy books were published during this early period: Klácel's *Básně* (Poems, 1841); his psychological study, *Mostek aneb Sestavení Skormných Myšlenek o Tom, na Čem Každému Záleželi Má* (Little Bridge or the Collection of Humble Thoughts which Ought to be Important to All, 1842); and his translation, *Bajky Bidpajovy* (The Persian Fables of Bidpai, 1846). In 1841 and 1842 the matica published two editions of Šembera's *Vpád Mongolů do Moravy* (The Mongol Invasion of Moravia) in connection with the sexcentenary of the saving of Moravia from the Mongols in 1240, and in 1843 *Básně* (Poems), of the most important Moravian poet, Vincenc Furch (1817–1864).[9]

1848–1853

The revolution of 1848 caused Šembera and several other patriots in Brno and Olomouc to come together and replace the private matica with a larger, more permanent, active, ambitious and public organization to fight Germanization, especially the Germanizing activities of Count Jan Antonín Arnošt Schaffgotsch (1804–1870), bishop of Brno and principal anti-Czech figure, to provide a society through which the individual efforts of patriots could be correlated, to develop among the people a taste for reading good Czech books, to foster Czech language and literature, and to work for the equality of both German and Czech, especially in the schools.

The results of their activity was the creation of the Jednota Moravská (Moravian Union) in June, 1848, as a scholarly and humanitarian society. According to its by-laws it intended to gather funds for the purpose of establishing a reading room and stocking it with journals appearing all over the empire, to establish a salon for literary conversation, the reading of literature, and other similar literary activities, to publish useful works for the Slavs of Moravia, to establish natural history collections, and to support libraries.[10] The Jednota was to be financed by small fees and contributions.

Among those who supported Šembera were Jan Ohéral (1810–1868) an important newspaper editor[11] and František Sušil (1804–1868), a poet, priest, editor, and the leader of patriotic Catholics.[12] Klácel, who also supported Šembera, said at one of its early meetings, "There is no more safe and sure way to lasting national liberty than through the equality and sincerity [*upřímé*] of education."[13]

The society was practically stillborn and lasted only long enough to publish one book in Czech and German—Šembera's *O Rovnosti Jazyka Českého a Německého v Moravě* (*Über die Gleichstellung der Beiden Landessprachen in Mähren*) before Vienna suppressed it. In this work Šembera argued that parity of language had previously existed in Moravia, but not in recent centuries. He pointed out that since the seventeenth century there had not been a Czech bishop or *hejtman* in Moravia, that many of the clergy and officials were trained only in German, a situation which created a gap between them and the people, and that Czech scarcely existed in public life. In conclusion he suggested a practical way of restoring this parity by using both languages in the schools.

The spirit of revolution and nationalism, however, was too strong during 1848–1849 for this first failure to discourage completely Moravian patriots. Shortly after Vienna suppressed the Jednota, members of the Moravian Club of deputies at Kroměříž tried in March, 1849, to reorganize as the Národní Jednota Moravská sv. Cyrilla a Methoda (National Moravian Union of SS. Cyril and Methodius). Ohéral, chairman of the Moravian Club, prepared the by-laws which were generally the same as the Jednota.

[8] All bibliographic citations in this chapter are from H. Traub, "Dějiny Matice Moravské," *Časopis Matice Moravské* **34**, 3 (1910): pp. 197–229; **34**, 4 (1910): pp. 313–341; **35**, 1 (1911): pp. 60–102; **35**, 2 (1911): pp. 154–192.

[9] Other publications of this period were a general collection of *Písne Vlastenské* (Patriotic Songs, 1843), an anonymous collection of poems, *Hlasy Moravanů u Příjezdu Jeho Cís. Výsosti Arciknížete Františka Karla do Holomouce* (Moravian Voices in honor of His Majesty Archduke Francis Karl's Visit to Olomouc 1846), *Adressa Poděkovací Císaři Pánu a Universitě Vídeňské* (Declaration of Gratitude to the Emperor and the University of Vienna, 1848) in thanks for the recently promulgated constitution, a collection of Silesian national songs (*Národní Písně*, 1848) by the minor poet Cyprian Lelek, and finally, the Lutheran minister Daniel Sloboda's *Populární Botanika* (Popular Botany, 1848). This phase of the history of the Moravian matica ended as it began—publishing national songs and handbooks for the people.

[10] Traub, "Dějiny Matice Moravské," *Časopis Matice Moravské* **34**, 3 (1910): p. 202.

[11] Ohéral is considered a renegade Czech by some (Jakub Malý for example) because after he moved to Prague in 1852 he went over to the German side and after his move to Vienna in 1864 he became a centralist.

[12] Considered by some to be the greatest of the awakeners in Moravia, Sušil consistently worked for a closer union between Moravia and Bohemia. Among his most important publications is *Moravské Národní Písně* published in 1835 (four years before Čelakovský published his *Ohlas Písní Českých* [Echoes of Czech Songs]).

[13] Albert Pražák, *Národ se Bránil* (Prague, 1945), p. 311.

These activities were to be financed by fees and donations paid into a fund called the "Komenský Treasury." Plans were prepared to begin activity in Kroměříž on March 9, 1849 (SS. Cyril and Methodius Day). Unfortunately, the dissolution of the parliament on March 7 wrecked this last attempt.

After the dispersal of the parliament the Moravian Club broke up and its members scattered. A few, however, among whom were Ohéral, Viktor Brázdil (1834–1901), who later became the official archivist of the province of Moravia, and Alois Pražák (1820–1901), a politician and lawyer, returned to Brno where they continued to work for reorganization. Within ten days they circulated 500 copies of an announcement calling for help and support. This time they were successful and on April 17, 1849, the National Moravian Union of SS. Cyril and Methodius was organized formally. Karel Havlíček-Borovský (1821–1856), the greatest Czech journalist of the nineteenth century, was present at this meeting and later wrote in his *Národní Noviny* (National News), "Each of us rejoices that finally in Moravia, where Slavic life is so limited, an important step has been taken to improve national life." [14]

The assembly approved almost the same goals as those worked out previously at Kroměříž. The main difference was, in deference to political realities, that the new by-laws stressed the educational rather than the nationalistic nature of the society's activities. Even so, Vienna called for several redraftings of the by-laws, each requiring further clarification of the strictly non-political nature of the society. Finally the National Union amended its by-laws to include the following statement:

> The National Union is a scholarly and humanitarian society aiming to publish books, support libraries, and reading rooms, natural history collections, and art works. The society rejects all kinds of political activity, and it will never concern itself with politics, not even by publishing newspapers, journals, or books connected with politics, nor will it in any way collect money for the purpose of distributing such political writings.[15]

After this complete and total surrender to Vienna, its by-laws were finally approved November 10, 1849. A new era in the Moravian national awakening began, that of official and public activity rather than the isolated activity of individuals. In commenting upon this Malý ecstatically wrote, "From that time on Moravia was again ours," that is, not totally German.[16]

There were three kinds of membership—supporting, active, and contributing, for 100fl., 50fl., and 2fl. respectively. All members were permitted to participate in all activities, to make suggestions, and to vote. Members of the first two classes received publications free and those in the third class received them at half price.

Among the officers of the National Union were Klácel as chairman, Šembera as a secretary, and Pražák as treasurer. Members of the governing board included Brázdil, Professor Helcelet, and Count Bedřich Sylva-Taroucca (1811–1881), whose Portuguese ancestors had served under Prince Eugen of Savoy and later settled in Moravia. The count was a priest and theologian and had studied in Prague, where he had been greatly impressed by the efforts of Count Sternberg to further the Czech national revival in Bohemia and he wished to do similar things for the Czechs in Moravia. All told, the board consisted of forty men from Brno and the countryside, nineteen of whom were clergymen.

Within a month after its by-laws had been approved the society had 245 members and at the end of its first year (1849) 303 members, many of whom were Catholic priests. Several members of the nationally minded nobility, such as Count Egbert Belcredi (brother of the statesman Richard) the leader of the moderately patriotic Moravian nobility; Count Emanuel Poetting-Persing (1820–1898), a patriotic priest; and the historian, Petr Ritter von Chlumecký (1825–1863), and some of the leaders of the Czech renaissance in Bohemia like Palacký, Havlíček, and Purkyně, also joined.

This initial success was blighted almost immediately, however, by the antipathy of Bishop Schaffgotsch of Brno. He took offense at the leadership of Klácel whom the good bishop thought entirely too liberal in his religious views. Klácel soon left his order, became a socialist, and in 1869 emigrated to the United States.[17]

In reference to this conflict of personalities Rieger wrote to his friend Karel Hušek that Klácel had been removed from his professorship "because of aspiring ideas," because he had lectured from books to which the bishop objected, because of his association "with people of incorrect sentiments and activi-

[14] Traub, "Dějiny Matice Moravské, *Časopis Matice Moravské* 34, 3 (1910): p. 205. Thereafter, however, Havlíček did not print much about Moravia. Once in 1850 a reader of his *Slovan* (The Slav) complained, "Each time your *Slovan* comes to hand I always look in vain for something about Moravia. Other than notes from the bishop of Brno and other important lords and one letter from Kroměříž you have given us nothing on Moravia. It is my belief that there is enough activity to warrant more coverage." *Slovan*, 1850: p. 1581.

[15] Traub, "Dějiny Matice Moravské, *Časopis Matice Moravské* 34, 3 (1919): pp. 209–210.

[16] Jakub Malý, *Naše Znovuzrození: Přehled Národního Života Českého za Posledního Půlstoletí* (Prague, 1880–1884), pt. 3: p. 81.

[17] Klácel accepted the invitation to edit a Czech newspaper, the *Slovan Amerikanský* (American Slav) in Iowa City, Iowa. There he changed his first name to Ladimír and hoped to realize his dream of a freer society by organizing in 1870 the Union of Freethinkers. Until his death in Belle Plaines, Iowa, he spent his years writing, editing, and organizing liberal movements.

ties"—especially Ohéral and Šembera, and also because of his *Slawomanie.*[18]

The bishop was also disturbed at rumors that the National Union was going to print the works of Voltaire, George Sand, Trollope, and Heine. Furthermore, several priests had allegedly "fallen," having joined the National Union. As a result of the bishop's opposition many of the clergymen resigned their membership, including Šusil and Count Sylva-Taroucca, and founded a new rival society in August, 1850, in direct opposition and competition with the National Union. This was the *Dědictví sv. Cyrila a Methoda* (Heritage of SS. Cyril and Methodius), a religious (even ultramontain) rather than national society for the purpose of publishing Catholic books of various sorts especially for the Catholics of Moravia. In 1852 they also began publishing an almanac, *Moravan*, to compete with *Koleda* which was published by the National Union (see below p. 37). This society was extremely successful. In ten years it had 10,254 members and a fund of over 73,000fl.[19]

Since in Moravia as well as in Bohemia the clergy represented the largest group of national supporters, such a rival organization seriously hurt the National Union. The clergy were not only the best writers, but also the largest group of book buyers and supporters of literary societies. So seriously was the Union hurt by this rival organization that only fifteen members attended its meeting in April, 1851. In spite of such difficulties, however, the National Union pushed ahead.

Since there was no institution to sponsor it the National Union had to fend for itself. To increase membership it organized some agents, about ten in all, throughout the countryside and also in Prague, to promote the National Union and its publications. At first its headquarters were in a room in the private apartment of Pražák, where it stayed until it moved into more suitable quarters in 1852.

The National Union apparently conceived of itself as some sort of an incipient academy, for it divided itself into five divisions—historical, philological, natural history, art, and humanitarian and economic—to organize better and foster scholarly work in Moravia. It also did what it could to work against Moravian separatism from Bohemia. In various ways it tried to spread education among the people by organizing libraries, publishing, and exchanging publications with other Slavic literary and scholarly societies.

In 1850, for example, it created a Library Council to build up existing libraries and to found new ones. It donated copies of its own publications to existing libraries and succeeded in establishing nine small libraries (usually consisting of about 100 books and a bookcase) in connection with schools. In 1850, following the example of the Czech matica, it began to exchange publications with other Slavic societies such as the Czech, Croatian, and Ruthenian maticas, and with the university libraries in Prague, Cracow, Lwów, Vienna, and Graz. Its chief activity, of course, was publishing and through 1853 it published or distributed twenty works, including its annual journal.

In October, 1849, some patriots pointed out that if the National Union wished to function like the Czech matica a journal would be requisite. Many, however, considered such a venture premature. They argued that there was not yet enough interest in Moravia to support such a journal, nor enough contributors to keep it going, and that the largest body of supporters of the National Union, the clergy, especially those of the clergy with writing talent, were already publishing in a Catholic journal, *Hlas Jednoty Katolické pro Víru, Svobodu, a Mravní Ušlechtilost* (Voice of the Catholic Union for Faith, Freedom, and Moral Nobility), founded by Sušil in 1840.

After two years of discussion a compromise solution was agreed upon which resulted in the appearance in 1851 of *Koleda* (Christmas Carol), an almanac edited by Helcelet. It was especially designed to appeal to a wide segment of the Czech population of Moravia, especially to the rural masses. Among other things it offered popular and useful articles on natural history, agriculture, technology, geography, travel, biography, and humor. About 3,000 copies of each issue were printed for distribution in Moravia, Bohemia, and Slovakia. It lasted until 1858.

Other than eight volumes of *Koleda* their most important publications at this time were three more works of Klácel: *Slovník pro Čtenaře Novin, v Němž se Vysvětlují Slova Cizího Původu* (Dictionary for Readers of Newspapers in Which Words of Foreign Origin are Explained, 1851), a second volume of *The Fables of Bidpai* (1852), and his translation of Goethe's *Reineck Fuchs* (called in Czech *Ferina Lišák z Kuliferdy*, 1852) based on the medieval beast epic of Reynard the Fox which is full of criticism and concept for the upper classes and the clergy.[20]

[18] Jan Heidler, ed., *Příspěvky k Listaři Dra Frant. Lad. Riegra* (2 v. in one, Prague, 1924–1926), 1: p. 15.

[19] While this society was in competition with the matica it was certainly not a national society as the titles of some of its early publications indicate—Dr. Jan E. Bily's *Dejiny Církve* (History of the Church), Professor Matěj Procháska's *Život bl. Sarkandra* (Life of the Blessed Sarkander, 1576–1620, a Catholic martyr from Moravia), and Fr. Sušil's translation of the Jewish Wars by Josephus (*Válka Židovská*).

[20] Additional publications included *Prostonárodní Výklad zákona Obecného od 17. Března 1849* (Popular Explanation of the Public Laws Since March 17, 1849) and *Pěstounka Čili Vychování Malých Dítek Mimo Školu* (The Governess or the Rearing of Small Children Outside of School) by the pedagogue František Mosner (1797–1876) both of which appeared in 1851. During the next two years they brought out a posthumous

In the hopes of lessening German opposition and of being able to accomplish more for the Czech revival in Moravia than the publication of a few rather unimportant books, the National Union sought some kind of association with the Agricultural Society such as the Czech matica had with the Czech Museum. The new law of societies of November, 1852, however, prevented this and restricted the activities of the National Union strictly to publishing. All other dreams of national activity, especially that of developing into an academy, were killed.

Given the political realities of the Bach era, it is surprising that the National Union functioned at all. It was kept under strict surveillance, an agent of the police attending all of their meetings. The Union, furthermore, was always in financial straits. When, for example, it was invited in 1851 by the Croatian matica to send delegates to a congress of Slavic philologists in Zagreb it could not afford to participate.

During the difficult time of the early 1850's, Helcelet wrote to the Czech matica (of which he was a member) suggesting that the National Union become the Moravian branch of the Czech society, but the Czechs were themselves having so much trouble under the Bach regime that such a merger seemed unwise.

In March, 1853, the National Union, giving up all higher aspirations, voluntarily reconstituted itself officially as the Matice Moravská. Its new by-laws defined its goal as simply that of supporting Czechoslovak literature by publishing good books particularly needed by Moravian Czechs.

1853–1869

The new by-laws of the Moravian matica were approved in December, 1853. Membership was open to all, former members the National Union becoming automatically members of the matica. Those who contributed 100fl. or more received two free copies of all publications and those who contributed 50fl. received one free copy. This new organization began officially in January, 1854, with a fund of only 4,364fl. Helcelet was its first president and was assisted by Pražák and Josef Chytil (1812–1861), a historian.

One of the few extant documents in Vienna pertaining to the various maticas is one about this reorganization of the Moravian matica.[21] In it the police in Brno briefly reviewed the activities of this society since 1848, recorded its name change and reorganization, and noted, that the society was so weakly endowed that it seldom had more than 600fl. a year to work with. The report also made rather slighting comments about some of the matica's members. Helcelet, for example, was described as a "calm person with an overpowering passion for Greek and Slavic literature." One Anton Muhsil, a bookbinder from Jihlava (Iglau), was called "*harmlos.*" A Dr. Fritz was termed an "eager lad" (*eifriger Bursche*), and a priest, Alois Jelínek of Jihlava, was described as one so taken up with Greek studies that "his passion for Slavic literature has declined." Withal the police assured Vienna that little was to be feared from the matica. The author closed, however, with the declaration that "My special task remains, that of continuing to watch the here-named individuals and to bring to your Excellency's attention any significant developments."

Even with little government harassment and a simple program of publication, however, the matica was able to accomplish very little. During the remainder of the 1850's its only activity was the annual publication of *Koleda* which, after its circulation slowly dropped from 3,000 to 1,800 copies, ceased altogether in 1858. *Koleda* was killed by a general lack of interest, competition from the Catholic-sponsored *Moravan*, lack of contributors as well as subscribers, and an increase in printing costs. For all intents and purposes the Moravian matica was dead. A change in the political atmosphere was needed to revive it.

The long awaited relative political freedom of the 1860's did not at first really benefit the Moravian matica or other similar societies. Many of the leaders of Slavic national and cultural societies before 1860 were frustrated politicians who had tried to achieve modest benefits for themselves and their people through the only means available to them, cultural activity. When, therefore, after 1860 it became legally possible to engage in political activities, many of the early cultural leaders, such as Helcelet and Pražák, were no longer particularly

edition of Professor Boček's *Přehled Knížat a Markrabat i Jiných Nejvyšších Důstojníků Zemskych v Markrabství Moravském* (Outline of Princes, Margraves, and Other of the Highest Provincial Officials of the Moravian Margraviate), and Volume Two of Klácel's *The Fables of Bidpai.* They also brought out the first and last issue of *Zpráva o Národní Jednotě sv. Cyrilla a Methoda pro Rok 1849* (News of the National Union of SS. Cyril and Methodius for the Year 1849), and cooperated with a commercial printer in the publication in 1850 of a map the *Korunní země Morava a Slezsko* (Crown Land of Moravia and Silesia).

In 1850 the National Union, following the example of the Czech matica, attempted to set up two regular publishing series: the *Domácí Poklad Nauk* (Domestic Treasure of Knowledge) and the *Domácí Poklad Zábavného Čtení* (Domestic Treasure of Entertaining Reading), neither of which was successful. Only one volume was ever issued—a translation in 1852 of Betty Paoli's *Die Welt und Mein Auge,* called *Čest Rodinná* (Family Honor) in Czech. Paoli was the pseudonym of Barbara Glück an Austrian writer of verse and fiction.

The National Union also marketed 400 copies of Helcelet's *Národní Zeměvidi Rakouské Říse dle Šafaříka* (National Maps of the Austrian Empire after Šafařík), 208 copies of Volume One of Klácel's translation of *The Fables of Bidpai* and finally 265 copies of Šembera's *The Mongol Invasion of Moravia.*

[21] Allgemeines Verwaltungsarchiv, Oberste Polizei-Behörde: Präsidiale I, 1091/1854.

interested in purely cultural pursuits as substitutes for political activity. In general it was not for some time, until the newness of the experience wore off, that pre-1860 cultural and national societies benefited very much from constitutionalism.

The Moravian matica, still the only Czech national, scholarly, or literary society in Moravia, entered the period of constitutionalism with only 134 members and less than 5,500fl. in cash and book-stock. Its first sign of new activity was on December 20, 1859 with a declaration attesting it was still alive. Thereafter for a few years it quietly went about its business and accomplished a few modest things such as financing in 1861 the publication of Šembera's *Paměti a Znamenitosti Města Olomouce* (Recollections and Sights of the City of Olomouc), and exhibiting copies of its most important publications in the London world's fair of 1862. Subsequently, interest waned.[22] Nothing significant was accomplished again until in 1866 it brought out two volumes of the writings of perhaps the most famous native son of Moravia, Karel of Žerotín (1564–1636), a nobleman, humanist, and leader of the *Jednota Bratrská*, (*Unitas Fratrum*, Union of the Brethern, or, incorrectly, The Moravian Brethren.) This was his *Zápisové o Soudě Panském* (The Records of the Court of the Lords).

Aside from these few publishing ventures, most of the 1860's were lost in talk and suggestions about what ought to be done. The only concrete thing that came of all this talk was the suggestion to publish a journal to take the place of *Koleda*, which had ceased in 1858. Fortunately, at about this time two important things took place which strengthened the matica and led to the founding of the proposed journal.

In 1867 the first Czech language secondary school in Moravia was founded in Brno. Its first director, I. Wittek, previously of Znojma, became a staunch supporter of the matica. The association between the matica and the gymnasium was further increased when Prof. Václav Royt (1827–1907), a school inspector and member of the matica, became one of the instructors of the school. In lieu of other Czech intellectual centers this secondary school played a very important role in Czech cultural and national life in Moravia (as the Serbian gymnasium in Novi Sad had previously advanced the Serbian revival in Hungary.)

The second important event took place in 1868 when Count Egbert Belcredi, a strong supporter of the matica since 1849, replaced Mathon as president. Belcredi, assisted by Brandl, Pražák, and Royt, provided spirited leadership. On the day he assumed office, June 4, 1868, he made the decision to proceed with the publication of a journal as soon as possible. He appointed Brandl, Royt, and Count Sylva-Tarroucca who, while still a member of the *Dědictví*, had rejoined the matica as a committee to execute this decision.

One month later this committee reported that, since there still was not a single scholarly or literary journal in the Czech language published in Moravia, the matica should found one which should also become the organ of the matica. The committee further recommended that this organ should publish popular as well as scholarly articles, particularly on history, topography, statistics, monasteries, cities, communities, source materials, philology, and the history of Moravian place-names. The journal was to be a quarterly beginning in January, 1869, and Royt was named editor.

There was, of course, some opposition to this decision. Šembera wrote from Vienna that it would be better for the matica to support the Czech *Časopis* and *Památky*. He pointed out that these journals were having a difficult time and questioned the chances for success a new journal in Moravia would have. The Committee, however, ignored his comments.

Of much more significance was the real fear on the part of other members that the matica would not succeed in such a venture until it had made peace with the Catholic church, which had officially withdrawn its support back in 1850. As a result the matica notified the church consistories in Brno and Olomouc in August, 1868, that "The Committee of the Moravian Matica which has as a goal the fostering of Czechoslovak literature by publishing or supporting the publication of good books wishes to present the high reverend consistory a copy of its by-laws and its proposal to begin publishing a journal on January first of the following year. . . . The Committee of the Moravian matica promises that it will never be found among the adversaries of the church's activities and rights, but will always support them." [23]

After this complete capitulation to the realities of religious and national life in Moravia the matica was rewarded by the issuance of a pastoral letter by Archbishop Friedrich Egon, Landgrave of Fürstenberg which, among other things said, ". . . and since the council of the matica has given the agreeable assurance that it will never join the opponents of the Church's aims and rights, we are favorably inclined to recommend the support of this society to our clergy." [24] Furthermore, the archbishop as well as bishop Schaffgotsch of Brno became not only members of the matica, but deigned to serve on

[22] In 1864 Helcelet, president, since 1853, was too busy in politics as a member of the Landtag and the Reichsrat, and was therefore replaced as president by the school director, Dr. František Mathon, who was assisted by Vincenc Brandl.

[23] Traub, "Dějiny Matice moravské," *Časopis Matice Moravské* 35, 1 (1911): pp. 75–76.

[24] *Ibid.*, p. 76.

the governing board. With this kind of assurance the committee now felt secure enough to proceed with the publishing of an annual, the *Časopis Matice Moravské* (Journal of the Moravian Matica) which first appeared January, 1869. Royt served as the journal's first editor until 1875. Then he was succeeded by František Bartoš (1837–1906), a philologist and director of the Brno gymnasium, who served until 1882. *Časopis*, which remained for years the only Czech learned journal published in Moravia, soon became, next to the Czech journal of the same name, the most important historical journal in Czech lands.[25]

Thereafter the matica became primarily a scholarly publishing house for this journal and a few sporadically published books for Czechs in Moravia. Its officially stated goal was "to support Czechoslovak literature with special attention to the needs of Moravia by publishing good writings or contributing to them. . . ." [26] The post-1868 history of this matica is therefore really an epilogue and not germane to the present study.[27]

The society still exists. In 1959 the journal was reorganized and renamed the *Sborník Matice Moravské* (Magazine of the Moravian Matica), and the organization itself was affiliated with the Czechoslovak Academy of Sciences.

V. THE CROATIAN MATICA, 1842: A SUCCESSFUL OUTGROWTH OF ILLYRIANISM

Through the freewill offerings of friends of the national literature a fund called the Matica ilirska will be founded...for the goal of publishing in the national tongue the old Illyrian classics and other generally useful books which the matica considers worthy.... The Zagreb Illyrian Reading Room will have the care and management of this fund.

From the By-laws

As a result of centuries of foreign domination by Turks, Germans, Italians, and Magyars, the Croats entered the nineteenth century territorially and socially fragmented, nationally and culturally weak, suffering from serfdom, ignorance, Magyarization, and with very small and largely Germanized noble and bourgeois classes. The official tongue was Latin. The Croatian language and literature was debased and not much national consciousness existed. There was, furthermore, almost no general consciousness of the tenth-century Croatian kingdom founded by Tomislav, nor of the Dalmatian-Croatian renaissance of the sixteenth and seventeenth centuries, nor of the Croat's affinity with other South Slavs.

In 1815 the Croats lived in four different areas—Croatia-Slavonia (the heart of old Croatia and center of the national revival), Dalmatia, the "Illyrian Kingdom," and Bosnia. The first three were incorporated into the Habsburg domain, but under different administrations, and the latter was ruled by the Ottoman Empire. The rule of Austria over the Croats began in 1526 when the Polish king of Hungary and Bohemia, Louis II, was killed fighting the Turks at Mohács. His brother-in-law Ferdinand I of Austria claimed and took Louis's lands including most of Croatia-Slavonia which had been a part of Hungary since 1102. The Austro-Turkish treaty of Karlowitz in 1699 gave more Croatian lands to the Habsburgs while Austria regained most of old Hungary from the Turks. The process was completed when Napoleon in 1787 forced Venice to surrender her Dalmatian territories (which she had bought from Turkey in the fifteenth century) to Austria.

Although the inclusion of Dalmatia into Austria brought most Croats under one rule, the process had been so long and complicated that they were still under three administrations and had no feeling of national unity. Dalmatia was incorporated into Austria and, along with Carinthia, Carniola, Gorizia, Gradisca, became the Illyrian Kingdom ruled from Vienna. Croatia-Slavonia was considered part of the Hungarian crown lands and was governed from Pest. The Croats in Bosnia remained under the Turks until occupied by Austria in 1878.

Despite centuries of political fragmentation and suppression, however, all national feeling had not died. Napoleon gave it a short but powerful charge when in 1809 he forced Austria to surrender to him a large part of Croatia, Dalmatia, Istria, Carinthia, Carniola, Gorizia, and Gradisca which he organized into the Illyrian Provinces. The French replaced the old Austrian feudal state organization with a modern centralized police state with a codified law, a unified customs system, and the French system of public education. The French also did away with the economically restrictive guilds and corporations and the rural *robota* (statute labor) system.

---

[25] During this early period the matica published a total of 245 articles, mostly on language and literature (40 per cent), history (26 per cent) and philosophy and religion (16 per cent), plus a miscellaneous group of articles on law, economics, foreigners in Moravia, and schools. These figures, based on Jinřich Šebánek's *Rejstřík Bibliografický k Časopisu Matice Moravské*, Brno, 1929.

[26] *Časopis Matice Moravské*, 1870: p. 49.

[27] As a result of the concordat with the Catholic church, membership took an upward swing. By the end of 1868, the matica had 300 members; during 1869, 365 new members came in, bringing the total to 665; by 1890 it had 805 members; and at the turn of the century it had grown to 1,321. About 55 per cent of these members were (as would be expected) either Catholic clergymen or teachers. The remaining 45 per cent consisted mainly of students, officials, lawyers, businessmen, large landholders, and institutional memberships.

Exact figures for 1877 show that the matica had 560 members: 210 priests (37 per cent), 91 professors (16 per cent), 60 students, 48 officials, 38 lawyers, 35 societies and institutes, 30 factories and businesses, 20 teachers, 11 M.D.'s, 10 estate owners, 8 farmers, and 3 ladies. As with the other maticas, the peasants and proletarians were hardly represented. From *Časopis Matice Moravské* 10 (1878): pp. 123–124.

After Austria retook the Illyrian Provinces in 1814 the French innovations were eliminated. One significant lasting effect of the French occupation however remained: for the first time since the Middle Ages Croatian lands had actually been reunited. This fact nurtured among a few patriots the growing idea that the future fortune of the Croats and of the South Slavs depended upon the restoration of the allegedly pre-existent "Illyrian union"—referring to the rule of the ancient Roman province of Illyricum by Slavic tribes from the sixth and seventh centuries to the coming of the Franks in the ninth century.

These Croatian patriots, centered around Zagreb in Croatia-Slavonia, were very much influenced not only by the semi-historic myth of ancient Illyria, but also by the reality of Tomislav's kingdom and the Dalmatian renaissance, and particularly by the recent experience and legacy of Napoleon's *Provinces Illyriennes*, and resented the fact that Austria wiped out the good features of French rule in Croatian lands.

They were also ashamed of the undeveloped condition of Croatian language, literature, and culture in general, and of the political and cultural domination of their territory by Magyars and Germans. Since the classical period of the seventeenth century in and around Dubrovnik (Ragusa) most literature was in the hands of the clergy and consisted largely of prayer books, legends of the saints, sermons, and didactic and religious pamphlets. Further evidence of the weakness of Croatian literature is that in 1810 a journalist tried to publish a Croatian newspaper, but could find no subscribers, and that to 1838 there was only one Croatian press in Zagreb. Inasmuch as they could expect little help from the conservative Croatian nobility and bourgeoisie (who were more interested in and jealous of their feudal privileges than nationalism or their countrymen), and since they themselves were politically impotent, these few patriots slowly evolved a national and cultural movement, the basic ideas of which were to effect a Croatian national unity and culture with a rejuvenated and standarized Croatian literary language.

They were also very much influenced by the broad pan-Slavic teachings of men like Kollár who taugth that the Slavs were one people with four dialects—Russian, Polish, Czech, and "Illyrian" or South Slavic, and therefore hoped for some kind of linguistic or political union of the South Slavs. This movement, the most important national movement in Croatian history, was given the name Illyrianism and lasted approximately fifteen years—from about 1832 to 1848.

At first the Illyrian movement was a form of Yugoslavism, but the very real historic and cultural differences among the South Slavs prevented any unity beyond the standarization of Serbo-Croatian grammar. While the Yugoslav proponents of Illyrianism were not successful, the more narrow-scale Croatian national movement flourished and endured beyond 1848. As with most of the other Austro-Slav national movements, the Illyrian movement was led by a small group of intellectuals inspired by self-denying patriotic zeal, who gave themselves fully, spoke out against what they considered to be injustices and inequalities, and resented the conservativism and apathy of many of the noble and wealthy. This small group, largely led by Ljudevit Gaj, succeeded in building up an atmosphere of enthusiastic Romanticism in Zagreb.

During this fifteen-year period the Illyrians accomplished many significant things. For the first eleven years to 1843 they had the support of Metternich, who hoped that the creation of an Illyrian language would wean the South Slavs (especially the Serbs) away from their close attachment with old Slavic and Russian pan-Slavism. When the Illyrian movement, however, turned out to be more separatist and anti-Austrian than anti-Russian pan-Slavism, Vienna abruptly curtailed it in 1843.

The Illyrians in Zagreb founded and supported the first Croatian literary journals and newspapers and the first Croatian national institutions such as reading rooms, a museum, a national hall, a matica, and a theater. They resurrected the "Illyrian classics" (the writings of the old masters of Dubrovnik), and fostered the idea of an academy of arts and sciences. Above all they strove to develop and spread national literature.

The chief ideologist and spiritual leader of the whole movement was Ljudevit Gaj (1809–1872) who was born near Krapina in Slavonia. He began publishing poems as early as 1826. Though he produced no outstanding literature himself, it was his orthographic reforms, his journals and newspapers, and his organizational ability which made possible the flowering of Croatian literature. At the beginning of the nineteenth century there were three major Croatian dialects—Štokavski, Čakavski, and Kajkavski, so named after their respective words for "what"—*što*, *ča*, and *kaj*. The first major problem facing Gaj was to decide which of these three dialects should be developed into a literary language. His native dialect was Kajkavski and his early poems were written in this dialect—the dialect of Zagreb and northern Croatia.

In 1830, however, Gaj concluded that it would be wiser to try to develop Štokavski into the literary language. This was a wise decision. Štokavski was not only the most widely used of the three major Croatian dialects, but it was the dialect which Karadžić was using and promoting among the Serbs. By coordinating his linguistic reforms with those of Karadžić, Gaj hoped to create a uniform "Illyrian language" for the Slovenes, Croatians, and Serbs.

Štokavski, moreover, was also the language of the "Golden Age of Croatian Literature," of the Dalmatian poets, and by adopting this inherited literary language Gaj's task of linguistic organizations, philological development, standarization, and popularization was greatly facilitated.

Gaj's first major work, a short essay on Croatian orthography published in Croatian and in his own German translation, was published in 1830. In this *Kratka Osonova Hrvatsko-Slavenskoga Pravopisanja* or *Brief Introduction to Croatian-Slavic Orthography* he advocated the use and development of the Štokavski dialect over the Kajkavski.

The next major step in the Croatian revival and the Illyrian movement was in 1835 when Gaj was allowed by Metternich to begin publication of his newspaper the *Ilirske Narodne Novine* (Illyrian National News) and its literary supplement the *Danica Ilirska* (the Illyrian Morning Star) which were published for the "illustrious and honorable gentlemen of all orders living in the South Slav countries—the Croats, Slavonians, Dalmatians, Dubrovnikians, Serbians, Carinthians, Styrians, Istrians, Bosnjaks and all other Slavs of our descent and lovers and defenders of our language. . . ."

The publication of these journals marked the real public beginning of the Illyrian movement,[1] and since there were few books of quality published in Croatian during that period these journals of Gaj were extremely important. Among those who followed and supported Gaj and contributed to his journals were writers and philologists such as Vjekoslav Babukić, Dimitrije Demeter, Ivan Mažuranić, Dragutin Rakovać, Pavao Štoos, Ljudevit Vukotinović, and one Slovenian, Stanko Vraz. Within a year or two these and most other Croatian men of letters had adopted Gaj's orthography, which was based on the simple rules of one letter for one sound, a few diacritical marks over some letters (č, ć, ž, š, ĕ, following the Czech practice), and Karadžić's idea of "speaking as you write and writing as you speak," and had given the Croats a single literary language and the foundations of a modern literature. Thus was solved the first problem of the Illyrians.

The movement produced three important writers—Mažuranić, Vraz, and Preradović. Ivan Mažuranić (1814–1890), the movement's greatest poet, had a varied career. Born of poor parents, he learned many languages, taught at the gymnasium in Zagreb, became a lawyer and finally a politician. He wrote for Gaj's *Danica*, but his greatest literary effort, and one of the most important productions of all Croatian literature, was *Smrt Smail-age Čengića* (Death of Smail-aga Čengić). This epic poem, about an event in 1840 when some Montenegrans ambushed and killed the Turkish Aga, Smail Čengić, was published in 1846. Mažuranić used this incident to describe the sufferings of his people and their heroic resistance to the Turks.[2]

Later Mažuranić turned to politics. In 1848 he became a deputy in the Croatian Sabor (Diet) representing the young progressives. In 1873 he became the first bourgeois to become *ban* (governor) of Croatia, a position he held until 1880.

A second important poet was Petar Preradović (1818–1872), a professional military man in the Austrian army who spent most of his life out of his homeland. His most important publications were a collection of poems, *Prvenci* (First-Born), in 1846 and *Nove Pesme* (New Poems) in 1851.

The last of the triad was Stanko Vraz (1810–1851), a Slovenian literary critic and lyric poet from Styria who tried to become a Croat—the only non-Croat to espouse fully the Illyrian movement. Vraz began to write in Croatian when he was twenty-five, and three years later, in 1838, he made his home in Zagreb. He published in Gaj's *Danica*. His chief work is represented by three collections of his poems, *Djulabije* (a Turkish word meaning a delicious apple), in 1840; *Glasi iz Dubrave Žerovinske* (Voices from the Žerovo Forest), 1841; and *Gusla i Tambure* (Gusla and the Tambouras, both are stringed instruments), 1845. He tried to raise Croatian literature to European standards. He believed that new Croatian literature should be based upon folk poetry and not upon the model of the Dubrovnik and Dalmatian writers who, he contended, imitated the Italians and were too much admired. From Zagreb the Illyrian movement soon spread throughout the Croatian lands and thence to the Serbs and the Slovenes. For a variety of reasons, however, including competing national programs and Magyar resistance, the movement was not exported successfully.

The Serbs had a firmer national tradition and better political position at the time and did not feel that they needed help from the Croats. They were pleased with their recent victories over the Turks, and with their independent state. Among the few Serbs who were interested was the director of the gymnasium at Novi Sad, Petar Jovanović, who supported Gaj and the movement through his literary magazine, *Bačka Vila* (Fairy of Bačka). Such support, however, was more than offset by the leaders of the Serbian matica in Novi Sad who wanted nothing to do with the Illyrians. Pavlović, secretary of the Serbian matica, for example, wrote to Gaj.

[1] Apparently the first faint literary expression of the Croatian national movement was in an anonymous German pamphlet, *Sollen wir Magyaren werden?* published in Karlovac in 1832 and variously attributed to Kollár or A. Vakanović. This denunciation of Magyarization created great interest and soon three editions were printed, but the government confiscated as many as possible.

[2] Available in English: Ivan Mazuranic, *The Death of Smail Aga*, trans. with notes, J. W. Wiles (2nd ed. London, 1932).

The Illyrian name, the Illyrian language, and the Illyrian people will never be adopted anywhere in place of the real historical name.... We do not want contributions written in Serbian distorted either in language or in sense; we do not wish the Serbs and anything that is theirs, even though it may be common to a certain extent, to be named Illyrian in our own or foreign newspapers and thus betrayed; in short, we do not want Ilyrianism at all![3]

The Slovene response was little better than that of the Serbs. The Slovenes refused to forsake their own literary language, which already had been rejuvenated by Kopitar and by the poetic genius, Francè Prešeren (1800–1849) (see below, chap. VII). The only important Slovenian support came from Vraz.[4]

In order to strengthen the whole movement in general and specifically to popularize the old Croatian Štokavski literature of Dalmatia for the purpose of acquainting their countrymen with the existence of this significant body of literature, Gaj and his followers decided to institutionalize their ideas and movement by founding some national societies, especially some sort of learned society. In this respect they were strongly influenced by the Czech and Magyar National Museums, the Johanneum in Graz, and especially by the Serb and Czech maticas. Accordingly in 1836, through the pages of *Danica*, he urged the Sabor to found and support a Croatian society of the friends of Illyrian culture (Družtvo Prijatelijah Narodne Izabraženosti Ilirske). This urging, however, was premature as there was not enough interest in Croatian culture among the upper classes and the Sabor did not enact Gaj's suggestion.

After this failure the Illyrians, forced to look to their own efforts, founded several small, modest, and non-political reading rooms (Sing. *čitaonica*) where patriots could assemble to read books and journals, to talk about politics and literature, to study the national language, to encourage one another, and to plan bigger and better national activities.

The first such reading room was organized in Varaždin in northern Croatia late in 1837 by a lawyer, Metel Ožegović.[5] Varaždin was at that time the largest city in Croatia but, since Zagreb was more centrally located and the real center of Illyrianism, Varaždin never became very important in the national revival. A year later, during March, 1838, a second reading room was set up in Karlovac by Antun Vakanović and Ambroz Vranjican. Finally during August, 1828, the third and most important of all these societies was organized in Zagreb and named the Illyrian Reading Room.

This society was led by Count Janko Drašković (1770–1856), a member of a distinguished noble family who favored the Illyrian movement. He considered himself a writer and published a few poems and two booklets: *Dissertacija Iliti Razgovor, Darovan Gospodi Poklisarom Zakonskim* (Dissertation on a Discussion Presented to the Honorable Delegates) 1832, a tract on economics and politics which was a kind of political program for Illyrianism; and in 1838 *Ein Wort an Illiriens Hochherzige Töchter über die Altere Geschichte und Neueste Regeneration Ihres Vaterlandes* (A Word to the Highhearted Daughters of Illyria Regarding the Previous History and the Newest Regeneration of their Fatherland), an attempt to interest Croatian women in the revival. His most worth-while contribution to the national cause, however, was his representing the movement before the public and in high society. Throughout the *Vormärz* period he lent his name, talent, money, and energy to the movement and was at the head of every important cultural activity.

As president of the Illyrian Reading Room, Drašković was assisted by a secretary, Vjekoslav Babukić (1812–1875), who held this post until the society succumbed to absolutism in 1854. Babukić was a grammarian and the first professor of Croatian at the Zagreb gymnasium. Among his many philological studies, probably the most important is his *Slovnica Ilirskoga Jezika* (Grammar of the Illyrian

[3] Zvane Črnja, *Kulturna Historija Hrvatske* (Zagreb, 1965), p. 424. *Cf.* Črnja's *Cultural History of Croatia* (Zagreb, 1962), pp. 304–305—a condensed English translation of the 1961 edition of *Kulturna Historija Hrvatske.*

[4] There was also some enthusiasm for the movement from the Croats in Dalmatia and Bosnia. After Gaj's visit to Dalmatia in 1840, Antun Kuzmanić founded the literary newspaper, *Zora Dalmatinska* (Dalmatian Dawn) in 1844. In Bosnia some young men like Marian Šunjić, Franja Jukić, and Grgo Martić supported Gaj.

[5] The Croats were the first among the Yugoslavs to develop these reading rooms. The Serbs founded their first one in 1842 in Novi Sad and the Slovenes not until 1861 in Trst (Trieste).

In 1853 the K. K. Polizei-Direktor in Fiume (Rijeka) sent a long and detailed report to his Direktor der Obersten Polizei-Behörde in Vienna about one of these Croatian reading rooms in Fiume. In this report, which is only partly readable because of fire damage, the author is visibly upset over the strength of Croatian nationalism. He recounts that "The Tricolor was flown in front of the building and over the entrance was written "Narodna citavnica" [*sic.*]. All the furniture, the curtains, and even the billiard tables were covered in these colors. The windows were all decorated with many portraits of Slavic notables. People conversed in Croatian and went to amateur Croatian theatrical productions. German was completely eliminated in conversation and the spirit of fanaticism and a form of *Terrorismus* visibly prevailed."

Another fact that disturbed the Polizei-Direktor was the number of government officials who were members of this society. He reported its membership of 195 as follows:

Active officers 13? (number burnt off), retired officers 14? (number burnt off), priests 30? (number burnt off), civil servants 46, teachers 12, M.D.'s 2, lawyers 3, businessmen 57, private (persons of independent means) 2, honorary 16.

These figures indicate that probably 73 or about 40 per cent of the members were imperial civil and military officers. (Allgemeines Verwaltungsarchiv, Oberste Polizei-Behörde: Präs. I: 462/1853.)

Language), which was printed in *Danica* in 1836 and had a great effect on the Illyrian movement.

The Illyrian Reading Room was opened to the public November 1, 1838, and offered more than twenty journals and newspapers in different languages including the Russian *Severnaia Pchela* (Northern Bee), the Serbian *Srbske Novine* (Serbian News), and *Narodni List* (National Paper), the *Polski Tygodnik Literacki* (Polish Literary Weekly), and the Czech *Pražské Noviny* (Prague News), *Včela* (Bee), and *Květy* (Flowers). Later it added the *Journal de Debats, Frankfurter Oberpostamts-Zeitung*, and the *Wiener Zeitung*. At first the reading room occupied temporary quarters, but in 1846 it moved into more suitable quarters in the National Hall, the erection of which the Reading Room Society had sponsored earlier as a center for the national revival and headquarters for other national societies.

As important as the reading room was in itself, its most significant role in the revival was as a seed bed for most of the subsequent national institutions and societies such as the museum, the matica, and the academy. At a meeting of the reading room members in March, 1839, it was decided that the national movement needed additional institutions, especially a matica as in Novi Sad and Prague, to publish useful books for the people in the "Illyrian Language." Accordingly, within three years, the reading room founded four additional societies.

In 1840 Mažuranić, who may have been influenced by the performance that year in Zagreb of a Serbian theatrical troupe from Novi Sad, presented a suggestion to the reading room to found a society for the promotion of the Croatian theater. At that time only German theater existed among the Croats and no plays had been presented in Croatian. As a result of Mažuranić's suggestion the first drama in Croatian was performed that same year in the theater on St. Mark's Square. This was *Juran i Sofija* (Juran and Sofia), a historical drama by Ivan Kukuljević (1816–1896) a writer, historian, politician, and outspoken Illyrian. Shortly thereafter the Croatian *Sabor* gave permission to the bishop (later archbishop) of Zagreb, Juraj Albert Haulik (1786–1869), a Croatian patriot of Slovak descent and an official of the *ban*, to conduct a national collection to build a national theater.[6]

In 1841 the reading room organized an economic society (Gospodarsko Društvo) which, through its *Gospordarski List* (Economic News), strove to improve agriculture and raise the standard of living among the peasants. Bishop Haulik was its first president. Also in 1841 the Reading Room Society founded a national museum and the above-mentioned National Hall.

The most significant act of the Reading Room Society, however, was initiated during February, 1842, when Count Drašković made a speech declaring that its most important work was to disseminate knowledge of science and literature among the masses in their own tongue, and especially to print the works of the Dalmatian authors. The Serbian and Czech maticas provided excellent models for the Illyrians.

1842–1848

During the following April the organization was effected and the Illyrian matica (Matica Ilirska) came into existence with the stated goal of printing "the old Illyrian classics and other useful books in the national tongue." [7] To this end over a period of thirty-two years the society succeeded in publishing four literary and scholarly journals and forty-four other items (most of which were scholarly, rather than literary) including five volumes of the Illyrian classics and eleven of a "useful" (*korisni*) character. Drašković assumed the title of honorary president and role of patron and protector, while Gaj was elected as the working president, assisted by Babukić as secretary. Among other Illyrians who served in the beginning were Mažuranić, Vukotinović, Dimitrije Demeter, and Štoos. Gaj's *Narodne Ilirske Novine* served as the organ and voice of the matica commonly called "Croatian" rather than "Illyrian."

The new society began immediately to solicit memberships and donations to finance its publications. The main source of income was from memberships, which were sold for a minimum of 50fl., payable at once or over five years, and which entitled members to all publications. By the end of 1843, in response to the first membership drive, the matica had about 450 members, living mainly in Croatia-Slavonia, among whom were Josip Kuković, bishop of Djakovo; Eduadro Jelačić, vice-zupan of Zagreb; Miloš Obrenović, former prince of Serbia, baron Mirko Ožegović, bishop of Senj, Gaj, Drašković, five canons, five members of the lesser nobility, and four institutions, who collectively contributed about 5,000fl.

If this modest success of the Croatian matica did not disturb Vienna, complaints that Gaj was stirring up the Slavs, Gaj's visit to Russia, and the growing Russophilism of some Serb nationalists did. Ferdinand, therefore, issued a *Reskript* in 1843 aimed directly at Illyrianism by forbidding the use of the name Illyrian throughout Croatia and Slavonia in schools, in public documents and debates, and in the newspapers. Gaj, for example, was required

[6] In 1861 the Sabor voted an annual subvention for this theater. The present National Theater on Marshal Tito Square was opened in 1895 and is considered to be the most beautiful theater of its period in southeastern Europe.

[7] From the by-laws printed in *Književnik* 1, 1 (1864): pp. 7–9.

immediately to drop the word Illyrian from his newspaper, which henceforth was known simply as the *Narodne Novine*. The decree claimed that Emperor Ferdinand was not opposed to the national language, but only the sowing of seeds of bitterness and dissension among his subjects.

This decree was a triumph for some Magyars and Germans who were becoming increasingly anti-Slav. Since the beginning of the Illyrian movement they had tried to hurt it by misrepresenting it to the emperor as a rebellious movement. In 1840, for example, Gaj had been accused by a bishop Schrott of Zagreb of stirring up the young people to create an Illyrian nation "which might become extremely dangerous for the monarchy on the occasion of its first clash with Russia," [8] and of inciting the Croats against the Magyars. And in January, 1843, the *ban* of Croatia had written to Sedelnizky about the necessity of closely watching all national developments like "Slavism, pan-Slavism, and Illyrianism." The *ban* also had reported on the "countless articles" on these movements which were appearing in Croatia, and especially raised the frightening question, "Whether it was possible that the notorious writer Gaj was working towards an agreement with Russia." [9]

This decree of 1843 and a law of the same year which made Magyar the exclusive language of legislation, government, and official business, marked the beginning of the end of the Illyrian movement. For the next six years it continued feebly until ended completely by the events of 1848 and the subsequent absolutism.

While 1843 signaled the demise of Illyrianism, it was by no means the end of the Croatian revival. After the successful killing of the Yugoslav phase of the Illyrian movement, Vienna and Pest relaxed somewhat and Count Drašković was able to save the reading rooms and the matica, which continued their efforts to advance the Croatian rebirth. One gauge of the success of Drašković and other patriots is that in one year (1848) the matica's fund increased from 5,000fl. to more than 28,000fl. and membership rose to 592, an increase of over 30 per cent. The idea of "Great Illyria" faded and its promotors turned to the more immediate and practical problems of Croatia proper. From its beginning through the founding of the Croatian Academy in 1867 the matica became and remained the most important institution of the Croatian revival.

Most of its members were of the clergy, the nobility, and the middle classes. That there were only seven institutional memberships—three reading rooms, two seminaries, one regiment, and the Economic Society—suggests how limited any kind of national, scholarly, or literary institutional activity was at that time. Of considerable interest as evidence of growing Slavic solidarity were the twenty members from other Slavic groups—one Slovak, one Pole, and nineteen Czechs. The lone Slovak member was bishop Stefan Moyzes, a one-time (1830–1847) censor and teacher in Zagreb who was then a Catholic bishop in Banská Bystrica, and who became the first honorary president of the Slovak matica in 1863 (see below, pp. 56–57). The single Pole was Count Ferdinand Bakowski from Galicia. The Czechs included Counts Jan Kolowrat and Lev Thun, Neuberg, Palacký, Rieger, Jungmann, Šafařík, Čelakovský, Purkyně, J. Frič, and Hanka.

The main, and almost only, function of the matica during the pre-1848 period was publication. During this seven-year period it published fourteen items, including three issues of a journal and four important contributions to the development of a national literature.[10]

In accordance with its aim of publishing the classics, the first major publication of the matica was a new edition in 1844 of *Osman* by Ivan Gundulić (1588–1638), the greatest writer of the seventeenth-century "Golden Age" of Dalmatia and one of the earliest important Slavic poets. Gundulić, a member of a patrician family in Dubrovnik, wrote lyrics and a number of plays, not all of which have come down to us. His fame rests on *Osman*, a pseudo-epic of twenty cantos about Croatian *bans* and Serbian kings, set during a war between Turkey and Poland and the defeat of the Sultan Osman II by the Poles in 1621. Gundulić, singing of freedom and patriotism, tried to inspire the Slavs of Turkey with the hope of eventual liberation. Republished more or less in honor of the 200th anniversary of his death, the edition was prepared by Mažuranić who also recreated its two missing cantos.

Three years later, in 1847, the matica published a collection of Gundulić's other known writings, *Različite Piesni* (Various Poems) including his three extant dramas, *Ariadna*, *Dubravka*, and *Proserpina*. Some indication of the growing importance of the matica and increasing strength of the national movement is the fact that whereas only 1,000 copies of *Osman* were printed, 3,000 copies of *Various Poems* were published.

In 1844 the matica had also printed a drama by the most important Croatian playwright of the Illyrian period, Dimitrije Demeter (1811–1872). Demeter, creator of the Croatian national theater, was one of the best representatives of Illyrian literature, which was similar to that of Western Romanticism, but not so sentimatal or mystic and full of a strong faith in the South Slavs and their future. This drama, *Teuta* (Queen Teuta) the first modern Croa-

[8] Črnja, *Cultural History of Croatia*, p. 303.

[9] Haus, Hof- und Staatsarchiv, Index der Polizei-Acten, 304/1843.

[10] All bibliographic citations are from Jakša Ravlić and Marin Somborac, *Matica Hrvatska: 1842–1962* (Zagreb, 1963).

tian tragedy, deals with the semi-legendary third-century B.C. queen of Illyria and her defeat by Rome as a result of the disunity and selfishness of her supporters and was a thinly disguised call for Slavic unity against oppressors.

As was customary during the early stages of all the Slavic revivals, the Croatians produced a dictionary, the *Ilirsko-Nemačko-Talanski Mali Rěčnik* (A Small Illyrian-German-Italian Dictionary) in 1849, with an outline of "Illyrian" grammar. In addition to these four publications the matica assumed in 1847 the publication of *Kolo*, the first Croatian literary journal.[11]

1849–1860

During the revolution period of 1848–1849 Croatia (under the leadership of Josip von Jelačić [1801–1859]), an imperial colonel of the Croatian border troops and a mild Croatian nationalist, whom Ferdinand appointed *ban*, *Feldmarshall Leutnant*, and commanding general in March, 1848) severed all ties with Hungary and established herself as an autonomous government in Austria with her own constitution. Fearing the success of the Magyar revolution against Vienna and the subsequent increase of the Magyarization of Croatia, Jelačić aided Vienna by leading a Croat army against the Magyars. He was, however, defeated. In fact, Russian help was necessary to subdue the rebellious Magyars.

Those Croats who had expected any consideration from Vienna for their pro-Austrian position during the revolution were greatly disappointed. After the many revolutions within the empire had been suppressed forcefully, the Croats were not rewarded for their efforts. As the old cliché goes, the Croats received as a reward from Vienna what the Magyars got as punishment. Under the regime of the new minister Bach they lost their autonomy and constitution. Jelačić remained as *ban* until his death in 1859, but following orders from Vienna and suffering from a decline of mental vigor, accomplished little for his people. Freedom of the press was abolished, progressive newspapers banned, the reading rooms were closed.[12] German was introduced into schools and administration, and the country was flooded with secret police and spies. Most Croatian intellectuals withdrew from public life or made their peace with absolutism. Mažuranić, for example, became the state prosecutor of Croatia in 1850.

Gaj, as a result of his Illyrian or Yugoslav ideals, was treated especially harshly and Jelačić, who considered Gaj as a rival, did little to mitigate his treatment. Gaj's paper was sold to the government, he went bankrupt, and was even imprisoned for a while in 1853. Not only did the government turn on Gaj, but many of his co-nationalists feared to associate with him and blamed him for the failure of 1848–1849. He was neither appointed nor elected to any position in the matica when it was reorganized in 1850–1851.[13] After 1848–1849, he did not figure prominently in the Croatian national revival. The matica, however, continued to use his press until at least 1860.

Absolutism had the same blighting effect on the Croatian national movement as it had on all the other Austro-Slavs. During this decade the Croatian national revival not only did not advance, it lost ground. The matica, however, apparently was considered too insignificant to suppress and remained relatively unmolested. With the demise of the reading rooms in 1850 the matica became completely independent and its first action was to effect a reorganization which was completed in 1851. Ambroz Vranjičan replaced Count Drašković as its president and Kukuljević became a vice-president in charge of the literary board. Also on the literary board were Mažuranić, Vraz (leaders of the old Illyrian movement) and Mirko Bogović (1816–1893), one of the leading literary figures of the period of absolutism and the first Croatian writer to be jailed for his writings. The matica received some significant support when Bishop Josip Juraj Strossmayer and Jelačić became members in 1851. The brightness of the Illyrian period, however, was over. Thereafter the matica was very conservative and academic.

During this decade it established exchanges of publications with the Czech, Serbian, and Ruthenian maticas, the Polish Ossolineum in Lwów, and the

[11] *Kolo*, originally founded by Vraz in 1842, was modeled on the Czech *Časopis*. Even after the matica took over this journal Vraz remained as chief editor. It appeared three times during 1847, not at all during 1848–1849. Finally in 1853 it was replaced by *Neven*—a more popular journal. Among the more important contributions published in *Kolo* were "Illyrianism and Croatism" by Ljudevit Vukotinović, "The Code of Vinodol" by Mažuranić, and "Croatian National Songs" by Vraz. Works by non-Croatians such as Štúr and Karadžić were also published. The journal also brought out some important translations such as Pushkin's story *The Queen of Spades*, Mickiewicz's poem *Forefather's Eve*, and Byron's poem *The Prisoners of Silom*.

[12] The loss of the reading room in Zagreb was balanced somewhat when Kukuljević founded in 1850 the Društvo za Povjesnicu Jugoslavensku (Yugoslav Historical Society) which published the first Croatian historical review, the *Arkiv za Jugoslavensku Povjesnicu* (Archive of Yugoslav History) in seven volumes between 1851 and 1863. This society hoped to advance the union of the South Slavs through the study of history as the former Illyrian movement had attempted to do through literature. In the main, however, it fostered only scientific research in the domestic history of the Croats and was not very successful as a unifying factor.

[13] In this respect Gaj's treatment after 1848–1849 resembles that of Palacký who was forced by Vienna to resign as the executive secretary of the Czech Museum and president of the National Theater Committee. Only two members of the museum protested this action and some of Palacký's friends for a while dared visit him only at night.

Serbian Grammatical Society in Beograd [14] and published twenty-two items of which six were official reports and by-laws, one was an appeal to writers for publishable manuscripts, two were volumes of the annual *Kolo*, six were volumes of the weekly *Neven*, and seven were books.

Kolo was one of the first literary casualties of absolutism. It ceased in 1851. The matica succeeded in replacing it, however, with a less pretentious publication. This was *Neven* (Marigold), an "entertaining and instructive" weekly founded in January, 1852. *Neven*, modeled after the Czech *Lumír*, became, *faute de mieux*, the most important Croatian literary journal of the 1850's. Its first editor and principal contributor was Bogović, who published articles on history, natural science, travel, and biography. It was never very secure or stable and during its short life of seven years it had four editors, suffered continually from a shortage of writers and subscribers, slowly went from a weekly to a monthly to a quarterly and ceased altogether in 1857.

Three of the seven books were of little significance (one on herb medicine and two religious works), but the remaining four helped fulfill the aims of the matica. In 1852 it published an anthology, *Cvět Narodnoga Knjižtva* (Selection of National Literature), a guide to poetic art, *Upta u Pjesmenu Umjetnost*, and *Kristiada* (Life of Christ) by Junije Palmotić (1606–1657), a contemporary of Gundulić and one of the greatest playwrights of seventeenth-century Dubrovnik. In 1854 it brought out a second edition of Gundulić's *Osman*. The fact that 2,000 copies of this second edition were printed (in contrast to the 1,000 copies of the 1844 edition) suggests the high hopes of the leaders of the matica. Apparently these hopes were not realized, for after this second edition of *Osman*, nothing other than *Neven* was published for the rest of the decade.

In an attempt to better the situation the matica was reorganized again in 1858. At that time Mažuranić became president and Matija Mesić, professor of law at the academy in Zagreb, was elected to succeed Mažuranić as the vice-president of the literary board. In spite of ambition and ideas about expanding and improving publications there was little that Mažuranić and Mesić could do, and the matica continued to limp along until the October Diploma and February Patent created a better atmosphere for national life.

[14] It was not particularly pan-Slavic however. Among the over 500 letters and other pieces of correspondence (to 1881) in the Archives of the Croatian matica in Zagreb I found only five with other Slavic institutions. Four of these concerned book sales and lists. The fifth was a suggestion from the Serbian matica regarding a dictionary to be published in Serbian, Croatian, Slovenian, and Bulgarian.

1860–1867

The end of absolutism and the beginning of constitutionalism brought new life and hope to Croatian patriots. To them the greatest political blessing of Schmerling's February Patent of 1861 was the granting of a government independent of Hungary and the giving of limited legislative and administrative powers to the Croatian Sabor. These concessions, however, did not entirely satisfy the political aspirations of Croatian leaders such as Antun Starčević (1823–1896), member of the literary board of the matica, a contributor to *Danica*, *Narodne Novine*, *Zora Dalmatinska*, *Neven*, and *Kolo*, and leader of the national rightist party in the Sabor. Their main political activity during the early 1860's was to try vainly to create an autonomous Croatian kingdom within the empire.

The February Patent also gave hope and encouragement to Mažuranić and other leaders of the matica who took immediate steps to increase both the quality and quantity of its publications and to add new members. Their success, however, was only moderate and the matica did not flourish during the early years of constitutionalism as would have been expected.[15]

The main reason for this rather disappointing and surprising lack of progress is the simple fact (noted above) that when national leaders found themselves politically potent they tended to jilt the arts for politics. Since most of the leaders of the Croatian matica (as of the Czech and Moravian) were as politically as culturally minded, and since they had from the beginning looked upon cultural activity as a substitute for stifled political ambitions and aspirations, they eagerly embraced their newly acquired opportunity for real political activity in the Croatian Sabor and in the Viennese Reichsrat, and began devoting an increasing amount of their time and energy in this manner. Kukuljević, for example, following the precedent of Mažuranić, turned to politics and became district prefect of Zagreb.

During these seven years the matica published twenty-two items, including six official reports, four translations, four issues of journals, and eight books—most of which reflected a shift from polite literature to the academic and useful. They published but one of the Dalmatian classics, only four Romantic works, and nothing of the new Realist school then developing. Perhaps the most important publication was a collection of old ballads about the Balkan

[15] Through 1860 the matica had published an overall average of two publications a year. Between 1860 and 1867 it increased this by fifty per cent to an average of three per year. Additional evidence of its modest growth is the fact that by the end of 1863 only twenty-nine new founding members had joined (bringing the total of such members to 294), including the poet Peter Preradović and two important political leaders, Starčević and Bogoslav Šulek.

Christian struggle with the Turks, written by another member of the Dalmatian school, the Franciscan Andrija Kačić-Miošić, to praise and glorify his people and to educate them regarding their past. This was *Razgovor Ugodni Naroda Slovinskoga* (Pleasant Discourse of the Slavic People), first printed in Venice in 1756. This extremely popular work, one of the most widely read books among all the South Slavs, is known to exist in at least forty-five editions. Between 1863 and 1866 four volumes of the collected works of Vraz were published posthumously: In 1863 a second edition of his *Djulabije, Glazi iz Dubraze Žerovinski* and *Gusle i Tambura* and volume I of some previously unpublished miscellaneous poems (*Razlike pjesme*) in 1866.[16]

Perhaps the most important act, however, of the matica was to found in 1864 the first Croatian scientific and scholarly journal, *Književnik*, a "journal for the language and history of the Croats and Serbs, and natural science." The matica edited and published this quarterly for three years, until the opening of the Croatian Academy in 1867. Its first editors were the famous Croatian historian Franjo Rački (1828–1894) and the philologist Vratoslav Jagić (1838–1923). Rački was the founder of modern Croatian historical research, and became the first president of the academy. Jagić, through his subsequent editing of the *Archiv für Slavische Philologie*, came to be considered one of the fathers of modern Slavic philology.

An interesting development during this period was the founding of the Dalmatian matica in Zadar in 1862 by Božidar Petranović, who served as its president until his death in 1874. Petranović had been a member of the Illyrian matica since 1853 and wished to found a similar society along the coast for the Serbs and Croats of Dalmatia. Its most important early publication was the annual *Narodni Koledar* (National Calendar). In 1912 it relinquished its separate existence and became a branch of the Croatian matica in Zagreb. During fifty years of independent operation it published several journals and about twenty-five books in Latin and Cyrillic characters.[17]

1867–1874

The *Ausgleich* or "compromise" of 1867 between Austria and Hungary restored Hungary's freedom under very favorable circumstances, making her an independent kingdom with her own constitution, diet, and government, while at the same time curtailing the national rights of the Slovak, Ruthenian, Rumanian, and Serbian minorities left in the Hungarian part of the dual monarchy. Only the Croatians received guarantees of autonomy by an additional agreement (or *Nagodba*) effected between Croatia and Hungary in 1868.[18] The *Nagodba* granted some restricted autonomy to Croatia which was to be ruled by an appointed *ban* responsible to the Croatian Sabor that would be generally autonomous in four areas—education, religion, internal administration, and judicial affairs. Croatian became the sole official language and was permitted in the joint diet in Budapest to which the Croats sent about forty delegates.

Many elementary and secondary schools were reorganized as Croatian schools, and intellectuals adopted as a motto "Through education towards freedom." [19] Great advances were made in culture, science, and scholarship, especially after the academy opened in 1867 and the university was founded in 1874. Increasing demands for more autonomy led to the appointment of Mažuranić (president of the matica 1858–1872) as *ban* in 1875, a post he held until 1880 when increasing Magyarization forced him out. He was replaced by the Magyar chauvinist Khuen Héderváry, whose twenty-year rule seriously curtailed Croatian political progress, although cultural and academic life, especially that of the academy and university, which was founded in 1874, continued to flourish.

The *Nagodba* affected the matica in two ways. In one way the resulting cultural autonomy permitted new important institutions to develop, causing the pioneering society of the matica to wane in importance. During 1867 and 1868 two new institutions were founded—the Croatian Academy and the St. Jerome Society—which, by taking over important aspects of the program, so weakened the matica that it eventually redrafted its by-laws and commenced a new and different phase of existence.

[16] In 1863 the matica made its contribution to the widely celebrated millenium of the coming of SS. Cyril and Methodius with a memorial volume including contributions by Kukuljević, Rački, and Preradović. The four translations were of a Polish work on popular science and three popular books by the German writer J. H. Campe about the discovery of America. Other books of lesser importance included two works in honor of the bicentennial of the death of Count Nikola Zrinski (Miklós Zrinyi, 1508–1566), a Magyar leader of Croat origin whom both peoples regard as a national hero. He was *ban* of Croatia 1542–1561, and was killed defending the fortress of Szigetvár (Szigeth, Siget) against Suleiman the Magnificent in 1566. Both publications, a biography and an honorific poem, were by Matija Mesić.

[17] Petar Karlić, *Matica Dalmatinska* I–III (Zadar, 1913), and Vjekoslav Maštrović, "Kalendarski Zbornici Matice Dalmatinske in Hrvatske Knižarnice u Zadru, 1863–1910," *Radovi* 3 (1957): pp. 271–315.

[18] Only the Croats of Croatian-Slavonia went to Hungary and were affected by the *Nagodba*. Dalmatia and Istria with the large Croatian city of Rovinj went to Austria where real power and influence was in the hands of the Italian bourgeoisie.

[19] The Czechs had a similar slogan, "Through enlightenment to freedom."

On the other hand it can be argued that the founding of the academy in 1867 represented the ultimate goal, success, and fulfillment of the matica. From the beginning the matica was an embryonic learned society which for a period of over thirty years functioned as best it could as a substitute for an academy, and was also the main sponsor of such an institution. Some of the important founders of the acedemy, including Bishop Strossmayer, Kukuljević, Mažuranić, Bogović and Šulek, were or had been members and officers of the matica. The matica further promoted the idea of the academy by publishing *Književnik*.

Probably the first practical step taken towards organizing the academy was in 1860 when bishop Strossmayer offered 10,000fl. to fund its establishment and presented the matter before the *Sabor* in 1861. Strossmayer (1815–1905), popularly known as the *Prvi sin Naroda* (First Son of the Nation), in 1849 at the early age of thirty-four became bishop of Djakovo, one of the oldest and largest sees in Europe. From then until his death nearly fifty years later, he devoted his enormous revenues to the furthering of the Croatian revival. His motto was *Sve za Vjeru i Domovinu* (All for Faith and Fatherland). In addition to his work to establish the academy, Strossmayer supported many students and schools and helped found a university in Zagreb in 1874.

After five years the by-laws of the academy were finally approved in March, 1866, and the Hrvatska Akademija Znanosti i Umjetnosti (Croatian Academy of Learning and Art) commenced activity during July, 1867. Rački was elected its first president and Strossmayer became its patron. Its main goal was "to foster and support science and art among the Croats, Serbs, Slovenes, and Bulgarians and to promote independent research and the universal advance of learning and art." It was organized in four divisions: historical-philological, philosophical-juridical, mathematical-natural sciences, and the arts. Its first home was in the National Home. In 1884 it moved into its present monumental structure on the Zrinski Square.

Its rapid rise to the most important of all South Slav scholarly institutions was hastened by the acquisition of the 18,000-volume library of Kukulejvić in 1868, of additional gifts of 60,000fl. and in 1885 an art collection of 256 paintings (mostly Italian Renaissance) valued at 200,000fl. from bishop Strossmayer, and by other gifts from other patriots.

The first important act of the academy was to begin in 1867 its own journal *Rad* (Proceedings), the Academy's oldest and best known publication, successor to *Književnik*. In 1868 the academy began a series devoted to South Slavic historical sources, the *Monumenta Spectantia Historiam Slavorum Meridionalium*. In 1869 appeared the first volume of *Stavinc*, also devoted to source materials. The academy also initiated a series of studies and monographs which by 1900 exceeded 200 volumes.

The realization of an academy eliminated the need for the matica to continue its attempts to publish scholarly and scientific things. The matica's sphere of activity was further reduced by the Society of St. Jerome (Hrvatsko Knježevno Društvo sv. Jeronima), founded in Zagreb in January, 1867, when about twenty friends of Croatian popular culture met to determine how to supplement and expand the attempts of the matica to distribute books among the Croat peasantry.[20] Under the direction of archbishop Haulik, by-laws were drafted and formal organization took place in March, 1868. St. Jerome (340?–420), its patron, was a native of Dalmatia and father of the Western Church who had become the patron saint of the Slavonic liturgy.

Because of the pioneering efforts of the matica and the reading societies, the relative freedom of the 1860's, and the grass-roots approach of the society, it was an immediate success and became and remained the largest and most important Catholic cultural institution in Croatia. It began with 160 members and about 3,300fl. (of which bishop Strossmayer contributed 2,000fl.). Its first patron was Archbishop Haulik and its first president was the canon Tomo Gajdek (1809–1886).

In ten years it had approximately 4,500 members and printed 30 publications. By 1898 it had a capital of 168,000fl., a membership of over 14,000, and had published over a million and a half copies of about 100 publications. It was governed by a president and a board. Its patron and protector was always the Archbishop of Zagreb, and its president was almost always a canon of the Zagreb bishopric. In 1890 the society acquired impressive headquarters on the King Tomislav Square, where it exists to this day under a different name (Society of SS. Cyril and Methodius) and with a greatly curtailed publishing program.

Its most important publication was the almanac *Danica* (named *Koledarek* during the first year), a typical miscellany of all sorts of popular material which was accepted with enthusiasm and rose by the end of the century from a circulation of 3,000 to over 50,000. Among its other publications, almost none of which were written by well-known authors, were prayer books, lives of the saints, histories, biographies, and many instructional books on beekeeping, cattle and hog breeding, viticulture, horticulture, brewing, personal health, natural sciences, and popular literature.

After the establishment of the academy and the St. Jerome Society, the matica went through a six-year period of adjustment before it decided how best to adapt to the competition presented by these two

[20] See various articles in the society's almanac, *Danica*, for the years 1928 and 1929.

societies. Meanwhile it accomplished very little. In 1869, after the academy's *Rad* supplanted *Knijževnik*, the matica began to publish *Vienac* (Wreath), a small "interesting and informative" weekly literary journal. Its first editor was August Šenoa (1838–1881), the foremost Croatian writer of the 1860's and 1870's. Under his editorship until his death in 1881, *Vienac* became the voice of the younger generation of writers and remained the principal Croatian literary journal into the twentieth century. The matica, however, published *Vienac* for only four years. Furthermore, with the exception of a second volume of Vraz's *Miscellaneous Poems* in 1868, this was the only publication of the matica for six years.

By 1874 it was clear that the matica must either disband or change its basic purpose. Under the leadership of Matija Mesić, who succeeded Mažuranić as president in 1872, the leaders of the matica decided to leave scholarly and scientific publishing to the academy and the distinctly popular type of material to the St. Jerome Society. Its by-laws were amended to read that its main purpose is "to spread useful knowledge, other than that which is specifically scientific and specifically popular." Its name was changed officially from the "Illyrian" to the "Croatian" matica. From this time on it ceased to be a significant national institution and became simply an important publishing house for the Croatian middle classes. Ivan Kukuljević, a vice-president from 1851 to 1858, was elected the first president of the reformed matica.

EPILOGUE

The Croatian matica's new program was initiated in 1875 with the publication of a translation of Jules Verne's popular *Around the World in Eighty Days.* Thereafter, the matica published each year about ten popular books by Croatian and non-Croatian authors. Among the many authors translated were Homer, Cicero, Plato, Plutarch, Pushkin, Turgenjev, Mickiewicz, Sienkiewicz, G. P. Moravský, Goethe, Fenelon, Macaulay, Hans Christian Andersen, and Washington Irving.

Apparently this reorganization and the leadership of Kukuljević was successful. By 1898 the Croatian matica had published more than 1,470,000 copies of 228 books and had over 11,000 members, and was housed in an impressive building on Strossmayer Square.

As has been pointed out above the pioneering efforts of the Illyrian matica—the most important institution of the Croatian revival from the beginning into the 1860's—were really over by 1860–1861. It still exists, however, and in modern Yugoslavia, with its sister societies the Matica Srpska and the Slovenska Matica, is an important literary institution which between 1946 and 1962 published over 350 volumes.

VI. THE SLOVAK MATICA, 1863: A SHORT-LIVED OPPONENT OF MAGYARIZATION

The Slovak matica is a union of the admirers of the Slovak nation and life. Its goal is to awaken, to propagate, and improve the moral and native cultural of the Slovak people; to cultivate and support Slovak literature and fine arts; to aid the material welfare of the Slovak nation and to work for its improvement.

From the By-laws.

The founding of the Slovak matica in 1863, while based largely on the models of other maticas in the empire, was actually the culminating act of a long series of similar efforts extending back over seventy-five years. Slovak Catholics and Protestants had already organized nine or more literary societies for the fostering of culture and education among the Slovaks. Unfortunately, since these literary societies had usually been sectarian, they had failed to unite the people and had had only very limited success.

The story of the Slovak national problem and the Slovak revival is complicated by serious problems of language and religion. After the destruction of the Great Moravian State in about 997 by the Magyars, the Slovaks slowly passed under the control and the heel of the Magyars. Since there was no strong Slovak state outside the Habsburg realm the Slovaks looked to themselves and to their cousins the Czechs for what national consciousness they maintained or generated.

At the beginning of the Slovak revival in the late eighteenth century the Slovak literary language was Czech. This was a result of three things: a weak native culture and literature, the much stronger culture and literature of their close neighbors and kinsmen the Czechs, and the activities of a dynamic and influential Protestant minority. Both Protestantism and Czech culture had been important in Slovakia since the fifteenth century, when the Hussites for a time controlled the area. Furthermore, many Slovaks studied at the university at Prague. This Protestant minority and its influence had been strengthened in the sixteenth century by the spread of Lutheranism and during the sixteenth and seventeenth centuries when many Czech Protestants found shelter in Slovakia. Since the counter-reformation was not so strong there, a number of printing presses were established by Czech Protestants for the purpose of printing Protestant books to be smuggled into Bohemia. Czech became the liturgical language of the Slovak Protestants, who used the sixteenth-century Czech translation of the Bible, the Kralice Bible, a Czech equivalent of the "King James Version," translated by Jan Blahoslav, bishop of the Moravian Brethren.

Although never amounting to much more than 15 per cent of the total Slovak population, the Protestant (largely Lutheran) minority was significant far beyond its numbers because of its close ties with the much stronger cultural and national movement of the Czechs. They clung tenaciously to their religious and cultural ties of over two hundred years with Bohemia and did all they could to strenghten the Hussite tradition. After Joseph II's *Toleranzpatent* of 1781 the position and influence of the Protestants of the Augsburg and Helvetic confession was considerably strenghtened. A special decree was issued one year later granting similar rights to the descendants of the Hussites and Czech Brethren—who were officially considered to be Lutherans. In less than ten years the number of Lutheran parishes more than doubled—from 205 in 1781 to 435 in 1790. Their cultural center was Bratislava which, with its faculty of theology and law and the Lutheran Lyceum, resembled a small German university town.

The Catholics on the other hand throughout the seventeenth and eighteenth centuries tried to develop a purely Slovak literature as a barrier between the Czechs and the Slovaks.[1] The Jesuits, especially, laid the foundation of a native literature to combat the influence of the Hussites. One of their efforts along this line was the publication in 1718 of a collection of sermons in the western Slovak dialect by a Paulinian monk, Alexander Máčaj, *Panes Primitiarum aneb Chleby Prvotin* (Breads of the First Harvest). Their religious, cultural, and intellectual center was in Trnava (Nagyszombat, Tyrnau), the "Slovak Athens," seat of the first Magyar university which was founded there in 1635 (when Buda and Pest were in Turkish hands). There was also a longstanding and fundamental question whether the Slovaks were a part of the Czech nation living in Hungary, or a separate nation.

As a result of these religious, linguistic, and ethnic problems and questions there evolved a dual literary tradition which was inherited by the second generation of nineteenth-century revivers and which was not finally settled until the language compromise in 1852 (see below p. 55). Thereafter, the Slovaks were united in their national efforts and the Slovak matica was the first important cultural institution in which Catholics and Protestants united their efforts.

Apparently it was the dynamic Protestants who under the spirit of the Enlightenment organized the first of a series of literary societies to advance Slovak culture and learning. In Bratislava and a three-county area in south central "Slovakia" (before 1918 "Slovakia" can only be equated to fifteen counties of Upper Hungary), they organized or attempted to organize between 1785 and 1810 at least seven literary societies. Their first attempt came hard on the heels of the Patent of Tolerance of 1781, and was accomplished by a Lutheran priest, Ondrej Plachý (1755–1810), with a few other Slovak writers in Banská Bystrica (Neusohl, Besztercebanýi) in Zvolen (Zolyom) County. There in 1785 he organized the Societas Slavica. The organ of this small and short-lived society was the *Staré Noviny Literaního Umění* (Old Journal of Literary Arts) which was published in Czech for two years, 1785–1786, and had only about sixty subscribers. Written for educated Slovaks, not the peasants, its spirit was one of progress and Christian humanity, not nationalism.

The Protestant spirit was also active in Malahont (Kishont) county. Here Matěj Holko, Sr. (1719–1785), a Lutheran minister and historian, had been trying for many years to found a learned society. Not, however, until his son, Matěj Holko, Jr., founded the Societas Lectoria in Valle Kis-Hontana (Čitatel'ská Spoločnost' Malahontská, Malahont Reading Society) in 1791 in Rimavská Sobota (Gross-Steffelsdorf, Rimasyambat) did anything come of the elder Holko's efforts.

One year later another Protestant society was organized by the Lutheran priest Samuel Ambróżу (1748–1806) in Hont County at Banská Štiavnica (Schemnitz, Selmec-es Belabanya), namely the Societas ex Totis Monarchiae Austriacae Eruditis Coacta (Society of the Learned from All of the Austrian Monarchy). To carry out its aim of spreading culture among educated Protestants through the whole of Austria, it founded a journal, the *Annales Novi Ecclesiastico-scholastici Evangelicorum August. & Helvet. Confessionis in Austrica Monarchia* (New Religious-Learned Annals of the Protestants of the Augsburg and Helvetic Confession in the Austrian Monarchy) which lasted for nine years—1793–1803. This society, often referred to as the Ambrózy Society after its founder, was never very important or national in spirit and it published in Latin which limited its reading audience to the educated, but, as will be noted below, it did lead to the founding of the much more important Banska Learned Society.

During the same year of the founding of the Ambrózy Society still another Lutheran priest attempted to found a literary group. This was Jiří Ribay (1754–1812), well educated in languages, literature, and history, and an important collector of old Slovak books and manuscripts. In 1793 Ribay and Martin Hamljar (1750–1812), another Lutheran minister and writer, tried to organize the Institutum seu Societas Slavo-Bohemica inter Slavos in Hungaria (Slavo-Bohemian Institute or Society Among the Hungarian Slavs) but nothing came of their efforts.

The real significance of their initial effort was that a few years later they did succeed, with the help of a few other Slovak patriots, in organizing in Bratislava in 1801 the Spolek Literatury Slovenské (Slovak

[1] For a Marxian challenge to this standard "bourgeois" interpretation of Bernolák and his work, see Ján Tibenský, "Bernolák's Influence and the Origins of the Slovak Awakening," *Studia Historica Slovaca II* (Bratislava, 1964), pp. 140–189.

Literary Society) in connection with the Lutheran Lyceum (an autonomous secondary school) there. The main purpose of their society, which became the Protestant answer to Bernolák's Catholic literary society (see below, pp. 51–52) was to print and distribute good Czech books. In this respect, however, it was not very successful. It main success came in 1803 with the establishment of a chair for the study of Slovak language and literature.[2]

The next literary society was the Erudita Societas Kis-Hontensis (Učená Spoločnost' Malahontská, Malahont Learned Society) founded in 1809 in Nižný Skálnik (Alsósziklas) by another Lutheran minister in the Malahont bishopric, Ján Feješ (1764–1813), and a small group of supporters, including Matěj Holka, Jr. The main activity of this learned group (often called the Feješ Society) was to meet annually and to present papers to one another on all kinds of subjects—religious, pedagogical, historical, geographical, philosophical, in Latin, German, and Slovak. Many of these papers were printed in the society's annual, the *Solennia Memoriae Anniversariae Bibliothecae Kishonthanae Evang. A. C.* (Yearbook of the Anniversary Celebration of the Library of the Malahont Protestants of the Augsburg Confession) which was published in twenty-two volumes during the period 1809–1830. This society and its journal, however, had little influence beyond the narrow circle of its members.

In 1810 a much more important society was organized in Banská Štiavnica (Hont County)—the Učená Spoločnost Banskího Okolia (Banska Society of Learning), the last strictly Protestant effort to found a viable literary society.[3] This group, in a way a successor to the Ambrózy Society was, however, modeled as closely as possible after the Institutum in Bratislava, which had been so successful in imparting Slovak nationalism that similar branches were set up by Protestants in a few other Slovak centers such as Prešov, Kežmarok, and Levoča. The most important branch was the one in Banská Štiavnica, organized by two pioneers of the Institutum in Bratislava—Tablic and Ribay. Two years later in 1812 they organized their own chair for the study of Slovak language and literature at the Lutheran Lyceum in Banská Štiavnica, and began work rather modestly with 4,000fl. and 20 books.

Beyond the financing of this chair, the Banská Society wanted to spread in all possible ways useful information among the Slovaks. To this end it proposed to publish a sort of a journal or annual of scholarly and useful things under the title of *Djla Učené Společnosti Banského Okolj* (Works of the Learned Society of the Banska Region). In 1824 Tablic sent some material to the censor in Vienna for approval. A few years later it came back with the notation "non admittitur." That was the end of any hope of a journal. The society did, however, publish a few books between 1812 and 1822, among which were Feješ's *Nezemanům Zemanstva Žádostivným* (For Non-Squires Who Desire to Become Squires), a Lutheran catechism, and Stanislav's *Gramatika*.

In addition to these modest publishing activities the society, made up primarily of Lutheran clergymen, tried to collect Slovak antiquities, manuscripts, poems and songs, coins, and to protect historic things such as castles and church bells. They also hoped to right erroneous opinions held by foreigners about the Slovaks and their lands, to search out the etymology of the names of Slovak areas, cities, castles, and villages, and also to distribute prayer books to the schools.

Analysis of its extant financial records for the years 1811–1822 indicate that the society flourished for only about five of those years. It did practically nothing after 1822 and when its secretary Tablic died. Ten years later, it was officially dissolved. While it lasted it was in close connection with the Feješ society and each group extended membership to the other. These six societies then were the main Protestant efforts to advance Slovak culture and language through literary institutions.

Although the Catholics founded their literary societies somewhat later than the Protestants, and though they founded only two, those were very important. The first was founded in Trnava by Anton Bernolák (1762–1813), a Catholic priest, philologist, and writer who favored a western Slovak dialect in place of Czech for national reasons and for the purpose of driving a wedge between the Slovaks and Protestant Czechs.[4] Bernolák believed that the Slovaks would benefit themselves by separating from the revolutionary and anti-Catholic

[2] Among those who helped were Bohuslav Tablic (1769–1832), a Lutheran theologian and writer who had studied at Jena; Juraj Palkovič (1769–1850), a professor at the Lyceum and writer who had also studied at Jena; and Ladislav Bartholomaeides (1745–1825), and educator and writer.

Later L'udovít Štúr (1815–1856), the most important Slovak national leader of this period, became an assistant to Palkovič and eventually the head of the society. In 1843, however, as a result of growing Magyar nationalism and anti-Slavic sentiment, he was dismissed from the post and the organization faded into insignificance. Thereupon Štúr began a new career as an editor and publisher.

In about 1803 the name of the society was changed to Institutum Linguae et Literaturae Slavicae. Under this title it lasted until the 1840's and even though the language of instruction was Latin, it became a great force in shaping the second generation of Slovak patriots and in making the Lyceum a center of the Slovak revival. Palkovič, the first holder of its chair of Slovak literature, greatly influenced the whole second generation of Slovak patriots including Hurban, Hodža, Francisci, and Štúr. Palacký, Kollár, and Šafařík also studied there.

[3] See Albert Pražák's "K Dějinám Učené Společnosti Banského Okolí," in his *Slovenské Studie* (Bratislava, 1926), pp. 13–26.

[4] See note 1.

Czechs, and that they would also be strengthened in their struggle for national identity if they had books and newspapers in their native tongue.

To this end Bernolák published in 1787 an essay on Slavic philology, *Dissertatio Philologico-critica de Litteris Slavorum*, and the first Slovak grammar, *Grammatica Slavica*, in 1790. He rightly believed that the Slovak language needed to be unified. Unwisely, however, he adopted an imperfect and illogical orthography and then compounded his difficulties by selecting a Western Slovak dialect which resembled the Czech spoken in Moravia. Consequently his innovation, often called "Bernoláčina," made slow progress among the Slovaks.

His next effort was to found in 1793 in Trnava the Literata Slavica Societas, a Slavic literary society, the first real cultural organization among the Slovaks. This may also have been a reaction to the Language Act of the Magyar Diet of 1791, which founded a chair for the Magyar language at the university in Pest, and made Magyar the official language and a regular subject of instruction. This seems to have been the first act of Magyarization of non-Magyars in the lands of the Crown of St. Stephen; it was itself a reaction to the preceding attempts at Germanization made by Joseph II. The basic aim of this literary society was to promote the writing and circulation of books written in the western Slovak dialect and to raise the cultural and material level of the Slovaks.

Among the most important co-workers with Bernolák were his pupils, the poet Ján Hollý (1785–1849) and Juraj Fándly (1754–1810) a Catholic priest and writer. Every one who joined the society had to take a pledge that he would support its goals. It soon had eighty-three members from the neighborhood of Trnava, and eventually grew to a membership of 451, all of whom with the exception of a few laymen and teachers, were Catholic clergymen.

Because so many of its members were priests who lived close to the people and who desired to improve the material lot of their parishioners, much of its published matter was on farming, animal husbandry, irrigation, and fertilization. Hollý became the society's chief poet. The canon, Jur Palkovič (1763–1835), and Alexander Rudnay (1760–1831), cardinal primate of Hungary, were also important contributors and supporters.[5] The society lasted over fifty years, and was successful enough to set up branches and book stores in five towns—Nitra, Rovna, Banská Bystrica, Rožňava, and Košice.[6]

As the influence of the "Bernolák Society" began to wane, one of Bernolák's followers, Martin Hamuljak, and Jan Kollár, a Slovak who belonged to the Czech tradition, tried to unite both parties of the Slovak language question by means of a Slavic reading circle (*Slovanské Čítanie*) in 1826 in Pest.

Hamuljak (1789–1859), a lay Catholic and one of the most important members of the second generation of the Slovak revival, was neither a scholar nor a writer, but played the role of a mediator in trying to bring the two conflicting language sides together.[7] He was envious of the cultural and economic development of Western European countries, studied their institutions which fostered this development, and tried to transplant them among the Slovaks. Kollár (1793–1852), the author of the famous poem, *Slávy Dcera* (Daughter of Glory, 1824) was at that time a Protestant minister in Pest.

Nothing much came of their efforts to found a reading circle, but a few years later, in 1834, with the help of two other followers of Bernolák, Anton Ottmayer and František Kampelík (1805–1872), they did found the Spolok Milovníkov Reči a Literatúri Slovenskej (Society of the Friends of the Slovak Language and Literature) in Buda to replace the "Bernolák Society." Although it was essentially a Catholic institution, this new society did attempt to bridge the differences between the two language traditions. It began with ten members, each of whom subscribed 30fl., and Kollár was elected its first president. During its short life it engaged in publication and in collecting manuscripts, pictures, and books for the Catholic gymnasium in Banská Bystrica.

Its publishing activity began with the almanac *Zora* (Aurora), which appeared irregularly four times (1835–1836, 1839, 1840), and was edited by Hamuljak. Each issue of about 300 pages printed a variety of contributions from Slovak patriots such as Hamuljak, Hollý, Ottmayer, and Karol Kuzmány, and tried to appeal to both religious and language groups by printing articles in Bernolák's Slovak and Kollár's Czech by both Catholic and Protestant contributors. Its only other important publications were four volumes of the poems (*Básně*) of Ján Hollý (1841–1843) and a Biblical history by Schmid (*Biblická Historie*).

In spite of the fact that this society was one of the first public rather than private cultural institutions among the Slovaks it lasted only ten years, for several reasons. Cultural and national conditions among the Slovaks were not yet advanced enough to give the society much financial support, it did not succeed in uniting the two language traditions, and it was frowned upon by the Magyars.

[5] Famous among Slovaks for his statement, "Slavus sum; et si in cathedra Petri forem, Slavus ero!"

[6] The Society was and is often referred to variously as the Bernolák Society, the Slowenské Učené Towarišstwo, the Towarišstwo Litterného Umeňá, or the Litterné Slowenské Towarišstwo.

[7] For a recent study of Hamuljak in English, see Jozef Butvin, "Martin Hamuljak and the Fundamental Problems of the Slovak National Revival," *Studia Historica Slovaca III* (Bratislava, 1965), pp. 135–172.

M. Godra has remarked on its significance,

The merit of the Zora Society lies in the fact that changes approved in it and published in its almanac... both as to language and orthography, although condemned at the beginning even by some Slovaks ... nevertheless began shortly after to acclimatize in Slovakia, until, at last, the most common language representing the best Slovak dialect, was formed for our tribe.[8]

None of these eight Catholic and Protestant pioneer societies had been very successful, but they at least had prepared the way for the more significant institutions which followed. Immediately after the demise of the Society of the Friends of Slovak Language and Literature the most important national effort of the Slovaks before 1848 and one of the most important cultural events in all nineteenth-century Slovak cultural and national history was effected. This was the founding of still another literary society, Tatrín, in 1844.

About 1844 several things occurred that finally led to the solution of the Slovak language problem, which, however, got worse before it got better. During the Hungarian Diet of 1843–1844 laws were enacted making Magyar the exclusive language of legislation, government, official business, and public instruction, leading, of course, to the suppression of Slovak language and literature. Shortly thereafter the gymnasium at Levoča was closed, the chair of Slovak language and literature at the Lyceum in Bratislava was abolished, and L'udovít Štúr was dismissed from his post as head of the language institute of the same school. Thereupon Štúr turned his considerable energy into a crusade for the use and development of the Central Slovak dialect which he considered a better instrument than either Czech or Bernolák's Western Slovak for adoption as the standard Slovak literary language.

To promote his ideas Štúr founded a society and two journals, and wrote several books. His first journal was the political newspaper, *Slovenskje Národňje Novini* (Slovak National Gazette) and its biweekly literary supplement, *Orol Tatránski* (Eagle of the Tatras) in 1845 in Bratislava, which until their demise in 1848 became the chief organs and repositories of his school of literature. In 1846 he also founded in Skalice the weekly *Slovenskje Pohl'adi na Vedi, Umeňja a Literatúru* (Slovak Views on Science, Art, and Literature), the first Slovak scholarly review, which lasted to 1852, when it was succeeded by Hurban's *Slovenské Pohl'ady.*

Also because of Štúr the second issue of Hurban's almanac, *Nitra*, in 1843 was published in Central Slovak; the first issue in 1842 had been in Czech. In 1846 Štúr published his theoretical and practical justification of the need to make Central Slovak the literary language. This was his *Nárečja Slovenskuo Alebo Potreba Písaňja v Tomto Nárečí* (Slovak Dialect and the Necessity of Writing in That Dialect), and also the first grammar of this dialect, *Nauka Reči Slovenskej* (Grammar of the Slovak Language).

To foster further Central Slovak, Štúr and some other likeminded Slovak patriots[9] founded the literary society, Tatrín, in September, 1844 in Liptovský Sv. Mikuláš (Liptószent-Miklós in Liptov Country). Hodža became its first president, Fejérpataky its secretary, with Štúr and Hurban as members of the executive committee. According to its by-laws, its goal was "by all legal ways to build a pure Slovak life without regard to religion, rank, or other differences among individuals, to create, support, foster, and spread this culture, and to arouse Slovak national consciousness."[10]

Although its founders and members were primarily Protestant, Catholics were invited to join. Each member was expected to contribute 80fl. over a two-year period or a minimum of 5fl. a year to the society. During its first year it gained twenty-three members, had sixty at the end of its second year, and eighty at the time of its dissolution in 1847. Most of the members were from the Liptov County area, but a few members were scattered over eleven other Slovak counties.

Tatrín, organized somewhat along the lines of the several maticas in the monarchy to which it was loosely related, was more closely connected with the Croatian matica (which was also in the Hungarian part of the realm) than with the Czech matica, with which it had no real connection at all, a fact largely explained by the existing language quarrel between the supporters of Czech and Slovak.

From the beginning, Štúr and his followers tried to establish close connections with the Croatian matica so that both national groups could become better acquainted with both languages and with each other, and could draw closer together to fend off Magyarization. He tried to work out a reciprocal arrangement in reference to publications and finance. The Croatian matica was willing to join in this form of cooperation as soon as Tatrín received official permission. Unfortunately this was never obtained, and nothing much came of its initial contacts with the Croatian matica.

[8] M. Godra, "Rozpomienka na Kriesitel'ov Narodnosti Slovenskej Pred Rokmi" *Slovenské Noviny* 6, 42 (1874), no. 42, as cited by Butvin, "Martin Hamuljak and the Fundamental Problems of the Slovak National Revival," p. 165.

[9] Such as Michal Miloslav Hodža (1811–1870), the future famous poet, philologist, and leader of the Slovak uprising in 1848; Jozef Miloslav Hurban (1817–1888), an important Lutheran minister, writer, and politician; Father Ondrej Radlinský (1817–1879), a Catholic priest and important editor; Karol Kuzmány (1806–1866), a Lutheran writer and professor of theology; Ján Francisci (1822–1905), a publicist and politician; Kašpar Fejérpataky-Belopotocký (1794–1874), a writer and educator, and Štefan Marko Daxner (1823–1892), a publicist and politician.

[10] Daniel Rapant, *Tatrín: Osudy a Zapasy* (Turčianský sv. Martin, 1950), p. 56.

The main activities and efforts of Tatrín during its short life were to foster and support Slovak culture publishing and distributing books, financially supporting promising young Slovak students, and sponsoring the Central Slovak dialect, often called Štúršina, which, partly through the quality of the works of its early poets, Andrej Sládkovič (1820–1872) and Janko Král' (1822–1876), ultimately became the standard Slovak literary language.

Tatrín attempted to found a collection of Slovak antiquities which might have been very successful if the society had lasted longer. Štúr was also greatly concerned over the problem of alcoholism and used Tatrín as an instrument to fight it, by organizing temperance societies (*spolky miernosti*) among the people and distributing pamphlets warning them against the evils of drink, especially brandy.[11] He also worked to establish Sunday schools and reading rooms, one of which in Bratislava had over 800 volumes.

In the area of financial support Tatrín, which was never affluent, did manage to give stipendia totaling over 600fl. to eighteen students. Most of the students so helped belonged to the Union of Slovak Youth then headquartered in St. Mikuláš.

The society, forbidden to acquire a press of its own, utilized, instead, printers in Levoča and Skalice. They had hopes of printing many books and even of starting a periodical. Five book-distribution centers were to be set up, in Bratislava, Pest, Banská Štiavnica, Banská Bystrica, as well as in St. Mikuláš to serve a wide section of the Slovak populace. Booksellers received from twenty-five to forty per cent commission and subscribers were to receive each seventh book free.

Magyar intransigence ruined most of these hopes and their actual publication program was quite modest, consisting of only four of five items which, however, were significant. The first was Štúr's *Grammar* in 1846. The same year they published Hodža's *Dobruo Slovo Slovákom, Súcim na Slovo* (Good Word for Slovaks Interested in Words) and a year later his *Epigenes Slovenicus, Liber Primus* (Theory of Slovak Grammar, Vol. I), and Josef Plech's translation of Zscholky's *Goldmacherdorf* which was called in Slovak *Zlatnica*. Finally in 1848 they published Hodža's *Dodávok k Větínu o Slovenčině* (Contributions to Slovak Style).

The first result, however, of all this furious activity by the Štúrists was to give the Slovaks three contending literary languages rather than two, for those who favored either Czech or Bernoláčina were not willing to give them up. This led to a bitter quarrel of which Tatrín became the focus. Štúr was opposed by three groups: by Czechs like Palacký, Rieger, and Havlíček, by the Bernolákists, and by most Slovak Lutherans such as Kollár and Šafařík who favored the use of Czech.

Palacký, for example, in 1846 published through the Czech matica a pamphlet, *Voices About the Need of One Literary Language for Czechs, Moravians, and Slovaks*, which cited a formidable list of thirty-three Czech, Moravian, and Slovak authorities who opposed the Central Slovak dialect. Palacký warned and entreated that it was not the time to divide further already weak forces, especially since Slovak was almost prescribed by law, for it was excluded from the Diet and administration, and the higher classes of Slovaks had mostly deserted Slovak for the Magyar cause. He argued that the nation must look for support to the middle and lower classes who were already divided and antagonized by several dialects.[12]

At first all appeals for harmony were in vain. The only thing that became clear was that a return to Czech was impossible. The real question was to which of the two contending Slovak dialects would they turn—to the western Bernoláčina, or to the central Štúršina. Finally in 1847 at the fourth (and last) general meeting of Tatrín in Čachtice the Slovak Lutherans agreed with Štúr. Then the Bernolákists and Štúrists both made concessions and decided that a special philological commission should be named to pass on Hodža's grammer. The most prominent members of the two warring factions were named to serve on the commission, among whom was Štúr himself.

Before this group could accomplish much, however, the revolution of 1848 broke out and the work of the commission was suspended—not so much because the revolution hindered it as because the Slovaks, like other Austro-Slavs, seized this opportunity to lay aside their cultural instruments for combating an alien and hated influence to take up political ones. After "spring of the peoples" proved to have no summer the Slovaks, like the other Austro-Slavs, were required to pick up again these same cultural tools.

As early as March 10, 1848, the Slovaks, led by Štúr, Hurban, and Hodža and the Slovenská Narodná Rada (Slovak National Council) met in Liptovský Sv. Mikuláš and adopted a manifesto of six articles. It spelled out the first formal "Demands of the Slovak Nation," and became the first Slovak

[11] Drink and usury (the result of intemperance) were the great social evils of the unsophisticated Slovak (and of most peasant groups, throughout the whole monarchies). It was a vicious circle. Apparently Štúr was not very successful, for the problem continued into the twentieth century.

[12] Although Palacký had good reason for linguistic unity, it is interesting to compare his anti-Slovak stand with the often-quoted statement from his autobiography: "Even if I were of gypsy birth and the last of my clan, I should still consider it my duty to strive with all my strength that at least an honorable memory of it might remain in the history of mankind." Apparently he felt political realities outweighed the honorable memory of the Slovak language.

public revolutionary manifesto and political program of modern times. This memorandum, beginning with a somewhat idealized picture of the brotherly harmony which had prevailed for centuries in Hungary between Slovaks and Magyars, went on to claim that the Slovaks were as much a nation as the Magyars and were entitled to equal rights. Among the rights claimed were the use of their language even in the debates in the Hungarian Diet, legislative assemblies for each national group, the establishment of ethnographic borders, use of the languages of the national groups for administration in those areas where a minority group predominated. They also demanded schools, the right to vote, freedom of the press and of assembly, the right to raise the national colors, protection of persons, and the creation of a Slovak academy of law and a chair of Slovak at the university in Pest, in return for which Magyar would be recognized as the diplomatic and official language of the central authorities.

Pest reacted with characteristic vigor and animus. "Upper Hungary" was placed under martial law and criminal proceedings were started against Štúr, Hurban, and Hodža, who fled to Prague for safety. Some Slovaks, however, took up arms against the Magyars as some Croats and Serbs had already done. The Slovak rebellion was crushed of course and many Slovaks were either imprisoned or hanged.

After the Magyars were defeated by the Russians at Világos in August, 1849, the Slovaks submitted another petition to Francis Joseph pleading for autonomy. But Vienna, treating the Slovaks no better than the Croats, returned them to the Magyars. Like the Czechs and other Slavs in the empire, the Slovaks had to confine their post-1848–1849 national and cultural activities rather strictly to literary activities, and the old quarrels over the proper literary medium for the Slovaks broke out again. Even during the revolutionary period the struggle continued. Kollár, for example, as an official of the government tried to make Czech the language of Slovakia. For this purpose he encouraged Daniel Lichard (1812–1882), a Lutheran minister, writer, and educator, and Father Ondrej Radlinský to found in 1849 the *Slovenské Noviny* (Slovak News) in Czech, or what they chose to call Staroslovenčina (Old Slovak). This newspaper was published biweekly and later triweekly in Vienna and lasted until 1861.

To counteract this revival of Czech among the Slovaks and to attempt to return to the language accord of 1847, Štúr effected the restoration of the philological commission of 1847 in the personages of three prominent Protestant Štúrists—himself, Hurban, and Hodža—and three equally renowned Catholic Bernolákists—Radlinský, the dramatist and editor Ján Palárik (1822–1870), and the priest Štefan Závodník (1813–1892). They met in Bratislava during October, 1851, agreed to unite their efforts for Slovak cultural autonomy, and agreed upon the use of the Central Slovak dialect for literary purposes. They also voted their approval of Professor Martin Hattala's *Grammatica Linguae Slovenicae* (Grammar of the Slovak Language), based on the Central Slovak dialect, and commissioned him to translate it into Slovak. It appeared the following year as the *Krátká Mluvnica Slovenská* (Short Slovak Grammar) with a preface signed by these same six men. In this manner the linguistic schism was ended and Štúr settled the problem Bernolák had raised sixty years earlier.[13]

Aside from a few publications such as the *Cyril a Method* (Cyril and Methodius) and *Slovenské Pohl'ady* (Slovak Views) there was not much other activity to give evidence of a Slovak national spirit. For the remainder of Bach's absolutism the Slovak national movement was very quiet. Only six Slovak books were printed during this decade and a monument was erected to Ján Hollý. Other evidence of the weakness of the Slovak national movement is the fact that the naturalist Dr. Gustáv Reuss (1818–1861) published his excellent work, *Květena Slovenská* (Slovak Flora) in 1853 in Czech. Even Štúr's *O Národních Písních a Pověstech Plemen Slovanských* (On the Folk Songs and Tales of Slavic Peoples) was published in Czech by the Matice Česká and other works by him were published in German.

Things took a turn for the better in 1858 when two new almanacs were published in Buda—*Concordia* by the priest Jozef K. Viktorín (1822–1877) and the dramatist J. Palárik (1833–1870), and *Lípa* (Linden Tree) by Viktorín. They both tried to revive creative writing, to function somewhat as literary magazines, and to further win over the hold-out defenders of Czech to the Slovak literary language. According to Rizner, however, there was apparently only one issue of *Concordia* ever published and *Lípa* lasted only until 1863.[14]

The first real waft of fresh air after the stifling period of absolutism was felt among the Slovaks shortly after the defeat of the Austrians at Solferino, June, 1859. The following July a *ukase* granted limited language rights in the schools and in September another gave the Protestants of Hungary complete religious autonomy. Both these concessions helped the Slovak national revival. One of the first results of this relative freedom was the founding by Radlinsky of a pedagogical newspaper called *Priatel' Školy a Literatury* (Friend of School and

[13] One year earlier in March, Palárik and Radlinský had already brought out a Catholic weekly for church and school, called *Cyril a Method* (Cyril and Methodius) which, with its literary supplement, *Príloha*, was printed in the new "corrected and revised Slovak."

[14] L. Rizner's *Bibliografia písomnictvá slovenského* (Turčianský sv. Martin, 1933).

Literature) in 1859. In 1860 Pavol Dobšinský (1828–1885), a poet and publicist in Banská Štiavnica, began publishing *Sokol* (Falcon), a thrice-monthly magazine for the arts and literature.

After the reforms initiated by the October Diploma of 1860 and the February Patent of 1861 Slovak national life improved more rapidly. Within a month of the February Patent, Ján Francisci founded in Buda the first Slovak political newspaper: a semi-weekly, the *Pešt'budínske Vedomosti pro Politiku a Literaturu* (Budapest News for Politics and Literature), which soon became the official interpreter of Slovak views. Among its important supporters and contributors were Daxner, Palárik, and Viliam Pauliny-Tóth (1826–1877), a writer and politician.

While Slovak cultural and national life improved, the political situation did not. There was not a single Slovak in either the Reichsrat of 1860–1861 or in the Hungarian Diet of 1861. In the former the Slovaks were represented only through the Croatian Bishop Strossmayer and in the latter by the Ruthenian, Adolf I. Dobriansky (or Dobrjanskij as he spelled his own name in Latin characters).

Since the Hungarian Diet of 1861 did nothing to advance Slovak national causes, some patriots like Daxner and Francisci through the pages of the *Pešt'budínske Vedomosti* called for a large national meeting or demonstration to be held June 6, 1861, in Turčiansky Sv. Martin (Thurócz Szent Martón, hereafter St. Martin)—the "Bethlehem of Slovak national life." At this time St. Martin was a rather unimportant village of about 3,000 on the River Turec, somewhat isolated in the mountains with no great advantages or attraction over other Slovak communities in Upper Hungary, such as Banská Bystrica where at the time more Slovak intellectuals were living. St. Martin did possess, however, many patriotic and hospitable citizens willing to do all they could to foster the national revival.

This demonstration, led by Daxner, attracted over 6,000 Slovaks of all classes and had to be held in the yard of the main church, since no building could accommodate the crowd. At this national rally a Memorandum drafted by Daxner was approved, which was much more dignified in tone and temperate in its claims than had been the Manifesto of 1848. In it the Slovaks asked for the same rights as other nationalities in the monarchy, that is, for language rights, schools, societies, periodicals, representation in public institutions, the abolition of statutes supporting Magyarization, and a chair of the Slovak language and literature at the University of Pest.[15] This Memorandum (the Slovak "Magna Carta") was taken by a delegation to Pest where it was not only not received, but was replaced by a pro-Magyar counter proposal signed by Slovak Magyarones (renegades who deserted to the Magyars), which was read and applauded. Later, protest meetings were organized against the Slovaks. At about the same time, however, Vienna dissolved the Hungarian Diet because of its attitude regarding the settlement of differences between Austria and Hungary. This resulted in a better situation for the Slovaks, who took the opportunity to send a delegation to Francis Joseph in Vienna with a slightly changed version of the Memorandum with the request that the emperor enact its demands of the Memorandum by a solemn imperial decree.

The delegation to Vienna, led by Bishop Štefan Moyses (1797–1869) and the Lutheran Bishop Karol Kuzmány, was actually received by the emperor, who accepted the Memorandum, but turned it over to Austrian officials. They in turn passed it on to the chancellery of the Court at Pest, which considered the document subversive. Unfortunately for the Slovaks, Vienna accepted this opinion and nothing came of the whole Memorandum movement.

As a result of this failure to gain any rights from Vienna or Pest the Slovaks were forced to turn to themselves. This decision led directly to the founding of the Slovak matica.[16]

Among the first things the Slovak national leaders undertook was the establishment of several Slovak private schools. The first fruit of this effort was a Protestant gymnasium established largely through Daxner's efforts. Later a Protestant gymnasium was set up by Kuzmány in St. Martin in 1866, and still later a Catholic one in 1869 in Kláštor pod Znievom, about twelve miles from St. Martin. Prior to this, Slovaks wishing to study in their own language at the secondary school level were restricted to the gymnasia in Bratislava and Levoča (which had been severely suppressed in the early 1840's) and in Banská Bystrica (from which Slovak instructors would be dismissed in 1868). These three new Slovak schools, however, had little money and, lacking text-books in Slovak, they had to utilize those in Czech.

Of more significance, however, were the steps taken to found the Slovak matica. Shortly after the failure of the Memorandum Ján Čipkay, a Slovak patriot and estate owner, sent 1,000fl. to the committee which had organized the national rally of June, 1861, to support the Slovak national movement. This contribution apparently caused the disappointed leaders of the Memorandum, who had failed in their political aspirations, to turn back to literary and

[15] See Daniel Rapant's *Viedeňské Memorandum Slovenské z Roku 1861* (Turčianský sv. Martin, 1943). For an English translation of this memorandum see Jozef Lettrich, *History of Modern Slovakia* (New York, 1955), pp. 285–286.

[16] The idea was actually first broached by Šafařík, who in a letter to Kollár in 1827 (one year after the Serbian prototype had been organized) wrote, "I have been thinking about a Slovak matica and how we could found our own." *Matica Slovenská* (Turčiansky sv. Martin, 1946), p. 6.

cultural means of promoting Slovak culture and nationalism. They therefore decided to establish their own matica or foundation as their kinsmen the Serbs, Czechs, Croats, and Moravians had already done. A steering committee was soon organized consisting of Francisci, Pauliny-Tóth, Palárik, Kuzmány, and others. By February, 1862, Francisci had prepared the by-laws, which after a few changes were accepted the following November by Vienna. According to these by-laws the purpose and aim of the Slovak matica was "to publish and distribute Slovak books and works of art, to give lectures on cultural subjects, to collect funds for the purpose of aiding literature, the arts, science, natural history, and researches in antiquities, and also to subsidize native scholars and artists, and to offer prizes and rewards for works on science and the arts."[17]

Immediately after the formal approval of the by-laws, announcements were sent out stating that contributions were to be sent to authorized agents in St. Martin, Pest, and Banská Bystrica. Among the earliest contributions was one of 1,000fl. from Francis Joseph himself, and a like one from Bishop Moyses.

So successful was this initial fund drive that six months later on May 1, 1863, Francisci was able to announce in his *Pešt'budínské Vedomosti* that the matica had received donations and pledges in excess of 50,000fl.

The significant activities of the Slovak matica during its brief lifetime of about twelve years can easily be summed up in one rather short paragraph. It was formally organized November, 1862, but did not hold its first general meeting until July, 1863, and it was dissolved officially April, 1875. It had, therefore, a life span of only eleven years and nine months. During this time it attracted about 1,100 members, held eleven general meetings in Martin, published eighty-two items, including nineteen volumes of its journal *Letopis*, helped standardize and promote Štúr's language reforms, granted financial aid to a few Slovak schools, to students and communities, developed many significant collections of coins, manuscripts, and other objects pertaining to Slovak culture and history, and erected a number of monuments and an impressive home for itself and its collections.

The purpose of this chapter is not to make these modest contributions seem more than they really are, but to assess their value and importance to a small culturally and nationally undeveloped people, to show their relation to the overall Slovak rebirth and to suggest the significance of the tradition and heritage of the Slovak matica after its dissolution in 1875.

The first general meeting was called during August, 1863, in St. Martin, when the Slovaks, as well as the rest of the Slavic world, were celebrating the millenium of Saints Cyril and Methodius. So many attended—more than 1,000—including almost every Slovak of importance, that as in 1861 the meeting was held in the churchyard.[18] At this gathering, over which Francisci presided, the matica was organized more formally with Bishop Moyses of Banská Bystrica as honorary president, Karol Kuzmány as vice-president (who actually directed its activities) and Ján Országh, Pavel Mudroň, and Tomáš Červen as members of the executive committee.

In the archives of the Slovak matica there are some flowery letters from other Slavic groups extending congratulations and encouragement to the Slovaks and their new venture.[19] The Czech matica, for example, officially send "brotherly love from the whole Czech nation on the Labe and Vltava rivers and from the Krkonoše to the Šumava mountains, to our dear brothers beneath the Tatra mountains on the Hron and Váh rivers." The letter, signed by Count Jan Harrach curator; and Václav Nebeský, secretary, closes with the wish, "May the Czech and Slovak maticas, sisters of the same mother, from today and for ever work together." Similarly the Serbian matica sent "brotherly love and heartfelt rejoicing."

Bishop Moyses was an excellent choice for honorary president for several reasons, not the least of which was the fact that he had lived in Zagreb and was personally familiar with the Croatian matica.[20] A governing board of leading Slovaks was also appointed at this time which included Daxner, Hurban, Hodža, Radlinský, Pauliny-Tóth, and the Ruthenian Adolf I. Dobriansky. Since May contributions and pledges had continued to come in and by August the matica had about 83,000fl. in pledges and donations.

One of the first acts of the new officers was to appoint a deputation to call upon the emperor to express thanks to him for permitting the matica to organize and to reaffirm the loyalty of the Slovaks to the throne. Francis Joseph received the deputation led by Moyses, Francisci, and Kuzmány, but he did not accede to their wish that he officially become their protector. The deputation also met with Count Anton Forgách, imperial Hungarian court chancellor, who surprised some of the deputation by his willingness and ability to converse with Bishop Moyses in

[17] Reprinted in Julius Botto's *Dejiny Matice Slowenskej* (Turčianský sv. Martin, 1913), pp. 126–138.

[18] An official police report on this meeting, sent from Pressburg to Vienna on August 16, estimated the gathering conservatively at from 600 to 700 and reported that there had been no disturbances of any kind. Haus-, Hof- und Staatsarchiv, Information-Index, 7178/1863.

[19] Archiv Matice Slovenskej, B. R. 79/I.

[20] Moyses had lived in Zagreb from 1830 through 1847. Although he was considered too liberal regarding Croatian nationalism, he did serve as an official censor from 1836 to 1843. See Rudo Brtáň, *Štefan Moyses a Chorvati* (Turčianský sv. Martin, 1949).

Slovak.[21] Nothing important, however, resulted from this trip to Vienna.

Also at this time some specific goals and projects for the matica were worked out, including the translation of good books into Slovak, a contest for a biography of Ľudovít Štúr, who had died in 1856, the collection of historic Slovak documents of all kinds, establishment of a numismatic collection, and the building of a national hall in St. Martin for its offices and collections.

1863–1867

Prior to 1867 the matica attained a membership of 1,112, the largest portion of which consisted of clergymen (365 or 32 per cent) and educators (123 or 10 per cent)—indicative of the important role these natural leaders of the common people played, not only in the Slovak revival, but in the whole Slavic rebirth. The next larger groups consisted of 93 officials of various kinds, 54 professional men, and a general group of 302 shopowners, craftsmen, and workers. The balance was made up of soldiers, women, landowners, and miscellaneous individuals and institutions such as schools, churches, libraries, and communities. Unfortunately only 14, or slightly more than one per cent of the membership, came from the mass of the peasantry—the very group the matica hoped to educate and waken to national consciousness—who were generally pathetically indifferent to their own national and cultural fate.[22] These two facts—the high percentage of intellectuals and urban classes and the low percentage of the common people as members—prevented the Slovak matica from effectively serving the whole nation. For the most part its literary activities were restricted to the educated classes.

Several honorary members were elected among whom were the Ruthenian bishop of Prešov (Eperjes), Jozef Gaganc, the Serbian bishop Nikanor Grujić, the Croatian *Župan* Ivan Kukuljević, the Slovenian philologist, Dr. Franjo Miklošić, and the Slovenian politician Janez Bleiweis, the Czech historian Palacký, and the Moravian lawyer Dr. Anton Beck. Apparently this bit of pan-Slavism did not bother Vienna. When, however, a rumor got out in 1864 that the Slovaks had requested "moral and material support" from Russia, a thorough investigation was conducted during October and November. The final report to Vienna, however, made it clear that all that had happened was that the Slovak matica had received from Russia in 1862, as had many other literary and learned institutions throughout the empire, a copy of an especially prepared book celebrating a millennium of Russian history, and that the matica had merely publicly acknowledged this gift, thanked the czar, and returned the compliment by sending the czar some of its publications.[23]

Among the objectives of this pre-1867 period which the matica tried to carry out were the building of a library to house its growing collection of books and manuscripts, publication of some Slovak readers for use in the two Slovak gymnasia, a few stipendia to be granted to students, and publication of a year book called *Letopis* (Chronicle).

Up to 1867 it was quite successful in carrying out these modest projects. During 1865–1866 it awarded twenty-four grants to students—twelve for 125fl., and twelve 50fl. Among the students who benefited were the future patriots Ambroz Pietor, J. M. Hurban, and F. Mráz. The matica also made grants of 200fl. to each of the two Slovak secondary schools. In the publishing field it printed up to 1867 twenty-six items including four issues of its journal *Letopis*, three almanacs, two readers for school children, works on agriculture, arithmetic, and grammar, a memorial to the great Croatian hero, Ban Nikola Zrinski, in connection with the three-hundredth anniversary of his death in 1566 while fighting the Turks, and miscellaneous reports and speeches.[24]

Of these early publications the most important was the journal *Letopis*. Its first two issues were uninspired miscellanea of minutes, membership and notation lists, speeches, and a bibliography edited, or better, "put together" (*sostavená*), by Michal Chrástek, one of the secretaries of the matica. The seventeen subsequent issues published through 1875 and edited by different persons, including Pauliny-Tóth and Sasinek were, however, much better. They averaged 115 pages and presented a total of 140 articles on all kinds of subjects such as history, ethnology, geography, philology, music, archaeology, botany, and annual bibliographies, plus detailed news

[21] Forgach (1819–1895), whose family was originally Slavic, had served previously as Statthalter of Bohemia. For part of 1861 he replaced the much disliked Karl Freiherr Mecséry and was known as somewhat liberal and pro-Czech. Unfortunately, during that same year he was replaced by the centralist Ernst Leopold Kellersperg.

[22] Figures from *Letopis* of 1867. A more recent breakdown of membership is as follows: Clergy 32 per cent, intellectuals 24.3 per cent, craftsmen and shopkeepers 21 per cent, juridical 7 per cent, women 2.3 per cent, peasants 1.8 per cent, and miscellaneous 5.6 per cent. *Dejiny Slovenskej Literatúry* (3 v., Bratislava, 1965) **3**: p. 43.

[23] Haus-, Hof- und Staatsarchiv, Information Index, 11891, 11911/1864.

[24] For a detailed list of all publications of the Slovak Matica see Peter Liba's *Vydavateľské Dielo Matice Slowenskej* (Martin, 1963).

During its short life the matica published in addition to nineteen issues of *Letopis* and four almanacs a total of sixty-six other items, forty of which were by-laws, speeches, and reports. The remaining twenty-six publications represent its serious book contribution: Belles-lettres and travel 4, school texts 4, history 3, geography 3, agriculture 3, philology 2, and one each in music, botany, geology, beekeeping, and three miscellaneous.

of the activities of the matica and its leaders. Each issue was published with the aim of helping the widest possible group, of fostering nationalism, education, and general culture, and promoting a better economic life.

In all, twenty-nine authors contributed materials. By far the most frequent contributor was one of its editors and a historian, František Viktor Sasinek (1830–1894), who wrote forty-one articles or about a third of the total. A distant second was Jonáš Záborský (1812–1876), a Lutheran minister and writer, with nineteen articles on various aspects of Slovak history. All others contributed four or less.[25]

Their first important book was Emil Černý's *Slovenská Čitanka* (Slovak Reader) a 344-page general collection of informative matter prepared especially for Slovak students in the secondary schools. Three volumes of this reader were published between 1864 and 1866. In 1865 Martin Čulen's *Počtoveda Čili Arithmetika* (Science of Reckoning or Arithmetic) was published.

These initial publications bear out the statement of Vlček that the publishing activities of the matica were mainly in technical, popular, and general cultural areas, rather than in belles-lettres. "In the creating of art, although it was a point of the matica program, the matica had no influence whatever. It can in no way be compared with the fresh, many-sided efforts of Štúr." [26]

The matica did, however, adopt, promote, and publish in Štúr's central Slovak dialect and the matica's greatest contribution to the Slovak national and cultural cause was the promotion and fostering of Štúršina as the standard Slovak language.

During this early period the matica also sent delegations to two important Slavic gatherings. The first was in 1866 when they participated in the tri-centennial of the death of Zrinski in Zagreb. To this they sent the Lutheran Hurban and Jur Slota (1819–1882), a Catholic priest, poet, and writer. At the same time they held a similar celebration in St. Martin in appreciation of which Bishop Strossmayer sent the matica a contribution of 1,000fl.

This festival was held on September 11 and 12. More than 250 individuals traveled to St. Martin to participate in the festivities, which included speeches, musical performances, and dramatic productions. The police reported that there was much evidence of Slovak loyalty to the monarchy and specifically noted a *Loyalitäts-Adresse* and an announcement that the matica would soon finance and present an exhibit of oil portraits of the imperial pair. The report also indicated that "in the restaurants and cafes, which were all quite full, the Slovaks made many toasts of loyalty and love to the monarchy and to their confederation brethern. On the other hand much distrust of the Magyars was evident. In no case, however, was there any trouble."[27]

The following year the matica sent three delegates to the famous Moscow Ethnographic Congress—two officers of the matica, Radlinský and Mudroň, and the lawyer Ján Jesenský.

1867–1871

After 1867 neither the future of the Slovaks nor the matica seemed inauspicious. Not only did the Slovaks enter the period of the *Ausgleuch* still unrepresented in the Hungarian Diet, but the political division among themselves which began about 1861 had by that time resulted in two well-defined and antagonistic parties which only resulted in splitting the Slovak vote and hurting their chances of gaining seats in the Diet.

Of the two parties the older one was the Národná Strana (National Party) which adhered to the claims of the Memorandum of 1861, had its headquarters in St. Martin and had the *Národné Noviny* as its mouthpiece. Its program was for a constitutional monarchy with autonomy for Slovaks, and its most important leaders were Hodža, Daxner, Francisci, and Pauliny-Tóth.

The other party was called the Nová Škola Slovenská (New Slovak School) and worked for some sort of cultural and ethnic modus vivendi with the Magyars. Its organ was the *Slovenské Noviny*, edited by Ján N. Bobula; its headquarters were in Pest. Its leaders were Bobula, Mallý, and Palárik, who followed the Magyar liberals.

Furthermore, the matica had not had time to make much headway in its hopes of culturally and nationally awakening the masses, many of whom were not only apathetic about the activities of the matica, but even suspicious of it and charged it with misuse of funds. That the matica accomplished as much as it did under such circumstances is noteworthy.

Although the compromise of the *Ausgleich* was the beginning of the end of the Slovak national revival, it was a few years before suppression began in earnest. During the five-year period, 1867–1871, the matica published twenty-five practical and popular items, including five issues of *Letopis*, two almanacs, Anton Penzel's *Ovocinár na Slovensku*, 1867 (Fruit Grower in Slovakia), the first volume of *Sborník Slovenských Národních, Piesní, Povestí, Prísloví, Porekadiel, Hádok, Hier, Obyčajov a Povier* (Almanac of Slovak National Songs, Stories, Proverbs, Folk Sayings,

[25] For a detailed index to this journal see Rizner's *Bibliografia Písomníctva Slovenského*.

[26] Jaroslav Vlček, *Dejiny literatúry slovenskej* (Turčiansky Sv. Martin, 1923), p. 351. Similarly the most recent study of Slovak literature says that the Slovak matica produced "casual publications rather than serious and artistic literature." *Dejiny Slovenskj Literatúry* (Bratislava, 1965) 3: p. 44.

[27] Haus-, Hof- und Staatsarchiv, Information-Index, 7171/1866.

Riddles, Games, Customs, and Superstitions) by Michal Chrástek, Emil Černý, and Pavel Dobšinský, in 1870; Dobšinský's *Úvahy o Slovenských Poviestach* (Treatises on Slovak Tales), and Ján Čajda's *Včelár na Slovensku* (Beekeeper in Slovakia) in 1871. Other publications were mainly speeches and reports.

The matica also created four committees of Slovak intellectuals to further the advance of language and literature; history, ethnography, and philosophy; mathematics, physics, and natural history; and economics and industry. It also acquired an impressive building in St. Martin for its headquarters, which enabled it to display properly its various large collections.

The matica was the first Slovak society to attempt on a large scale to locate, collect, and care for manuscripts, books, pictures, coins, maps, natural history objects, and such things pertaining to Slovak history, culture, and life. In response to a general solicitation individuals responded by sending in thousands of items of all kinds, each of which was acknowledged in *Letopis*. Its most important collection was its library which began with a gift from Martin Hamuljak of his personal library of more than 2,000 volumes. At the time of its dissolution in 1875 the museum-library of the matica had a collection of 10,629 scholarly books plus about 4,500 other volumes, 332 manuscripts, 12,957 coins and banknotes, 2,261 engravings and pictures, and hundreds of archeological specimens, minerals, maps, pieces of music, and collections of the papers of Hollý, Král', Sládkovič, Šafařík, and Štúr.

The biggest problem and failure of the matica were in attracting of peasantry to its ranks. Up to 1867 it had less than twenty members of the peasant class and few joined thereafter. In fact, membership plateaued off around 1,100 and remained rather constant for the rest of its life, a situation reflected by the fact that over its twelve-year life the number of copies printed of *Letopis* was never increased beyond the 1,300 copies of the first issue. Nor did its financial position improve dramatically. The matica ended 1867 with cash on hand of 58,200fl. and 1872 with 82,000fl.

In spite of this and the negative features of the *Ausgleich*, the matica wanted to continue to move ahead and urged its members to keep on working for their national rights. Its leaders had plans and ideas that would have required several hundred thousand gulden to execute, but at no time did they ever have as much as 100,000fl. to work with.

In 1868 the expectations of the patriots rose somewhat after the promulgation of the Law of Nationalities which, while it emphasized the privileged position of Magyar, also recognized the limited use of other tongues in districts where the non-Magyar tongues predominated. Paragraph twenty-six of article forty-four of this act provided that

> every inhabitant of the land irrespective of nationality, and every commune, religious denomination, and parish has the right to establish at his or its own cost and expense elementary, middle, and higher schools, and to found societies having for their aim the promotion of philology, arts, sciences, agriculture, commerce, and industry under proper state supervision, to formulate its own by-laws, if not inconsistent with the laws of the land... the language to be used in managing the affairs of such private associations being determined by the founders thereof.[28]

Furthermore, litigants and taxpayers were to be served in their mother tongue and judges were obligated to conduct the trial and examine witnesses in the language of the parties to the action.

These liberal provisions, however, were seldom, if ever, enforced. In practice the act made Magyar the official language and only under certain circumstances were individuals, not national groups, granted the rights promised in the law. Even these slight concessions were soon vitiated by the Magyar State Idea. (See below p. 62.)

Other than the passing of the language act the first direct interference by Magyars, after 1867, in the activities of the matica was during the August, 1868, general meeting when an official in the Turec county, in which St. Martin lay, protested that the matica was going beyond its main purpose as strictly a literary society. Surprisingly, the Hungarian minister of the interior, Baron Bela Wenckheim, did not agree and left the matica in peace. Thereafter the matica and its leaders functioned rather freely until 1872 when the enlightened Baron Jozsef Eötvös, who died in February, 1871, was replaced as minister of education and culture by the anti-Slovak August Trefort. (See below p. 62.)

Among the successes of the Slovaks during 1869 was the securing of three seats in the Hungarian Diet, one of which was held by Pauliny-Tóth. They also purchased an impressive and permanent home in St. Martin for their operations. A third Slovak gymnasium, a Catholic one, was set up in Kláštor pod Znievom, not far from St. Martin. Martin Čulen, former director of a Magyar gymnasium in Banská Bystrica, was appointed its first director. Ján Bobula founded a new publication in Pest, an almanac called *Minerva*. Bishop Moyses died in 1869 and was replaced as honorary president by Jozef Kozáček, a leading patriot and Catholic priest. Kuzmány continued to serve as the real head of the matica.

The year 1870 was also full of significant accomplishments. It was, however, the last good year the Slovaks enjoyed for the remainder of their dismal relationship with Hungary. It was a year particularly significant for the number of new publications and societies which were founded. Mikuláš Štefan

[28] Thomas Čapek, *The Slovaks of Hungary* (New York City, 1906), p. 94.

Ferienčik (1825–1881), an important Slovak journalist who had assumed control of Francisci's *Pešt'-budínske Vedomosti*, moved this political newspaper to St. Martin where it remained into the twentieth century and changed its name to *Národné Noviny* (later *Národnie Noviny* or National News).[29] Ján Kalinčák (1822–1871), an important Slovak writer, founded *Orol* (Eagle), a magazine of entertainment and learning in St. Martin where it lasted for ten years (1870–1880) until it was succeeded by the *Slovanské Pohl'ady*. Ferienčik also founded the monthly *Národní Hlásnik* (National Herald) in Budapest which lasted into the twentieth century.

Several other publishing concerns and national societies were also set up during 1870. In St. Martin a Joint Stock Publishing Society (Kníhtlačiarsky Účastinársky Spolok), was organized and became the official printer for the matica. It also published such Slovak newspapers as the *Národnie Noviny*, *Orol*, and *Národní Hlásnik*. It was neither a literary nor a national society, but a publishing firm founded and operated by the same men who controlled the matica, and as such was in reality the publishing division of the matica.[30]

Similar societies were founded by Samuel Ormis, gymnasium professor in Revúca, primarily for the purpose of publishing pedagogical works, and by some Catholic Slovaks in Pest, to print the *Slovenské Noviny*, the almanac *Minerva* and the dramas of Palárik.

The most important publishing concern which was set up in 1870 was, however, the Society of St. Adalbert (Spolok Svätého Vojtecha) which was organized by Radlinský in Trnava for the purpose of publishing and distributing good religious, moral, and educational books among the Slovak Catholics and of helping to support Catholic schools.[31] Its founders did not organize it in opposition to the matica, but only to supplement the work of the matica which published few strictly religious books. They also hoped to initiate a new translation of the Bible into Slovak.

At its first meeting in September, 1870, Bishop Henrik Szajbely was elected president and Radlinský, who had been working for such an organization since 1857, an honorary vice-president. At first it had no special organ of its own, but used the *Katolické Noviny* (Catholic News) as its mouthpiece.

The name of the society was well chosen. St. Adalbert (Adelbert or Vojtěch) became the first Czech bishop of Prague about A.D. 976 and suffered a martyr's death at the hands of the pagan Prussians in 997. Through his efforts Hungary was Christianized and the future patron saint of Hungary, Stephen, was baptized. Since St. Adalbert is also considered a patron saint of Hungary, the Slovaks did well to name their society after him. This society grew rapidly and by July, 1871, it had 1,485 members from all over Slovakia and a few from Austria, Bohemia, and Moravia.

Because of its strictly religious character it was allowed to function after the dissolution of the matica in 1875 and lasted into the twentieth century. Up to 1900 it had printed seventy-three items including twenty-nine issues of its annual, the *Pútnik Svätovojtešský* (St. Adalbert Pilgrim), a dozen "moral readers," a history of the Bible, hymn books, a catechism, and some lives of the saints.

Also of interest and importance was the organization of a Slovak women's society, *Živena*,[32] in 1870 which was brought about largely through the efforts of the publicist and editor Ambrož Pietor (1843–1906). This society, which soon had branches in every community in Slovak areas, offered courses in domestic hygiene and the care of small children, advocated temperance, and fostered and dignified womanhood and motherhood. It began to publish a journal to promote these objectives, an almanac also called *Živena*, the first issue of which appeared in 1872. It was edited by Pietor, who was also secretary of the society, but it was not very successful and its second and final issue did not appear for thirteen years, in 1885. The society itself endured, however, into the twentieth century.

After the successes of 1870 the hopes of the Slovaks were further raised by the appointment of the pro-Slav ministry of Hohenwarth in 1871 and by the founding of a journal for youth, *Napred* (Forward) in Skalica by Hviezdoslav (pseudonym of the famous poet Pavol Országh, 1849–1921). Furthermore, the matica's museum was visited and inspected by an official of the Magyar National Museum in Budapest who pronounced the Slovak collection to be excellent.

Also during the early 1870's the matica erected monuments to Hodža, Štúr, Hamuljak, and Sládkovič, and supported financially hospitals and reading

[29] Writers and publishers had to be careful. Just before the move to Martin, Hurban had been sentenced to six months in prison for an article he wrote in this paper. The article was "Čomu Naš Učia Dejiny" (What History Teaches Us).

[30] For a detailed study of this press see Pavol Halaša and Jozef Špetko, *Knihtlačiarsky Účastinársky Spolok v Martine* (Martin, 1958). After the dissolution of the matica in 1874 this firm continued to operate and published original works by Pauliny-Tóth, Hurban, Sasinek, Daxner, Francisci and other Slovaks, and also some translations of Turgenev, Tolstoj, Pushkin, A. Fredro, and Shakespeare, and became the most important press in Slovakia. After 1918 it gradually lost ground to other presses and societies and finally ceased operation in 1949.

[31] For the early history of this organization see *Spolok sv. Wojtecha, Založený a do Života Uvedený 1870* (Skalica, 1872). See also a new study by Sister M. Emma Hvozdovič, "History and Accomplishments of the Society of Saint Adalbert, Trnava, Slovakia," *Slovak Studies* 5 (1965): pp. 205–238. This society is still in existence although its religious activities were greatly curtailed after 1948.

[32] The Slovak (and Czech) name for Ceres. *Život* means life.

rooms (Slovanské čitárne). Some 150 of the latter were set up in Slovak areas. In 1873 the matica celebrated its tenth anniversary by deciding to inaugurate a program which would make books available to anyone for as little as fifty kreuzer, and by sending a delegation to Prague for the 100th anniversary of the birth of Jungmann. Such small successes, however, were soon totally obscured by the consequences of the appointment of Treford as minister of education.

1872–1875

The fateful year of 1872 began positively for all ethnic minorities in Hungary when Ferencz Deák in parliament on January 23, 1872, made a speech about the opening of a new Serb Gymnasium in Novi Sad, in which he said:

> Let us remember what difficulties we had to contend with in our youth, when we had to study in a dead and alien language, and how greatly the studies of the younger generation have been simplified by the use of their mother tongue as the language of instruction. The same is true of the nationalities. If we sought to compel their children, who know little or no Magyar, to pursue their studies in Magyar, then we should make their progress in the gymnasia impossible; the parents would spend their money to no purpose, the children would simply waste their time. Indeed, if we wish to win over the nationalities, we must not seek at all cost to Magyarize them; this can only happen if we create in them a love and attachment for Hungarian conditions. For two things are clear to me; to exterminate them would be a godless act of barbarism, even if they were not in any case too numerous for this to be possible; and to make them our enemies is not to our interest.[33]

Such a liberal outlook was not, however, held by the new minister of education, Treford, by the fanatic vice-commissioner of Zvolen County, Béla Grünwald, still less by the anti-Slav Kálmán Tisza who would soon (in 1875) become prime minister, succeeding Andrássy who was called to Vienna to become minister of foreign affairs. Their concept of the "Magyar State Idea" soon ruined the Slovak national movement.[34] The sixty-nine year old Deák stood alone in his liberalism. His like-minded colleagues Széchenyi and Eötvös were both dead.

Thanks to Treford, the matica was able to accomplish very little during its last four years. Its most important activity was publishing and for the period 1872–1875 it managed to bring out thirty items, most of which, however, were mere reports, speeches, and pamphlets. The most significant publications were the four volumes of *Letopis*, the three volumes of Sasinek's *Archiv Starých Česko-slovenských Listín, Písomností a Dejepisných Pôvodín pre Dejepis a Literatúru Slovákov* (Collection of Old Czecho-Slovak Letters, Documents and Historic Sources of Slovak History and Literature), 1872–1873, volume two of Chrástek, Černy, and Dobšinský's Collection of Slovak National Songs . . ., 1874, L. A. and J. G. Reuss's *Základné Pravidlá Súzvuku* (Fundamental Rules of Harmony), 1873, and finally *Hospodár na Slovensku* (Farmer in Slovakia) by the botanist and archaeologist, Andrej Kmeť (1841–1908) in 1875.

Treford, always fearful of pan-Slavism and the 1,000-year-old ghost of Svatopluk, was not satisfied merely to restrict the activities of the matica. He intended to destroy it and the whole Slovak revival. In 1873, incited by Grünwald's *Svornost* (Concord)—a rabidly anti-Slovak bi-weekly published in Banská Bystrica—which attacked the Slovak secondary schools as nests of pan-Slavism, Treford ordered a thorough investigation of these schools for this alleged "crime." The following year, in 1874, the gymnasia in St. Martin and Revuca were quickly closed. The one in Kláštor pod Znievom, however, successfully passed a four-and-one-half-day intensive inspection, but it was closed in 1874 anyway on the grounds that the building was too old.

The loss of these three schools was great. Budapest, of course, refused to provide state supported Slovak schools and therefore the Slovaks were left without any secondary education in Slovak for the rest of the life of the empire. Students had the choice of foregoing education beyond primary schools or of attending Magyar schools. On one occasion Pauliny-Tóth made an effort to reopen the school in St. Martin and in response to his appeal for funds in one month 100,000fl. poured in, but Treford would not allow the school to be reopened even with Slovak financing.

During the same year of the closing of the gymnasium the matica sent a delegation to the opening of the Croatian University in Zagreb. Sasinek, leader of the deputation, made a speech in which he declared, "Date nobis ex oleo vestro, quia lampades nostrae exstinguuntur" (Give us of your oil so that our lamps do not go out), a statement as prophetic as pathetic, for during the following year a greater national tragedy befell the Slovaks—the dissolution of the matica by Tisza and Trefort on the grounds that in spite of its constitution it engaged in political activities, was pan-Slavic (the sending of the delegation to Zagreb was given as an example), that some of its publications, especially the historical works of Záborský and Sasinek, were false and anti-Magyar,

[33] G. L. Oddo, *Slovakia and Its People* (New York, 1960), p. 136.

[34] This notorious "Idea," an old concept of Magyar chauvinists, was best spelled out by Grünwald in his book *Felvidékiek* (Highlanders) in 1878. It was that to have a safe future Hungary must become a homogeneous nation. The Magyars must rule, others must follow. The national awakening of the Slovaks as well as of the other minorities was dangerous. There was no Slovak nation, only a horde speaking that language which must be Magyarized. An educated Slovak who remained true to his people was deficient in patriotism and was a traitor to his country. The Slovaks must be Magyarized or eliminated, no compromise was possible.

and that its funds and property were improperly and carelessly administered.

A typical example of the Magyar point of view at this time is the following quotation from *Hon* (Fatherland), a major Magyar newspaper: "The Slovak matica consists of about 100 coarse individuals without property or purpose who simply like to hold office, but who have no real cultural mission. . . ." [35]

In 1875 its charter was annulled, the matica's library and rich collections were first sealed and then later transferred to another museum in Nitra (Neutra, Nyitra), a Magyar stronghold, its funds and other assets, totaling over 140,000fl. were confiscated by the government, and its building was turned into a district court. In 1883 salt was plowed into the soil of the Slovak national movement by assigning the confiscated monies of the matica to FEMKE, a Magyarizing society in Nitra.[36]

Hurban and Pauliny-Tóth went to Vienna to seek help and to swear allegiance, but, since Vienna was seldom adverse to the centralizing activities of the Magyars, they were not received, nor were their letters answered. When Dr. Mihajlo Polit-Desančić (1833–1920), a Serbian deputy to the Hungarian Diet, defended the Slovaks and insisted that the money be returned to the donors or to the "Slovak nation" as the charter of the matica stipulated, Tisza said on the floor of the Diet on December 15, 1875, that "there is no Slovak nation." The suppression of the gymnasia and the matica opened the floodgates of Magyarization which seriously curtailed and suppressed Slovak cultural and national life for the rest of the duration of the Dual Monarchy.

EPILOGUE

In 1879 Magyar was made mandatory in all elementary schools, even in Church-maintained schools. By 1910 there was not a single secondary school in Hungary where Slovak was either taught or used in teaching. Nor was it taught at the university in Budapest even though there was a Croatian chair there. In 1875 there had been 1,805 elementary schools in which Slovak was used along with Magyar, but by 1905 chauvinism had reduced this figure to 241.

Politically the Slovaks were seldom represented in the Hungarian Diet and could not effectively protest such harsh practices as the systematic Magyarization of place and family names [37] or the even worse forcible removal of Slovak children from their families to Magyar counties, a practice which lasted for eighteen years from 1874 to 1892 and which involved over 850 children. Justice was administered only in Magyar and there was no railroad, postal, or telegraph service save in Magyar.

Denied the use of their secondary schools and their main cultural-national society, former members and leaders of the matica struggled on as individuals to ward off total Magyarization through the press, portions of which remained unfettered and effective, and a few societies.

Between 1875 and the end of the Dual Monarchy there were three Slovak newspapers of significance. The most important was Ferienčik's *Národné Noviny* which remained the main voice of Slovak national consciousness. In 1881 Svetozár Hurban Vajanský (1847–1916), the famous son of J. M. Hurban, and Jozef Škultéty (1853–1948) revived the *Slovanské Pohl'ady* (Slovak Views) of Hurban in 1845. In 1886 Anton Zatopek in Budapest founded and edited the thrice-weekly *Slovenské Noviny* (the third paper of this name).

Several important institutions managed to stay in existence in spite of Magyarization—Živena, the women's society, the Joint Stock Publishing Company, and the Slovenská Muzeálná Spoločnost' (Slovak Museum Society). The latter was founded in 1895 in St. Martin largely through the efforts of Andrej Kmeť to collect and preserve things connected with Slovak life, and had a publication, the *Sborník Muzeálnej Slovenskej Spoločnosti* (Journal of the Slovak Museum Society). The most important of these institutions, however, was probably the St. Adalbert Society, which functioned in the field of religion as the matica had in national, cultural and instructional areas.

Through the quiet work of a few individuals and institutions the heritage and traditions of the Slovak matica were not lost. When it was revived in 1918 it soon had 1,275 members and became—and remained to this day—one of the most important cultural and educational institutions in all Czechoslovakia. In 1954 it became an official institution of learning and was designated as the Slovak National Library and library science center.

Throughout its short early life the matica had not been able to accomplish or realize anywhere near its full ambition or plans. But without its twelve years of activity the Slovaks would have been much more demoralized and torn apart by Magyarization than they were and much less capable of cultural development after 1918.

[35] Botto, *Dejiny matice slovenskej*, p. 118.

[36] Felvidéki Magyar Kozmüvelödési Egyesület (Upper Hungarian Educational Association). *Cf.* the EMKE (Erdelyi Magyarság Kulturális Egyesülete), the Magyar Cultural Association of Transylvania which was organized among the Rumanians.

[37] Kossuth's name was derived originally from the place of his birth, Kosuty, a village only several miles from St. Martin. Hungary's famous lyric poet, Sándor Petöfi, was Serbian—born Petrović. He Magyarized his own name out of respect for the Magyars.

VII. THE SLOVENIAN MATICA, 1864: A MODEST, ENDURING YOUNGER SISTER

The goal of the matica is to propagate with all its might the culture of the Slovene nation and, consequently, to support Slovene literature. The society will also publish or aid in the publishing of good scientific books which are suitable for the people.

From the By-laws.

In 1863, during the widely celebrated millennium of Saints Cyril and Methodius, the Slovenes took the requisite steps to found their matica, something which had been advocated for nearly twenty years. This society soon became the most important institution of the Slovene national revival.

Prior to the founding of the matica in Ljubljana, the Slovene national movement had neither an institution to foster it, nor a recognized center. Nor was there much feeling of unity among the scattered Slovenes. Society and culture were dominated by Germans and the peasants had no political rights or power. Furthermore, they had fewer schools and members of the noble and middle classes than probably any other Austro-Slavic group and almost no significant, political, or national movement before the early 1840's.

Since their appearance in history during the sixth century, they had almost never been independent. In fact, they are often characterized as a "non-historic" people, meaning that they had never had their own independent state. This is not quite true, for there was a Slovene state called Carantania during the eighth and ninth centuries. Shortly thereafter, however, they fell to Charlemagne and finally to the Habsburgs during the fourteenth and fifteenth centuries.

In 1815 they were the smallest group of Austro-Slavs (totaling about 1,000,000) and were even more scattered and disunited than the Croats. They lived in six areas of the monarchy—Carinthia, Styria, Carniola, and three parts of the Littoral (Gorizia, Trieste, and Istria). Only in Carniola and Trieste, however, did they form a majority of the population. Not only were the Slovenes divided by geography, but by political administration, economic interests, ecclesiastical jurisdiction, and dialectical and orthographic differences as well. Their whole national program rested almost exclusively on ethnic and linguistic ties, not history.

Prior to the matica period the Slovene renaissance had gone through at least six phases in one Slovene center or another. The earliest important phase of their revival was during the late eighteenth and early nineteenth centuries in Carniola (Krain, Kranjska, the most industrially and culturally advanced of all South Slav territories) in Ljubljana (Laibach) the provincial capital and administrative center, which was mainly Germanized save for the lower classes and the nationally minded members of the bourgeois and intellectual classes. Here the revival was fostered by the "Zois Circle" (Zoisov Króžek). Baron Žiga Zois (Sigmund Zois, Žiga Cojs, Žiga Cojz, 1747–1819), born in Trieste of an Italian father and Slovene mother, was a nationally minded Slovene industrialist who helped and encouraged other nationalists. The most important member of this circle was probably the poet, Valentine Vodnik (1758–1819), a one-time Franciscan friar who laid the foundations of modern Slovene poetry. In 1797 he founded an important newspaper, the semi-weekly *Ljubljanske Novice*, the first Slovene newspaper, through which he preached Slovene mutuality and tried to combat German and Italian influence. This paper lasted for only four years.

Other important members of the Zois Circle were the first Slovene historian and playwright Anton Linhart; the first Slovene pedagog, Blaž Kumerdej; the writer Jurij Japelj; and the famous Slavist Jernej (Bartholomaeus) Kopitar (1780–1844), the "first teacher" of the Slovenes. Kopitar's *Grammatik der Slawischen Sprache in Krain, Kärnten und Steiermark* (1806–1809) did much to foster and standardize Slovene and laid the foundation for the national revival.

Most of this same circle were also connected with the small, scholarly group called the Academia Operosorum (Academy of [Learned] Works) a society originally founded in Ljubljana during the late seventeenth century (it lasted from 1693 to 1701). This society had been re-established in 1781 to promote science and Slovene literature, but neither in the seventeenth nor eighteenth century was it very effective. By 1785 it was inoperative again.

After this modest beginning the center of the Slovene revival shifted from Ljubljana to a second center at Graz, Styria (Steiermark, Štajerska) whither many South Slavs gravitated to attend the university (founded in 1586) and the Theologenseminar located there. According to Matl, during the late eighteenth century the main cultural center of the fragmented Slovenes was this seminary from which came the early Slovene prayer books, catechisms, grammars, and some primitive poems.[1]

Of even more importance, however, during the nineteenth century was a third phase led by a group of students at the University of Graz which included many of the early Slovene national leaders such as Stanko Vraz, and Janez Nepomuk Primic. Primic, for example, founded in 1810 the Societas Slovenica, the earliest Slovenian literary society for the development and fostering of Slovenian speech among the Slovene students at the university. He later became an important writer and philologist and held the first

[1] Josef Matl, "Leistung und Bedeutung Erzherzog Johanns für den National-kulturellen Fortschritt der Slowenen und Kroaten," *Südost-Forschungen* 22 (1963): p. 357.

Lehrkanzel für slowenische Sprache at the university in Graz.

These young intellectuals who desired to become clerks, teachers, journalists, and lawyers, rather than clergymen, absorbed the German and Western ideas offered by Graz, but remainded nationally and consciously Slovenes. They tried to raise the academic and cultural level of their people, and also to establish ties with other Slavs. Graz early became the Slovene and South Slav window to the outside world. Some of its graduates remained there and worked for the good of their people, others returned to Slovene lands to form the nucleus of a Slovene bourgeois society.

Those who stayed in Graz were aided and supported in their national efforts by the benevolent Archduke Johann, brother of Emperor Francis, who in 1811 founded the famous Johanneum, a museum in Graz, which became the model for the Czech museum (see above p. 24). Later, in 1823, some Illyrian-minded students organized an Illyrischer Klub and in 1838 others founded the Slavischer Verein. Because of these institutions and the support of Archduke Johann, Graz remained for over thirty years the main cultural and national center of the scattered Slovenes.

Although Graz was the leading center of the Slovenian revival at this time, a fourth phase of the revival commenced when some attempts were made to further the work and goals of the old Zois circle and to make Ljubljana again a center of Slovene culture and national development.[2] To this end Miha Kastelic, a writer and librarian, and Matija Čop, also a man of letters and a librarian, founded and edited the first Slovene almanac in 1830—the *Krajnska Zhbelica* (*Krajnska Čbelica*, the *Carniolan Bee*). The principal poet of this annual was Francè Prešeren, the greatest of all nineteenth-century Slovene poets. Through his efforts the *Carniolan Bee* became the foundation of modern Slovene literature.

At about this time, during the 1830's, Illyrianism began to spread from Croatia to Slovene regions. With the exception of Stanko Vraz, however, the Slovene intellectuals were not enthusiastic Illyrians. The work of Vodnik and Prešeren had raised Slovene to a high artistic level and had given the people a literature of which they could be proud. After 1830, lyric and epic poetry flowered, and the Slovenes, Prešeren in particular, were not interested in submerging their language and literature into South Slavic Illyrianism. Although the Slovenes did adopt in 1846 the Illyrian orthography of Gaj, they preferred and preserved their linguistic individuality.

Unfortunately, the era of the *Bee* was short-lived and it ceased publication in 1834 after four volumes.[3] One of the main reasons for its demise was the opposition of the conservatives, especially the clergy, to some of Prešeren's poems, particularly to his love lyrics. Among those working against Prešeren and the *Bee* was Kopitar who was probably also motivated by the fact that Prešeren was eclipsing him as a national and cultural leader.

After the end of the *Bee*, no significant advance was made in the Slovene revival for nearly a decade, not until 1843 when Janez Bleiweis, in order to stimulate national consciousness, founded a newspaper in Ljubljana called *Novize* (*Novice*, *News*). Bleiweis (1808–1881), in spite of his Germanized name (the Slovenian form is Blavec) is often called the "father of the Slovene nation," compared favorably to the Czech journalist Havlíček, and generally considered to be the most influential Slovene during the 1840's. He had received degrees in medicine and veterinary medicine from Vienna and by 1840 was a professor of the latter subject at the Ljubljana Lyceum.[4] With the publication of *Novize*, Ljubljana became the uncontested center of the national movement. The period of this publication, up to 1854, is often referred to in Slovene historiography as the "Novice Period," and was (according to my reckoning) the fifth phase of the Slovene national movement.

As a physician and a veterinarian, rather than a man of letters, Bleiweis was convinced that, because of the small middle class and a large body of peasants and craftsmen, the Slovenes needed popular literature more than belles-lettres. Therefore, as secretary of the Imperial and Royal Agriculture Society (C. K. Kmetijska Družba) in Carniola, he convinced this group to publish the *Kmetijske in Rokodelske Novize* (Farm and Handicraft News), the first popular Slovene journal. This weekly, of which he was also editor, commenced in 1843. As would be expected, it was very popular and full of literary pieces, tendentious poems, and pious verse. As a result, the high-level literary efforts of Prešeren were neglected and the more simple, earlier tradition of Slovene literature was fostered.

During the revolution of 1848–1849, the Slovenes made few attempts to advance their cause. In April, 1848, they issued a manifesto to the emperor in which they made three main requests: they wanted to be joined into one land and nation, to receive national and linguistic rights, and to effect closer

[2] This desire of the Slovene nationalists was facilitated by Bishop Augustine Gruber (1763–1835) when he founded in 1821 the Landesmuseum im Herzogthume Krain. Though the good bishop was German and the museum was devoted to provincial patriotism, it was a center of learning and Bishop Gruber was sympathetic enough to the Slovenes to begin to study their language at the age of fifty-three.

[3] A fifth volume was published in 1848.

[4] In Austria, where horses and cattle were so important not only to the economy, but to the military, *Thierärzte* were very important and often better trained than ordinary physicians. Bleiweise received his degree in veterinary medicine as the famous Thierarzenei-Institut, founded in Vienna in 1823, which was the best in Europe.

economic and cultural union with their kinsmen in Croatia, Slavonia, and Dalmatia. Withal a modest proposal, but one which was refused by Vienna anyway.

Of more success was the founding of a semi-weekly newspaper in Ljubljana in July, 1848. This was *Slovenija*, the first Slovenian political journal. It was edited by Matej Cigale, a lawyer and linguist, and lasted until March, 1850. The Slovenes also organized a political club, Slovenija, in Vienna and Graz, which fostered union and equality, and the use of Slovene in the schools and public offices. Nothing much, however, came of such efforts, and after the "spring of the peoples" the Slovenes were still divided into six groups. The only positive and enduring result of 1848 to the Slovenes was the emancipation of the peasantry, resulting in the growing political and cultural consciousness of that class. The events of 1848, though never fully realized, bequeathed the Slovenes a strong desire of cultural and political unity of all "Slovene lands."

After the pall of Bach's absolutism settled over the monarchy, the program for Slovene national movement was curbed. The early, "first generation," national leaders—Zois, Vodnik, Kopitar, Primič, Čop, and Prešeren—were dead, and Bleiweis was quiescent. During the 1850's the center of the Slovene national movement shifted to a third and new center—to Klagenfurt (Celovec) in Carinthia, (Kärnten, Koruška).

The driving force behind this movement (the sixth and final phase of the Slovene revival prior to the matica era) was Bishop Anton Martin Slomšek (1800–1862). By 1846 he had become bishop of a diocese in eastern Carinthia and the Slovene area of Styria. Because of his national interest he is often called the "Apostle of the Slovenes," and is compared with the Croatian Bishop Strossmayer.

One of his first acts after becoming bishop was to found in 1846 a yearbook, *Drobtince* (Miscellany), for the instruction of the Slovene members of his church, especially for the teachers and students of his seminary. To further advance the literary and cultural standards of his see, he and a few other nationally minded Slovenes founded in 1852 in Klagenfurt an important publishing house.

This was the Družba sv. Mohorja (the Society of St. Hermagoras)—a publishing concern for the purpose of putting good Slovene books with a Catholic spirit into the hands of Slovenians where numbers were so small that few commercial publishers printed books for them. This society, modeled after the earlier Czech Society of St. Jan Nepomuk (see above p. 23), was significant in helping unify the scattered Slovenians.[5] The good bishop received much help in founding this society from Anton Janežič, a teacher of Slovenian in the Klagenfurt gymnasium who later became an important editor and writer, and from Andrej Einspieler, a chaplain in Klagenfurt who later became an important editor, theologian, and political leader. Membership was available from 2fl. for which members received up to six publications a year.

This publishing venture, the only significant national movement of the 1850's, was very successful. By 1860 the Society of St. Hermagoras had 1,116 members, in 1870 it had 16,175, and in 1880 over 25,000 members and its own building and press. By 1918 it had over 90,000 members to whom it distributed in that one year alone over 543,000 books—a figure which brought the total of books distributed since its beginning to 19,000,000. Considering the fact that there were so few Slovenes such figures are very impressive and indicate an unusually high rate of literacy—in fact, the highest rate of the South Slavs. Throughout the period of absolutism this society was the bulwark of Slovene nationalism and made an enormous contribution to Slovene unity and literature. The society is still in existence. After the plebiscite of 1920, which left Klagenfurt in Austria, it moved its headquarters for a few years to Prevalje and then in 1927 to Celje where it is today. An important branch, however, still exists in its original home of Klagenfurt.

After 1860, the new constitutionalism, even in the curtailed version permitted by the February Patent, allowed much greater political and cultural advances to the Slovenes even though they were still fragmented into six areas and ruled largely by a German bourgeois minority. The main political developments during the latter half of the nineteenth century were two, the growing strength and cleavage of the Old and Young Slovene parties, and the clarification of the central political issue. This issue was that "Slovenian nationalists were not willing to regard as lost those Slovenes who were indifferent to their appeals or who were consciously attracted to the German world, while the German nationalists vigorously opposed any efforts made by the Slovene pastors to pull their flocks from the abyss of Germanization." [6] Various programs to effect a pan-Slovenian political union were proposed, but were unsuccessful.

Bleiweis, Etbin H. Costa, and Lovro Toman were the leaders of the moderate and conservative Old Slovene party (sometimes called the Slovene Peoples' party). Costa was a politician and lawyer who later became mayor of Ljubljana and a deputy in the imperial diet. Toman was a prominent writer and politician. Their party had the motto "All for religion, country and the emperor!" and a program of

[5] See Janko Moder, *Iz Zdravih Korenin Močno Drevo: Iz Zgodovine Družbe Sv. Mohorja* (Celje, 1952).

[6] Thomas Barker, *The Slovenes of Carinthia: A National Minority Problem* (New York City, 1960), p. 66.

limited, compromising efforts for the improvement of the Slovenian situation in the empire.

They were increasingly opposed by the Young Slovene party which had evolved during the 1850's. This party, led by Fran Levstik, an important writer and philologist, usually designated as the founder of modern Slovenian prose, fought against foreign influence in Slovene society, conservatism in culture, and compromise in politics. After 1860, the ranks of the Young Slovenes were swelled by lay (in contrast to clerical) intellectuals emerging from the peasant class. This conflict became the basic political problem for the remainder of the century.

The *Ausgleich* of 1867 affected the Slovenes but little, for all Slovenes remained in Austria except a few who lived in a small area north of the Mura river. The new constitution of 1867, however, did permit public gatherings and the Slovenes, following the example of the Czechs, organized mass outdoor meetings (*tabori*) to explain their political goals, to increase national and self-consciousness, and to foster pan-Slovenianism—a program called the Yugoslav Program, to unite all Slovene regions into an autonomous Slovenian unit within the empire to be ruled by a governor appointed by the emperor. Article XIX of the 1867 constitution also required the provincial government to issue announcements in Slovenian as well as in German, and the Primary School Law of 1869 benefited most of the Slovenes by extending the use of Slovene in the primary schools.

Both political parties, taking advantage of the relative leniency of constitutionalism, worked to advance the national cause by organizing cultural societies. The Young Slovene leader, Levstik, took the lead and founded in Trst (Trieste) in January, 1861, the first Slovenian reading room (*čitalnica*). The following July another was opened in Maribor (Marburg) and in August Bleiweis organized the Narodna Čitalnica—the National Reading Room, in Ljubljana. The idea spread—by 1865 there were fourteen reading rooms, by 1869 there were fifty-eight, and seventy-seven at the end of the century in all Slovenian territories.[7]

These reading rooms had great influence on Slovenian intellectuals and politics. They fostered in all ways Slovenian language, literature, and the growth of national consciousness. Whenever possible, they built their own quarters, which were called National Halls (sign. *Narodni dom*). These societies became centers of national and cultural life, not only because of the reading materials provided, but because of the various other national activities they sponsored, such as dances, dramas, and lectures in the national interest. Many of them also organized choral, dramatic, and orchestral groups. Bleiweis's reading room in Ljubljana, for example, founded the Dramatično Društvo (Dramatic Society) in 1867, which evolved its own publication, the *Slovenska Talija* (Slovenian Thalia) for dramatic Literature and the Glasbena Matica (Music Foundation) in 1872, which also had a publication. Previously in 1863 it had sponsored the organization of the Južni Sokol (Southern Falcon)—a patriotic gymnastic society modeled on the Czech Sokol, to promote national consciousness among the South Slavs.

1863–1881

The most important organizational effort of the Ljubljana reading room, however, was also in 1863 when it established the Slovenska Matica—the single most influential step toward the institutionalizing of the Slovenian national movement.[8] The organization of such an institution was not a new idea. Many had suggested it. As early as 1845, for example, Bishop Slomšek had suggested through the pages of *Novize* that a society be established to publish inexpensive national and popular books in Slovenian to unite the scattered Slovenians. In 1850 a Dr. Jurij Šubic also tried through *Novize* to advance the idea. Still another attempt was made in 1858 at the time of the centenary celebration of the birth of Vodnik. In 1860 Ferdo Kočevar complained that "The Serbs have such an institution, the Czechs and Croats also, why not us? How much this would advance our literature! Many individuals would write if they had a publisher." [9] Nothing came of these various attempts, for several reasons. Not only were most Slovene intellectuals thoroughly Germanized, but the Slovene Illyrians considered Slovenian culture inferior to the South Slav cultural synthesis they were attempting to forge. Furthermore, many conservative Slovene patriots considered the St. Hermagoras Society sufficient for the task of publishing books in Slovenian.

By 1863, however, the Slovenes were more nationally conscious; political, national, and cultural life was more free, and all the other Austro-Slavs already had, or were setting up, their own maticas. Since the Slovenes had no academies, universities, literary societies, or even a Slovene gymnasium, the idea of a matica appealed to Slovene intellectuals. At the celebration of the millennium of Saints Cyril

[7] See E. H. Costa, "Statestični Pregled Sevh Slovenskich Čitalnic," *Letopis Matice Slovenske* 1869: pp. 282–296. Many of these reading rooms are described in Ivan Prijatelj, *Slovenska Kulturnopolitična in Slovstvena Zgodovina, 1848–1895* (Ljubljana, 1956) 2: pp. 135–239.

[8] The year 1863 was very important in Slovene national and cultural development. Not only was the matica founded, the millennium of SS. Cyril and Methodius honored, the Južni Sokol founded, but there was also a Bleiweis festival. Prijatelj, in his *Slovenska Kulturnopolitična in Slovstvena Zgodovina, 1848–1895* devotes seventeen pages to this one year.

[9] Prijatelj, *Slovenska Kulturnopolitična*, p. 250.

and Methodius which was sponsored by the Ljubljana reading room during March of 1863, the idea of a Slovene matica was advanced again. It was particularly pushed by several leaders of the Maribor reading room, who mailed to the Ljubljana reading room a tentative set of by-laws based on those of the Czech matica. Their suggestion was enthusiastically received, and at the time of the celebration a steering committee consisting among others of Baron Anton Zois, Costa, and Levstik was organized. *Novize* gave full coverage to the idea and its propagation which resulted in many cash contributions. Thus encouraged, the steering committee sought permission from the emperor to organize and its request was granted the following February. The Slovenian matica had come into existence, and although it was slow in developing it became and remained the principal Slovene literary, cultural, and scientific association to 1914 and also rivaled the St. Hermagoras Society as a publishing concern.

The matica was actually organized and controlled for nearly twenty years by "second generation" Slovene national and political leaders, most of whom were members of the Old Slovene party. Among them the most influential was certainly Bleiweis, who in addition to being editor of *Novize* and *Kmetijske in Rokodelske Novize*, a physician and veterinarian, secretary of the Agricultural Society, leader of the conservative Old Slovene party, and president of the Ljubljana reading room during the years 1863–1881, was also a board member of the matica from 1865 to his death in 1881, editor of its journal *Letopis* (Chronicle) 1867–1868, 1877–1881, and its president from 1875 to 1881. By his death in 1881 most of the original aims of the matica and the early national leaders had been attained and its pioneering days were over; this study does not go beyond that date.[10]

Other important national leaders who served as president of the matica during this first eighteen-year period were Baron A. Zois, Toman, and Costa. In addition Levstik, Einspeiler, and Josip Vošnjak, an M.D. and national leader, served as officers and board members during this period.

Most of these and other leaders were members of the Old Slovene group. The main exception was Levstik, but since he served as secretary only until 1865 and was not re-elected he and the Young Slovene party had little influence on the policy and activities of the matica.

The unfortunate split between the Old and Young Slovenes not only cost the matica the support and help of Levstik, but also of most of the important Slovene writers of the latter half of the nineteenth century such as Josip Stritar, Josip Jurčič, and Simon Jenko, who furthered the Prešeren tradition of belles-lettres as against the Old Slovene inclination towards the popular and the practical aspects of literature. These writers, instead of contributing to *Letopis*, supported Anton Janežič's *Slovenski Glasnik* (Slovenian Herald, in Klagenfurt 1858–1868), Stritar's literary monthly *Zvon* (Bell, in Vienna 1870, 1876–1880), and continually criticized the politics and publications of the matica.

Membership in the matica, available for as little as 2fl. and giving members a free copy of all publications, grew rapidly from 712 during the first year, to 1,200 two years later, to 2,291 in 1874, to over 2,500 in 1881, including members from over 100 communities throughout Slovene territories.[11] Typically most of these members were clergymen and middle-class intellectuals, businessmen, and lawyers. Its treasury grew at a commensurate rate—from 7,679fl. during the first year, to 27,765 two years later, to 59,887fl. in 1874, to more than 67,000 in 1881. Most of these monies were made up of small membership fees, but there were several significant large gifts. Dr. Lovro Toman donated the largest amount, 10,000fl. The next largest was 8,243fl. from Matija Debeljak, a wealthy patriot, and a bank in Ljubljana donated 3,000fl. Two clerics gave 1,000fl. each—Dekan Rozman of Konvice, and Bishop Strossmayer.[12] Baron A. Zois contributed 500fl. The *Haus, Hof und Staat* was represented by a 500fl. contribution from Francis Joseph himself. Some made donations in kind. Peter Kozler, a lawyer and amateur cartographer, for example, donated over 700 maps. Others gave books for a library, which by 1874 totaled over 2,000 volumes.

Ordinarily the society held general meetings only annually, while the administrative and literary boards and various committees met several times a year or as often as necessary. As soon as finances permitted, the matica acquired its own headquarters, first in 1869. In 1879 it purchased more adequate accommodations for 28,000fl.

According to its by-laws, drawn up largely by Lovro Toman, its main purpose was "to help the

[10] In spite of his great contributions Bleiweis has been severely criticized for opportunism, for compromising with the authorities, for claiming too much, and for being excessively critical of others. For example, see Antun Barac, *A History of Yugoslav Literature* (Beograd, 1955). Arnez, however, claims that his moderation was "motivated by sound political realism." See John A. Arnez, *Slovenia in European Affairs* (New York City, 1958).

[11] Membership and financial figures taken from the 1874 and 1881 issues of *Letopis*.

[12] Strossmayer's "pan-Slavic" activities were closely watched by Vienna. His contribution to the Slovene matica, for example, was duly noted by the police. (Haus-, Hof- und Staatsarchiv, Information-Index, 7178/1860). Later in August of 1863, at the time of the opening of the Slovak matica, Vienna telegraphed Pressburg and Agram asking whether Strossmayer was a member of the Slovak matica and whether he intended to attend the Slovak celebrations. The police minister in Vienna was no doubt relieved when Agram telegraphed that on August 3, Strossmayer had entrained for Trieste and not St. Martin. (Haus-, Hof- und Staatsarchiv, Information-Index, 7168/1863).

Slovene people develop true culture by publishing appropriate books in Slovene or by lending all support to their publication." [13] To this end it brought out books and journals, administered trusts, made book grants, and established book-exchange programs throughout the Slavic world. Some of these activities were never very successful or important. Not until 1881 and 1883, for example, did it acquire any trusts to administer, and even then they only amounted to about 10,000fl., a very small sum when compared with the several hundred thousand fl. administered by the Serbian matica.

It was, however, much more successful in its book grant and exchange programs. The matica leaders were especially sensitive to the needs of the secondary school students and for this reason not only presented many books for them, but put them into the hands of native students by donating them to Slovene secondary schools. By 1884 the matica had contributed over 10,000fl. worth of such books.

The most important activity of the matica, of course, was its publishing program. As had the other maticas, it began publishing by bringing out a literary-almanac, *Letopis*, in 1867 which devoted itself to educational and entertainment works. *Letopis* appeared annually and carried many articles on Slovene and general Slavic history and geography, as well as on scientific and practical economic matters. It also carried news about members and contributions, of the matica and other similar societies, holdings in the matica library, bibliographies, and other such general information. *Letopis* also ran biographic studies on Slovenes and non-Slovenes such as Slomšek, Krempl, Zois, Alexander II, Innocent III, Palacký, and Karamzin. Furthermore, many translations from German, French, Italian, Russian, Polish, Czech, and Croatian authors such as Dante, de Maistre, Bernardin de Saint-Pierre, Korner, Gogol, Lermantov, Turgenev, Czajkowski, Pol, and Havlíček, were published.

Letopis differed from similar journals published by other maticas in one significant way—it published very little about Slovene language and literature. The main reason for this is that by the time it came into existence, the problems of Slovene literary language and literature had been solved.

During this first period there were four editors of *Letopis*—Bleiweis, 1867–1868 and 1877–1880; Costa, 1869–1874; Ivan Tušek, 1875; and Maks Pleteršnik, 1876. It was first issued in quantities of 1,200 averaging about 100 pages each. One measure of the success of the matica is that *Letopis* soon expanded to 500 pages and that 2,500 copies were printed by the end of its first decade, and 3,000 in 1881.

Through 1881, the matica published a grand total of seventy-two items. In addition to the sixteen volumes of *Letopis* and fifteen small, miscellaneous items such as by-laws and membership lists, it published forty-one books of four categories: fourteen in history and geography, ten on philology and belles-lettres, nine in science, and eight popular works.[14] As has been indicated above, however, few of the best Slovene authors were published by the matica. With the exception of one publication each of Levstik, the scholar Janez Trdina, and the novelist Janko Kersnik, all publications of the Slovenian matica were either translations or by second-rank authors of popular and practical literature.

From the national point of view it is not surprising that works on history and geography should lead the list, for these were best suited to foster pan-Slovenianism and to further kindle the fires of nationalism. Appropriately the first book published by the matica was a history, *Zgodovina Slovenskega Národa* (History of the Slovene Nation) by Trdina brought out in 1866. In addition to this it published *Slovanstvo* (Slavdom, a General Survey of the Slovenes, Croats, Serbs, and Bulgarians) in 1873, *Zgodovina Avstrijsko-ogrske Monarhije* (History of the Austro-Hungarian Monarchy) by Janko Kersnik in 1874 (2nd ed. 1877), and *Grmanstvo in Njega Uplív na Slovanstvo s Srednjem Veku* (Study of German Influence on the Slavs During the Middle Ages) by Ivan Vrhovec, a popular writer and historian, in 1879.

In 1866 the matica published two geographic studies, *Vojvodstvo Koroško* (Corinthian Dukedom in Maps: A Statistical and Historical Survey), and *Vojvodstvo Kranjsko* (Carniolan Dukedom in Maps: A Statistical and Historical Survey), both of which were adapted and translated from works by the Czech geographer, Josef Erban. In 1874 it brought out *Prirodoznanski Zemljepis* (Physical Geography) by Janez Jesenko; it also published a six-part *World Atlas*.

The first of the philological and belles-lettres works was *Slovnica Českega Jezika z Berilom* (Dictionary of the Czech Language with a Reader) by Franjo Marn in 1867, which was followed in 1869 by Levstik's edition of *Vodnikove Pesni* (Poems of Vodnik), a volume of *Razne dela Pesniške in Igrokazne Jovana Vesela-Koseskiga* (Various Poems and Plays of Ivan Vesel-Koseski), a popular Slovene poet who imitated German styles, in 1870; a biography of Lovro Toman by Andrej Praprotnik in 1876; and a biography of E. H. Costa by Viljem Urban in 1877. In 1879 there appeared a translation of Jules Verne's *Around the World in 80 Days* and in 1879 another volume of the works of Koseski and a Croatian Dictionary (*Hrvatska Slovnica za Slovence*) by Marn. In 1880 there appeared a volume in honor of Kopitar, also

[13] *Letopis* 1868: pp. 2–4.

[14] All the following bibliographic citations are from Jože Munda, *Bibliografija Slovenske matice: 1864–1964* (Ljubljana, 1964).

edited by Marn, and finally in 1881 a Slovene Dictionary (*Slovenska Slovnica*) by Josip Šuman.

The matica's publications in science were mainly translations of German and Czech works including Schoedler's four-part *Das Buch der Natur* (1869–1875), Fellocker's *Die Mineralogie* (1861), and two volumes on natural history by the Czech Pokorný (1872).

In the popular or informative category the matica commenced with a translation of a popular German work, Rossmassler's *Die vier Jahreszeiten* (1867) which was followed in 1868–1870 by a general study by several authors of Slovenian Styria (*Slovenski Štajer*), Koseski's *Olikani Slovenec* (Cultured Slovene, 1868), a gymnastic instruction book for the *južni sokol* (1881), a work on the Eye and Vision (*Oko in Vid*, 1880), and finally a tract on the influence of alcohol on individuals and society (1880).

In spite of the modesty and paucity of such a publication list, Slovenian book publication was so undeveloped that the matica was considered an important publishing house and continued to grow in membership and influence. Its leaders made many book grants to prisons, workhouses, charitable institutions, also to military organizations, to Catholic and political societies, and especially to students and secondary schools.

In 1870 the matica proudly presented Francis Joseph with all eighteen publications to that date, and also sent some to a Slovenian reading room in San Francisco. The matica sold its publications in all Slovenian centers such as Ljubljana, Ptuj, Trst, Celje, Celovec, and Maribor, and in Prague, Zagreb, and other Slavic cities.

One of the most interesting and important activities of the Slovenian matica was its many and varied attempts to foster Slavic mutuality. In this sphere of activity it led all the other maticas. As has been noted above, its journal, *Letopis*, carried biographic studies of important Slavs other than Slovene, published translations of other Slav authors, sold its publications in other Austro-Slav centers, and exhibited its publications at various fairs such as that in Zagreb in 1871.

In addition the matica bestowed honorary membership on Slav notables—for example, on Rački of the Croatian Academy, and on Czechs such as Count J. Harrach, Palacký, Jan Purkyně, and Rieger.

They also sent deputations to or observed many Austro-Slav celebrations. Among their more significant activities in this respect was the observation of the eightieth birthday of the Czech scientist, Purkyně, in 1867; the sending of one of their board members, Dr. Josip Vošnjak, to represent the matica at the laying of the foundation stone of the Czech National Theater in Prague in 1868 [15]; and attending the festival occasioned in Prague by the centennial of the birth of Jungmann in 1873.

Similar delegations were sent to Zagreb in 1874 at the opening of the university there, again in 1879 in honor of the poet Peter Preredović, and again in 1881 to attend the funeral of the famous novelist August Šenoa. Furthermore, the death of the Slovak Bishop Moyses was observed in 1869, the Russian Pogodin's fiftieth year of literary activity in 1872,[16] and Strossmayer's twenty-fifth anniversary as bishop in 1875.

Perhaps more important was the matica's systematic and thorough building up of exchanges with other Austro-Slav literary and scholarly institutions. Among the thirty-one such programs worked out by 1881, the following were the most important: with the Serb, Czech, Dalmatian, Slovak, Moravian, Ruthenian, and Croatian maticas; the Czech Artists' Union, the Croatian Academy, St. Jerome Society, the Serbian Literary Society in Beograd, the Bulgarian Literary Society in Brajle, the Imperial University in Warsaw, the Ruthenian Society of St. Basil the Great in Uzhhorod (Užhorod, Ungvár) and the Russian Anthropological Society, the Rumiantsev Museum of History, the Slavic Literary Committee, the Imperial University, the Association of Lovers of Russian History and Antiquities, the Association of Archeologists (all in Moscow), and also with the Imperial Academy, and the Imperial Russian Geographic Society in St. Petersburg. Exchange programs were also set up with the Lithuanian Community for the Publication of National Memorial in Vilna, the Royal University of Oslo, and the Smithsonian Institution in Washington.[17]

[15] In Prague Vošnjak spoke about the Slovenian lack of historic rights, about the grave which the Germans had dug for them, and how the Magyars and Italians were dancing around it. "But," he concluded, "they are mistaken! The Funeral bells will call us to life!"

Gliša Geršić represented the Serbian matica at this event and the Slovak and Dalmatian maticas sent congratulatory telegrams. See chapt. VI of my study, *Czech Nationalism: A Study of the National Theater Movement, 1845–1883*, Urbana, Ill., 1964.

[16] The only extant document in the Viennese archives regarding the Slovenian matica is a *Tages Bericht* (Daily Report) of the Vienna Police which reflects the constant German fear of pan-Slavism. This document, dated March 15, 1872, reported that "At a private meeting of the members of the Slovenian matica in Laibach an elaborate, pompous, and affected address was dedicated to Pogodin, the famous Russian pan-Slavist in Moscow. This scheming document will shortly be sent to Vienna so that it may be signed by South Slav societies here in Vienna before being presented to Pogodin." (Haus-, Hof- und Staatsarchiv, Information-Index, 240/II/1872.)

[17] The only reference to this exchange with the Smithsonian Institution was in a document (182/1867) in the archives of the Slovenian matica which merely stated that some books were being sent to Washington. Even though this exchange took place two years after the fire which destroyed the official records of the Smithsonian, correspondence with this society has failed to turn up additional information. (See note 20, chap. III for similar problems relating to correspondence between the Czech matica and the Smithsonian.)

TABLE 1

A Comparison of the Activities of the Various Maticas

	Serb	Czech	Moravian	Croat	Slovak	Slovene
Period studied	1826–76	1830–60	1836–69	1842–74	1863–75	1863–81
Maximum number of members	600	4,800	665	600	1,100	2,500
Maximum wealth in fl. (gulden)	500,000	80,000	5,500	28,000	82,000	67,000
Publications (total)	160	112	37	59	82	73
books	52	63	26	24	19	42
misc. publications	52	3	2	20	44	15
journals, number of	2	3	2	3	1	1
" number of volumes	56	46	9	15	19	16
" maximum circulation of	1,500+	6,300	3,600	3,100+	1,300	3,000
Membership fee, minimum	40fl.	5fl.	5fl.	5fl.	3fl.	2fl.
Supported authors	√	√	√	√	√	√
Promoted language reforms	√	√			√	
Fostered national language	√	√	√	√	√	√
Awarded literary prizes	√	√				
Made book grants		√				√
Exchanged journals	√	√	√	√		√
Managed trust funds	√					
Granted stipendia to students	√				√	
Fostered Slavic mutuality	√	√	√	√	√	√
Collected for museums	√	√			√	
Erected monuments	√				√	
Had honorary members		√			√	√
Reading rooms, promotion of	√	√		√	√	√
National halls, connection with				√	√	√
Founded libraries			√		√	√
Organized scholarly activity	√	√	√	√	√	√

After the death of Bleiweis in 1881, the control of the Slovenian matica passed to the Young Slovenes, among whom some of the most important were at that time Peter Grasselli and France Levec. Grasselli was one of the leaders of the Dramatic Society and Levec was an important writer and editor of the *Ljubljanski Zvon* (Ljubljana Bell), a literary review which succeeded Stritar's *Zvon*. Thereafter the pro-Slav ministry of Taaffe permitted the Slovene political and cultural revival to advance rapidly. By 1884 there were thirty-five Slovene newspapers (in contrast to only twenty-two in 1874), the Slovenes were in control of not only the administration of Ljubljana, but of the Carniola Diet as well, and some new cultural and national societies were organized. Especially important was the Družba sv. Cirila in Metoda (Society of SS. Cyril and Methodius) founded in Ljubljana in 1885 for the purpose of creating and maintaining private primary schools for Slovene children in areas where instruction was normally in Italian or German. By 1890 it had fourteen branches. Under Taaffe the Slovenes also built their own national theater, museum, and art gallery, and the Slovenian gymnasium was divided into German and Slovenian sections.

While the Slovenian matica was no longer necessary as a pioneer and while it no longer remained the sole barometer of Slovene nationalism, it did indeed remain as the single most important Slovenian national and scholarly institution. It continued to publish *Letopis* and about four other publications annually into the twentieth century. It still exists today as one of the most important of Slovene publishing houses.

CONCLUSIONS

The foregoing has been an attempt to show how the Austro-Slavs through literary institutions—especially through the maticas—worked to foster nationalism, spread knowledge, and raise the standard of living of the masses during the early phase of the national rebirth; to evaluate the success of the maticas, to indicate their common activities, and to demonstrate the extent of mutuality, or cooperation these institutions engendered among the Austro-Slavs. So similar were these societies in outlook and activity that, in spite of their many differences, it is possible to speak of and characterize a "matica movement" which commenced with the Serbs in Hungary in 1826 and thence spread to the other Austro-Slavs.

Although they were never really popular or wealthy and although most of their publications were more academic and practical than belles-lettres, the maticas in general were very successful pioneers and showed considerable imagination and variety in their activities. Individually and collectively, they did more for the Austro-Slav national revivals than any other groups or societies.

TABLE 2

JOURNALS PUBLISHED BY THE VARIOUS MATICAS

Ethnic group	Name of Journal	Dates	Frequency of publication	Type	Maximum number of copies printed during period studied	Chief editor(s) during period studied
Serb	*Ljetopis*	1825-date	quarterly-annual	scholarly	1,000	Magaraševič, Hadžić-Svetić, Pavlović, Subotić, Hadžić.
	Matica	1865–70	3 × monthly	popular	500 (?)	Hadřić
Czech	*Časopis*	1827-date	quarterly	scholarly	4,000	Palacký, Šafařík, Vocel, Nebeský
	Pamatky	1855–63, (then taken over by Czech Museum)	annual	scholarly	800	Zap
	Živa	1853–78	annual	scholarly	1,500	Purkyně, Krejči
Moravian	*Koleda*	1852–58	annual	popular	3,000	Helcelet
	Časopis	1869-date	annual, quarterly	scholarly	600	Royt
Croat	*Kolo*	1847–51	irregular	popular	1,000	Vraz
	Neven	1852–57	weekly, monthly	popular	700+	Praus, Bogović
	Književnik	1864–67, (then taken over by Croatian Academy)	quarterly	scholarly	700 (?)	Rački, Jagić
	Vienac	1869–1903	weekly	popular	700 (?)	I. Perkovac
Slovak	*Letopis*	1864–75	annual	popular	1,300	Pauliny-Tóth, Sasinek
Slovene	*Letopis*	1867–1907	annual	popular	3,000	Bleiweis, Costa

The leaders of these six foundations who devoted their time and talent to advancing nationalism reads like a list of "Who was Who" of famous Slav political and cultural leaders: there were the Serbs Mušicki, Magaraševič, Hadžić-Svetić, Pavlović, Tekelija, Subotić, Hadžić, Miletić, and Jovanović-Zmaj; the Czechs Palacký, Jungmann, Presl, Hanka, Frič, Tomek, Čelakovský, Erben, Purkyně, and Vocel; the Moravians Šembera, Helcelet, Ohéral, Sušil, Brázdil, Pražák, and Royt; the Croats Babukić, Mažuranić, Vukotinović, Demeter, Vranjican, Kukuljević, Bogović, and Starčević; the Slovaks Šafařík, Francisci, Pauliny-Tóth, Palárik, Kuzmány, Bishop Moyses, Országh, Mudroň, Daxner, Hurban, Hodža, and Radlinský; the Slovenes Vraz, Vančura, Costa, Levstik, Bleiweis, Toman, Einspieler, Miklošić, and Vošnjak.

Their most important single activity was publishing and collectively they published 523 items, including 226 books, 161 volumes of 13 journals, and scores of membership lists, by-laws, announcements, and other official items. Among the authors whose works were fostered and published were many of the most important of that time as well as of preceding generations. This list included the Serbs Vidaković, Magaraševič, Obradović, Subotić, Mušicki, Nikolić, Kostić, and Ignjatović; the Czechs Jungmann, Kornel of Všehrd, Tomek, Presl, Čelakovský, and Palacký; the Moravians Klácel, Šembera, Furch, and Karel of Žerotín; the Croatians Gundulić, Demeter, Palmotić, and Kačić-Miošic; the Slovaks Šafařík, Sasinek, Štúr, Čulen, and Pensel; and the Slovenes Vodnik, Levstik, Kersnik, and Vesel-Koseski. Among the authors translated were Voltaire, Kotzebue, Lessing, Horace, Demosthenes, Milton, Shakespeare, Virgil, Goethe, and Jules Verne.

Their thirteen journals were not only the most important and influential periodicals of that era, but in some cases the only significant journals in some of the Slavic lands. They had a combined circulation of over 18,000 and were edited by some of the outstanding national and political leaders of the century, including Magaraševič, Palacký, Šafařík, Purkyně, Vraz, Rački, Jagić, Sasinek, Bleiweis, and Costa.

Another important activity common to all was the cultivation of Slavic mutuality for the purpose of more effectively advancing their goals and resisting German and Magyar suppression. In this respect they were of course influenced by the heady doctrines of pan-Slavism and Austro-Slavism.

Their contributions to mutuality varied in intensity from the simple granting of a few honorary memberships and attendance at celebrations in Zagreb and Moscow by the Slovaks, to the enthusiastic activities of the Slovenes which included exchange of journals, honorary memberships, promoting each others' national activities, selling their publications in other Slav capitals, attending one another's celebrations, translating and publishing other Slav authors, joining each others' societies, and publishing articles and books on Slavic literature, literary activity, history, and ethnography.

As would be expected, the maticas engaged in other activities not common to all. For example, only the Serbs and Slovenes managed trust funds; only the Serbs and Slovaks granted stipends to needy and worthy students; only the Serbs, Czechs, and Slovaks collected materials for museums; only the Czechs, and Slovenes made book grants, and only the Moravians, Slovaks, and Slovenians founded libraries.

Two tables are provided to show the common and the unique activities of these societies, their time periods, wealth, size, and number of publications, and to suggest the relative importance of the most important single activity of all the maticas—the publication of their journals. The bulk of all their publications suggests a higher level of literacy than is generally attributed to the Austro-Slavs.

APPENDIX

THREE OTHER MATICAS AND RELATED SOCIETIES: RUTHENIAN, POLISH, AND LUSATIAN

The Ruthenians lived in three areas—in Galicia, the Bukovina, and the sub-Carpathian part of northern Hungary. Those in Galicia came into the monarchy during the first and third partitions of Poland in 1772 and 1795 and were centered around Lviv (Lwów, Lemberg) and Ternopil (Tarnopol').[1] Those in the Bukovina were added to the monarchy when they were taken from Turkey in 1775 and their center was Chernivtsi (Czernowitz, Cernăuţi or Chernovtsy in present day Russia). Between 1786 and 1849 the Bukovina was joined to Galicia, thereafter it became a separate crown land. The Ruthenians in northern Hungary had filtered across the Carpathian Mountains looking for land in northern Hungary during the Turkish wars beginning in the sixteenth century and settled mainly in Uzhhorod (Ungvár or Uzhgorod in present-day Russia), in Priashiv (Eperjes or Prešov in present-day Czechoslovakia) and in Mukachiev (Munkács or Mukachevo in present-day Russia).

The Ruthenians were a people primarily of masses and Orthodox priests. Since they had been systematically Germanized, Polonized, Magyarized, or Rumanianized, the early national leaders (usually Orthodox clergymen) were Russophiles who looked to Russia for help in the preservation and fostering of Ruthenian culture. Most of the early societies, therefore, were Russophile, conservative, clerical, and designed for a small group of intellectuals. Like most Austro-Slavs, however, who originally expected help from Russia in their national revival, they were disappointed. The next generation of national leaders turned from Russia and looked to themselves for succor.

The heart of the whole Ruthenian as well as Ukrainian national revival was in Galicia (where they had long been favored by Vienna as a check against the Poles) and not in Kiev or Kharkov in the Russian Ukraine. Especially was this true after the demise in 1847 of the Kievan national society, The Brotherhood of SS. Cyril and Methodius, and after 1876 when Czar Alexander II forbade the printing of books in the Ukrainian language.

In Galicia the national revival was centered in Lviv and led by the Rus'ka Triitsia (Ruthenian Trinity) of Jakov Holovatsky, a poet and folklorist; Markian Shashkevych, a Uniate priest and poet; and by Ivan Vahylevych, also a poet. In 1837 they edited and published the first literature (in Ukrainian) for the Ruthenians in Galicia—the *Rusalka Dnistrovaia* (Dniester Nymph) an almanac which is usually considered to mark the beginning of the Ruthenian revival.

Further advance was made in 1848 when a political body, the Holovna Rus'ka Rada (Central Ukrainian Council), was organized to represent the Ruthenians of Galicia. Its primary goal was to divide Galicia into two provinces—a Polish and a Ruthenian. It was never successful politically and was dissolved in 1851. It did, however, bring one important national society into being—the Halytsko-rus'ka Matytsia (Galician-Ruthenian matica). This foundation, organized to print cheap, useful books in Ukrainian and to help standardize the language (as distinct from Church Slavonic, Russian, and Polish), was similar to the other maticas in the monarchy. By 1850 it had about 200 members and, during its most active period, 1849–1885, it published about eighty books and pamphlets (most of which were text and prayer books). The journals were *Naukovi Sbornik* (Scientific Collection) which was published for the years 1865–1868 and the *Literaturni Sbornik* (Literary Collection) which was published during 1860–1873, and 1885–1890.

Since this matica was very conservative and Russophile, a younger generation of national leaders, the "populists," organized in 1863 a society called Prosvita (Enlightenment), a popular cultural and educational institution to support the national literature and to advance national consciousness among the masses. The police in Lviv, who closely watched all "populist" activities and who attended the first general meeting of this society during December, 1868, must have been relieved when they were able to report to Vienna on the "true, moderate, and loyal speeches" made on this occasion.[2]

Prosvita soon replaced the matica as the center of cultural activities of the Ruthenians in Galicia. Between 1868 and 1912 it published 3,115,000 copies of 445 books. It also organized credit societies, trading and economic societies, founded vocational schools and libraries, and sponsored lectures, choruses, and theatrical groups. By 1912 it had 35,000 members, 74 branches, and 2,000 reading rooms with a collective membership of over 130,000 in Galicia. The importance of these reading rooms was augmented by the practice of members reading aloud to illiterate non-members.

---

[1] As far as possible I have tried to solve the vexing problem of nineteenth-century Ruthenian orthography and its proper transliteration by reference to the *Ukraine: A Concise Encyclopaedia* 2 Vol. (Toronto, 1963–1971), which unfortunately is itself not consistent.

[2] Haus-, Hof- und Staatsarchiv, Information-Index, 2161/1868.

The success of Prosvita among the masses caused another society to be organized in 1873 for academic studies. This was the Society of Shevchenko, which began as a literary group, but in 1892 it changed its name to the Scientific Society, in 1898 to the Naukove Tovarystvo Imeny Shevchenka (Scientific Society of Shevchenko), and became the unofficial Ukrainian academy of arts and sciences.

In the Bukovina, although the Ruthenians represented about 40 per cent of the population, the Germans and Rumanians dominated cultural and political life. The Ruthenian cause was further weakened after 1849 when the Bukovina was separated from Galicia. Their most important national society was the Ruskaia Besida (Ruthenian Club) organized in 1869 in Chernivtsi by Basil Prodan. It published an almanac and a newspaper, the *Bukovynskaia Zoria* (Bukovinian Star) in an attempt to preserve and develop the national traits of the people. This society was dominated by the Russophiles until 1884, thereafter by the populists. It should be noted in passing that when in 1875 a university was opened in Chernivtsi it had a chair for Ukrainian language and literature.

The Ruthenians in Hungary were the most exploited, miserable, and nationally unconscious of all minorities in the monarchy.[3] Although only about 100 miles from Lviv and Chernivtsi, they were shut off from their fellows in Galicia and the Bukovina by mountains. The people were 98 per cent illiterate and thoroughly Magyarized. Their most important awakener was a Moscowphile priest, Oleksander Duchnovych (1803–1865). He founded their first national society in 1850 in Priashiv. This was the Literaturnoie Zavedeniie Priashovskoie (Priashin Literary Institute). It had about seventy members and for a few years published school texts, folktales, songs, and three almanacs.

Although Duchnovych died in 1865, his efforts led to the founding of another publishing and literary society in Mukachiev. This was the Obshchestvo sv. Vasiliia Velkeho (Society of St. Basil the Great) which was modeled somewhat on the Czech matica. Though thoroughly Russophile its founding day was a national celebration in which over 500 participated. It became the cultural center of the sub-Carpathian Ruthenians and published mainly schoolbooks and almanacs. During its first four years, for example, it brought out three texts in arithmetic, geography, and world history, and a newspaper, *Svit* (World) which, however, ceased in 1871 because of lack of subscribers. For years it was led by Dobriansky, mentioned earlier as a representative of the Slovaks in the Hungarian Diet. In 1896 it was reorganized as a more public and popular institution. In 1902 it changed its name to Unio and continued to play a leading role in Ruthenian development until World War II.[4]

As has been mentioned above, the Polish situation differed markedly from that of the rest of the Austro-Slavs. Since their national culture had never been completely suppressed it did not have to be revived by a cultural renaissance. Their nineteenth-century national program was political, not cultural.

As a result of the eighteenth-century partitions the Poles in 1815 were divided among Russia, Prussia, and Austria. So much more favorable were the circumstances in Austria that Galicia became the "Piedmont" of reconstituted Poland after 1918. In 1869 Polish became the official "internal" language and there were many Polish cultural institutions. In Lwów for example they had a university (Polonized in 1873), an engineering college, a music conservatory, and the famous Ossolineum—a private foundation and museum to promote research which was set up as early as 1817 by Count J. M. Ossoliński. In Cracow there was the Jagiellonian University, Polonized in 1879, an academy of science (the Towarzystwo Naukowie Krakowskie founded in 1815, which changed its name in 1871 to the Akademia Umiejętności). In Warsaw there was the Towarzystwo Przyjaciół Nauk (Society of the Friends of Science) founded in 1800 and a university, founded in 1818; in Poznan there was since 1857 also a Society of the Friends of Science.

Later, in 1882, the Poles also established a matica, the Macierz Polska. This idea had been advanced as early as 1848 by young Prince Jerzy Lubormirski, who hoped to attach a Polish matica to the Ossolineum as the Czech matica was connected with the Czech museum. The failure of 1848–1849, however, ruined this idea and it lay dormant for thirty years. In 1878 the famous Polish author, Józef Ignacy Kraszewski and two priests, Kazimierz Hulanicki and Jan Swicki, again took up the idea which was effected in 1882 with Kraszewski as president.

The Polish matica was organized for the usual reasons of spreading culture among the masses and publishing popular books of various kinds. It was supported, however, more by the Polish Sejm or diet in Galicia and rich benefactors than by popular subscription. Its leaders met with considerable success. By 1902 its fund, the Kosciuszko Fund (Fundacja im. Tadeusza Kościuszki) totaled about 100,000fl., and by 1911 it had printed over a million copies of 169 moral, religious, historical, literary, scientific, and economic books. In order to make these publications as accessible as possible some of them, such as Mickiewicz's famous poem *Pan Ta-*

[3] Variously known as sub-Carpathian Ruthenians, sub-Carpathian Ukrainians, Carpathian Russians, Hungarian Ruthenians, or Hungarian Russians.

[4] See Ivan Žeguc, *Die nationalpolitischen Bestrebungen der Karpato-Ruthenen: 1848–1914* (Wiesbaden, 1965).

deusz (Mr. Tadeus), were sold for as little as 20 kreuzer.

Even the Lusatian Serbs (Wends) in Saxony founded their matica. These Slavs, the last remnant of the various groups of Polabian (along the Elbe River) Slavs, by the eighteenth century had been all but Germanized into extinction and their language was nearly dead. At the beginning of the nineteenth century they formed two tiny islands in a German sea, Upper Lusatia with a center at Budyšín (Bautzen) and Lower Lusatia with a center in Chóśebuz (Cottbus). Their nobility, clergy, and middle classes were largely denationalized and they had few nationally minded intellectuals.

Their national revival probably started around 1830 when one of their poets, Handrij Zejler (Seiler, 1804–1872), began to study the Lusatian language and grammar and, more particularly, in the 1840's with the publication of his newspaper, the *Tydźenska Nowina* (Weekly News), which he founded in 1842 in Budyšín.

The most important step in the Lusatian revival, however, was taken in 1847 when the political leader and philologist, Dr. Jan Arnošt Smoleŕ (Schmaler, 1816–1884), organized the Maćica Serbska, also in Budyšín. Smoleŕ, who remained its president until 1882, with the help of Palacký and Čelakovsky modeled this society after the Czech matica.[5]

By 1863 this organization grew to a membership of over 100 (mostly teachers and priests) who received publications free. It had published, by 1865, 20,000 copies of forty-five "useful and entertaining" books and by the end of the century 200,000 copies of over 100 books. It also brought out the *Časopis Maćicy Serbskeje* (Journal of the Lusatian Matica from 1847) which became and remained the most important Lusatian learned and literary journal. Also by 1900 it had its own quarters where it maintained not only its offices and a press, but also a bookstore, library, museum, theater, and concert hall.

Since the reorganization of Eastern Europe after 1945, its activities have been taken over by the Institut za Serbski Ludospyt w Budyšinje (Institute of Serbian Ethnology in Budyšín) which is a part of the East German Academy of Science in Berlin.

[5] Throughout the nineteenth century the Lusatians, as a result of having belonged to the Czech crown up to the Thirty Years' War in the seventeenth century, maintained close connections with and sought succor from the Czechs. See Peter Brock, "Jan Ernst Smoler and the Czech and Slovak Awakeners: A study of Slav Reciprocity," *The Czech Renascence of the Nineteenth Century*, eds. Peter Brock and H. Gordon Skilling (Toronto, Canada, 1970), pp. 74–94.

BIBLIOGRAPHY

Primary Sources: Unpublished

The main repositories of primary sources are in the archives of the various maticas in Novi Sad, Prague, Brno, Zagreb, St. Martin, and Ljubljana. Some documents are still extant in Vienna in the Polizei-Hofstelle and Oberste Polizei-Behörde collections of the Allgemeines Verwaltungsarchiv and in the Index der Polizei-Acten and Information-Index collections of the Haus-, Hof- und Staatsarchiv.

Primary Sources: Published

Most of the maticas have published various official histories many of which contain documents. The most important of these are: 1927. *Matica Srpska: 1826–1926* (The Serbian Matica: 1826–1926) (Novi Sad); Milisavać, Živan. 1965. *Matica Srpska* (The Serbian Matica) (Novi Sad); Tieftrunk, Karel. 1881. *Dějiny Matice České* (A History of the Czech Matica) (Prague); Traub, H. 1910–1911. "Dějiny Matice Moravské" (A History of the Moravian Matica). *Časopis Matice Moravské* **34**, 3: pp. 197–229; **34**, 4: pp. 313–341; **35**, 1: pp. 60–102; **35**, 2: pp. 154–192; Smičiklas, Tade and Marković, Franjo. 1892. *Matica Hrvatska od Godine 1842 do Godine 1892* (The Croatian Matica: 1842–1892) (Zagreb); Ravlić, Jakša and Somborac, Marin. 1963. *Matica Hrvatska 1842–1962* (The Croatian Matica: 1842–1962) (Zagreb); Botto, Julius. 1923. *Dejiny Matice Slovenskej, 1863–1875* (A History of the Slovak Matica: 1863–1875) (Turč. Sv. Martin); Mráz, Andrej. 1935. *Matica Slovenská v Rokoch 1863–1875* (The Slovak Matica: 1863–1875) (Turč. Sv. Martin); Bernik, Francè (ed.). 1964. *Slovenska Matica: 1864–1964* (The Slovenian Matica: 1864–1964) (Ljubljana); Costa, E. H. 1874. "Prvo Desetletje Matice Slovenske" (The First Decade of the Slovenian Matica). *Letopis Matice Slovenske* pp. 5–9; Lah, Evgen. 1885. "Matica Slovenska: 1864–1874–1884" (The Slovenian Matica: 1864–1874–1884). *Letopis Matice Slovenske* pp. 392–414; Lah, Ivan. 1921. *Začetki Slovenske Matice* (The Beginnings of the Slovenian Matica) (Ljubljana); and Žigon, Joka. 1935. *Veliko Pismo Slovenske Duhovne Združitve* (The Great Charter of Slovene Cultural Unity) (Ljubljana).

The early issues of the various journals published by the maticas also contain many primary sources. (For a list of these journals see Table 2.) The most important bibliographies of matica publications are: 1950. *Bibliografija Izdanja Matice Srpska: 1826–1949* (A Bibliography of the Publications of the Serbian Matica: 1826–1949) (Novi Sad); Grund, Antonín. 1931. *Sto Let Matice České: 1831–1931* (One Hundred Years of the Czech Matica) (Prague); Ravlić, Jakša and Somborac, Marin. 1963. *Marica Hrvatska 1842–1962* (The Croatian Matica: 1842–1962) (Zagreb); Liba, Peter. 1963. *Vydavateľske Dielo Matice Slovenskej* (Publications of the Slovak Matica) (Martin); Munda, Jože. 1965. *Bibliografija Slovenske Matice*: 1864–1964 (A Bibliography of the Slovenian Matica) (Ljubljana); and Šlebinger, Janko. 1940. *Publicacije Slovenske Matice: 1864–1930* (Publications of the Slovenian Matica: 1864–1930) (Ljubljana).

Also useful are Kneidl, Pravoslav. 1963. *Časopis Národního Musea 1827–1956—Rejstřík 125 Ročníků Muzejního Časopis* (The Journal of the National Museum 1827–1956—A Register of 125 Years of the Journal of the Museum) (2 v., Prague); and Šebánek, Jindřich. 1929. *Rejstřík Bibliografický k Časopisu Matice Moravské* (A Bibliographic Register of the Journal of the Moravian Matica) (Brno).

Secondary Sources: A Selected List of Specialized Studies

In addition to the official histories of the various maticas listed above there are many other studies. Among the more important in chronological order are:

(Serbian) 1864. "Matica Srbska." *Ost und West* **3–4**: pp. 882–885; Klíma, Hanuš. 1884. "Matice Srbská: Kapitola z dějin Kulturního Života Srbů Uherských" (The Serbian Matica: Chapter from the History of the Cultural Life of the Hungarian Serbs). *Slovanský Sborník* **3**: pp. 308–312, 372–376, 405–412, 473–482; Stajić, Vaša. 1927. "Sto Godinâ Matice Srpske" (One Hundred Years of the Serbian Matica). *Nová Evropa* **16**: pp. 189–202; Stajic, V. 1927–1928. "The Centenary of the Matica Srpska." *The Slavonic and East European Review* **6**: pp. 593–602; 1928. "Storočné Jubileum Matice Srbskej v Novom Sade" (The Centennial Jubilee of the Serbian Matica in Novi Sad). *Bratislava* **1-2**: pp. 295–298; 1931. "Matice Srpska: 1826–1926" (The Serbian Matica: 1826–1926). *Časopis Národního Museum* **105**: pp. 342–343; Nečas, Jaroslav. 1946. "120 let Matice srbské" (One Hundred and Twenty Years of the Serbian Matica). *Slovanský přehled* **32**: pp. 497–500; 1951. "Jubilarno Godište Letopisa Matice Srpske" (Jubilee Anniversary of the Serbian Matica's Letopis). *Hrvatsko Kolo* **4**: pp. 191–193; and Kimball, Stanley B. 1969. "The Serbian Matica—Prototype of Austro-Slav Literary Foundations: The First Fifty Years 1826–1876," *East European Quarterly* **3**: pp. 348–370.

(Czech) Hanuš, Josef. 1921. *Národní Museum a Naše Obrození* (The National Museum and our Rebirth) (2 v., Prague); Prokeš, Jaroslav. 1931. "The Centenary of the Matice Ceska." *Slavonic and East European Review* **10**, 29: pp. 420–427; Prokeš, Jaroslav. 1931. "Z Těžké Doby 'Matice České' 1850–1860" (From the Difficult Times of the "Czech Matica": 1850–1860). *Časopis Národního Museum* **105**: pp. 1–40; 1931. "Storočina Matice Českej" (The One Hundredth Anniversary of the Czech Matica). *Slovenské Pohľady* **47**, 5: pp. 335–336; Kop, František. 1941. *Národní Museum* (The National Museum) (Prague); Grund, Antonín. 1949. "Matice Česká" (The Czech Matica). *Národní Museum: 1818–1948* (The National Museum: 1818–1948) (Prague), pp. 231–235; Hroch, M., and Veverka, A. 1957. "K Otázce Sociální Skladby České Obrozenské Společnosti: Rozbor Společenského Složení Vlastenců Kolem Českého Musea a Matice České v Letech 1827–1848" (On the Question of the Social Composition of the Czech Societies of the Rebirth: An Analysis of the Social Make-up of the Patriots Around the Czech Museum and the Czech Matica During the Years 1827–1848). *Dějepis ve Škole* April 4: pp. 153–159; Vrchotka, Jaroslav. 1967. "Matice Česká a Národní Muzeum" (The Czech Matica and the National Museum). *Národní Museum* (Prague), pp. 83–90; and Kimball, Stanley B. 1970. "The Matice Česká, 1831–1861: The First Thirty Years of a Literary Foundation." *The Czech Renascence of the Nineteenth Century*, eds. Peter Brock and H. Gordon Skilling (Toronto), pp. 53–73.

(Croatian) Hudec, J. 1882. "Matice Hrvatská" (The Croatian Matica). *Slovanský Sborník* **2**: pp. 50–52; 1942. "Hundert Jahre Matica Hrvatska." *Volkstum im Südosten*: p. 56.

(Slovak) Hujer, O. 1923–1924. "Matica Slovenská" (The Slovak Matica). *Slavia* **2**: pp. 782–783; 933. "Matica Slovenská" (The Slovak Matica). *Bratislava* **7**, 4: pp. 449–450; Hruska, Miroslav. 1943. "Achtzig Jahre Matica Slovenska," *Slowakische Rundschau* **4**, 8: pp. 239–241; Telgársky, Jozef.

1957. *Matica Slovenská* (The Slovak Matica) (Martin); Kučera, Ondrej. (ed.). 1943. *Matica Slovenská* (The Slovak Matica) (Martin); Mat'ovičík, A. and Liba, P. 1963. *Sto Rokov Matice Slovenskej* (One Hundred Years of the Slovak Matica) (Martin); Mésároš, Július and Kropilák, Miroslav. 1963. *Matica Slovenská v Našich Dejinách* (The Slovak Matica in Our History) (Martin); Paška, Juraj. 1963. "Ein Bedutendes Jubiläum der Slowakischen Kultur." *Zentralblatt für Bibliothekswesen* 77, 8: pp. 337–347; Kvetko, Martin. 1963. "Storočné Výročie Založenia Matice Slovenskej" (The One Hundredth Anniversary of the Founding of the Slovak Matica). *Kalendár 1963: Kanadského Slovenského Podporného Spolku:* pp. 40–43; Horecky, Paul L. 1964. "Centenary of the Matica Slovenska." *Quarterly Journal of the Library of Congress* 21, July: pp. 203–206; Vongrej, Pavel. 1969. "Matitsa Slovachka (1863–1968) [The Slovak Matica (1863–1968)] *Glasnik na Institutot za Natsionalna Istorija* 13, 3: pp. 135–154.

(Slovene) Ušeničnik, Aleš. 1912. "Slovenska Matica in Krščánstvo" (The Slovenian Matica and Christianity). *Čas* 6: pp. 145–158; Prijatelj, Ivan. 1923. "Predzgodovina Ustanovitve 'Slovenske Matice'" (The History of the Founding of the 'Slovenian Matica'). *Razprave* 1: pp. 1–34; and 1954. "Prasnovanje Devetdesetletnice Slovenske Matice" (Celebrating the Ninetieth Anniversary of the Slovenian Matica). Glasnik *Slovenske Matice* 1: pp. 33–37.

Several short surveys of the Austro-Slav maticas have also been attempted. The most important are: 1865. "Slovenska Drushtva 'Matice'" (Slavic Societies: 'Maticas'). *Ljetopis Matice Srpske* 110, 39: pp. 308–331; 1866. "Matice" (The Maticas). *Slovník Naučný* (11 v., Prague) 5: pp. 166–179; and Budilovich, Anton. 1869. "Slavianskiia Maticy i Uchenyia Druzhstva" (Slavic Maticas and Learned Societies). *Zhurnal Ministerstva Narodnago Prosvieshcheniia*, pp. 459–475.

The essential literature regarding the lesser maticas is as follows:

(Dalmatian) Ilešić, Fr. 1909. "O Početkih 'Matice Dalmatinske' 1848/49" (The Beginnings of the "Dalmatian Matica" 1848–1849). *Hrvatsko Kolo* 5: pp. 131–137; Karlić, Petar. 1913. *Matica Dalmatinska* (The Dalmatian Matica) (3 v., Zadar); Maštrović, Vjekoslav. 1957. "Kalendarski Zbornici Matice Dalmatinske in Hrvatske Knjižarnice u Zadru, 1863–1910" (The Almanacs of the Dalmatian Matica in the Croatian Publishing house in Zadar: 1863–1910). *Radovi* 3: pp. 271–315; and Maštrović, Vjekoslav. 1960. "Matica Dalmatinska" (The Dalmatian Matica). *Narodni Kalendar* pp. 53–56.

(Polish) 1910. "Macierz Polska we Lwowie" (The Polish Matica in Lwow). *Wielka Encyklopedia Ilustrowana* (Warsaw) 45: pp. 152–154.

(Ruthenian) Kachala, S. 1865. "Halytsko-rus'ka Matystia i ii tsil" (The Galician-Ruthenian Matica and its Goal). *Meta* 4: pp. 111–120, 5, pp. 135–146; Kachala, S. 1865. "Iaka ie tsil Halystko-Rus'koi Matytsi" (What is the Goal of the Galician-Ruthenian Matica). *Slovo* 21: pp. 1–3; 22: pp. 1–3; and Didistkii, V. 1885. "Rospis Izdanii Halytsko-Rus'koi Matytsi ot 1848 do Konsta Marta 1885" (List of the Publications of the Galician-Ruthenian Matica: 1848–1885). *Literaturni Sbornik* 1: pp. 48–54.

(Lusatian) Hornik, M. 1872. "Rozprawa při 25-lětnym Założeńskim Jubileju Mácicy Serbskeje" (The Twenty-fifth Anniversary of the Founding of the Lusatian Matica). *Časopis Mačicy Serbskeje* 25: pp. 81–87; Muka, Ernst. 1898. "Złoty Jubilej Maćicy Serbskeje" (The Golden Jubilee of the Lusatian Matica). *Časopis Mačicy Serbskeje* 51: pp. 13–52; and Páta, Josef. 1929–1930. "Matice lužickosrbská" (The Lusatian Matica). *Slavia* 8: pp. 183–186.

Useful studies on related literary and learned societies and institutions:

(Czech) Kaloušek, Josef. 1885. *Dějiny Král. České Společnosti Nauk* (History of the Royal Bohemian Society of Sciences) (Prague); Teich, Mikuláš. 1960. "The Royal Bohemian Society of Sciences and the First Phase of Organized Scientific Advance in Bohemia." *Historica* 2: pp. 161–181; Zacek, Joseph F. 1968. "The *Virtuosi* of Bohemia: The Royal Bohemian Society of Sciences." *East European Quarterly* 2, 2: pp. 147–159; Kraus, Arnošt. 1936. "Kdy Byla Založena 'Sourkomá společnost v Čechách'" (When was the "Private Society in Bohemia" Founded?). *Český Časopis Historický* 42 (April): pp. 56–76; and Borový, K. 1885. *Dějiny Svatojánského Dědictví* (History of the St. John Heritage) (Prague).

(Croatian) Deželić, Velimir. 1929. "Šezdeset Godina Jeronimskog Napredovanja" (Sixty Years of the St. Jerome Society). *Danica*, pp. 35–40; Lončarić, Jos. 1929. "Društvo Sv. Jeronima Budi i Diže u Narodu Hrvatsku Svijest" (The St. Jerome Society and the Awakening of the Croatian National Consciousness). *Danica*, pp. 45–49; Markulin, Stejepan. 1929. "Jeronimske Palače" (The St. Jerome Palace). *Danica*, pp. 52–56; 1931. *Rad i Uspjesi Društva Sv. Jeronima* (The Work and Success of the St. Jerome Society) (Zagreb); and Ravlić, Jakša. 1963. "Ilirska Čitaonica y Zagrebu" (The Illyrian Reading Room at Zagreb). *Historijski Zbornik* 16: pp. 159–215.

(Slovak) Pražák, Albert. 1926. "K Dějinám Učené Společnosti Baňského Okolí" (On the History of the Banska Learned Society). *Slovenské Studie* (Bratislava), pp. 13–26; 1872. *Spolok sv. Wojtecha, Založený a do Žiwota Uwedný 1870* (The St. Adalbert Society: Its Founding in 1870) (Skalice); Hvozdovič, Emma. 1965. "History and Accomplishments of the Society of St. Adalbert, Trnava, Slovakia." *Slovak Studies I: Historica* 5: pp. 205–238; Rapant, Daniel. 1950. *Tatrín: Osudy a Zápasy* (The Tatrin Society: Its Fortune and Struggles) (Turč. Sv. Martin); and Halaša, Pavol, and Špetko, Jozef. 1958. *Kníhtlačiarsky Účastinársky Spolok v Martine, 1869–1949* (The Joint Stock Printing Society in Martin: 1869–1949) (Martin).

(Slovene) Moder, Janko. 1952. *Iz Zdravih Korenin Močno Drevo: Iz Zgodovine Družbe Sv. Mohorja* (From a Healthy Root a Strong Tree: From the History of the St. Hermagoras Society) (Celje); and Costa, E. H. 1869. "Statistični Pregled Vseh Slovenskich Čitalnic" (A Statistical Survey of all Slovenian Reading Rooms). *Letopis Matice Slovenske* pp. 282–296.

(Ruthenian) 1924. "The Shevchenko Society in Lemberg, 1873–1923." *Slavonic Review* 2 (March): pp. 563–566; and Rudlovčak, Olena. 1965. "Literarischer Verein Duchnovycs und Literarische Problems von Prešov um die Mitte des 19 Jr." *Duklja* 1: pp. 88–95.

(Polish) Hulewicz, Jan. 1958. *Akademia Umiejętności w Krakowie*, 1873–1918 (The Academy of Science in Cracow) (Warsaw); 1930. *The Polish Academy of Sciences and Letters: 1872–1930* (Cracow); Tyszkowski, Kazimierz. 1928. "Das Ossolinskische Nationalinstitut in Lemberg, 1827–1928." *Jahrbucher für Kultur und Geschichte der Slaven*, N. F., 4, 1: pp. 43–45; Dyboski, Roman. 1928. "The Centenary of a Great Home of Research in Poland." *Slavonic Review* 7 (Jan.): pp. 361–370; 1951. *Ossolineum* (Wrocław); 1956. *Zakład imienia Ossolińskich: 1827–1956* (The Ossolineum: 1827–1956) (Wrocław); and Wistocki, Władysław T. 1936. "Instytucje Kulturalne Galicji w Pierwszej Połowie XIX Wieku" (Cultural Institutions in Galicia During the first Half of the Nineteenth Century). *Pamiętnik Literacki* 33: pp. 642–663.

(Other useful studies are listed in the footnotes to this work.)

INDEX

GENERAL SUBJECTS

CITIES, COUNTRIES, AND REGIONS

INDIVIDUALS

INSTITUTIONS

JOURNALS AND NEWSPAPERS

www.ingramcontent.com/pod-product-compliance
Lightning Source LLC
Chambersburg PA
CBHW081139300726
48982CB00006B/1006

* 9 7 8 1 4 2 2 3 7 5 4 4 0 *